全国特色专业建设项目

2014 - 中国保险市场论丛

中央财经大学中国精算研究院
中央财经大学中国保险市场研究中心

中国商业出版社

图书在版编目（CIP）数据

2014中国保险市场论丛／中央财经大学中国精算研究院，中央财经大学保险市场研究中心著．—北京：中国商业出版社，2015.12
ISBN 978-7-5044-9190-9

Ⅰ.①2… Ⅱ.①中… ②中… Ⅲ.①保险市场-中国-文集 Ⅳ.①F842-53

中国版本图书馆CIP数据核字（2015）第273800号

责任编辑：刘洪涛

中国商业出版社出版发行
010-63180647 www.c-cbook.com
（100053 北京广安门内报国寺1号）
新华书店总店北京发行所经销
北京书林印刷有限公司印刷
*
787×1092毫米 1/16开 13印张 298千字
2015年12月第1版 2015年12月第1次印刷
定价：39.00元
* * *
（如有印装质量问题可更换）

目 录

新农保政策变量及人口增长率的优化 …………………………… 杨再贵　曹　园　1

养老保险缴费率与个人账户实账率的优化 ……………………… 高　彦　杨再贵　9

保险告知义务规则的最新发展及其启示 ………………………………… 张　虹　17

Delaying Retirement Strategy with Longevity Risk and Social Welfare

　　Maximization in China ……………………………………… Qiang Cui　27

Comparison of Two kinds of Bonus – Malus Systems in Environmental

　　Impairment Liability Insurance ………………………… Dan Yao　Sujin Zheng　37

Collective Credit and Behavior Restriction: the Analysis and Improvement

　　of the Credit Village Assessment for Risk Control in Liuyang, China

　　……………………………………… Lanfeng Li　Duo Fang　Yuling Wu　50

Central Financial Subsidy of Agricultural Insurance in China: the Efficiency and

　　Improvement for the Government ………………… Lanfeng Li　Yaoyuan Zhang　65

Indicators Analysis of Ping An Insurance Group

　　………………………………………………… Huiran Ma　Yumeng Zhou　89

Intuitive Chartist and Chart Intuition ……………………… Yidian Liu　Shuainan Du　108

Research on Underwriting Cycle of Chinese Commercial Property

　　Insurance and the Affected Factors …………………………………… Jing Kang　129

Insurance Group Risks Transmission Mechanism and Risk Management

　　Between the Head Firm and Its Subsidiaries ………………………… Meiyi He　140

An Empirical Investigation of Impact Factors for the Profit Performance of

Regional Life Insurance Market of China ·················· Xiao Wei　Jun Yang　162

Addendum for Three Formulae in Section 3.2 of Lectures on Macroeconomics
·· Zaigui Yang　Mengjie Zhang　177

Rural Consumption, Capital Accumulation and Pension Benefits in China
·· Zaigui Yang　Yuan Cao　183

Effects of China's Enterprise Employee Public Pension on Investment and Consumption ·························· Yan Gao　Zaigui Yang　195

新农保政策变量及人口增长率的优化[①]

杨再贵[②] 曹 园[③]

中央财经大学中国精算研究院/保险学院

【摘要】 本文用外生 OLG 模型,从社会福利最大化的角度,考察新农保政策变量与人口增率的最优政策组合,为今后新农保及城居保合并后城乡居民养老保险的发展提出合理政策建议。结果显示,村集体补助率与地方政府补贴率为互补关系,当人口增长率保持不变时,基础养老金率与缴费补贴率同向变动,且缴费补贴率相对基础养老金率弹性较大。当基础养老金率保持不变时,人口增长率小幅增加会大幅降低缴费补贴率;反之,人口增长率小幅下降会大幅增加缴费补贴率。因此,以调整财政支出结构的形式提高缴费补贴率,使基础养老金率只是略有提升,控制人口增长,确保人口平稳缓慢的下降是利大于弊的。

【关键词】 新农保;政策变量;人口增长率

一、引言

2014 年 2 月 21 日,《国务院关于建立统一的城乡居民养老保险制度的意见》(国发〔2014〕8 号)决定在总结新型农村养老保险(以下简称新农保)和城镇居民社会养老保险(以下简称城居保)试点经验的基础上,将新农保和城居保两项制度合并实施,在全国范围内建立统一的城乡居民养老保险。城乡居民养老保险将沿用新农保的制度模式,坚持和完善社会统筹与个人账户相结合的制度模式,进一步巩固和拓宽个人缴费、集体补助、政府补贴相结合的资金筹集渠道,完善基础养老金和个人账户养老金相结合的待遇支付政策。截至 2012 年底,全国城乡居民养老保险参保人数已达 4.83 亿人,其中城居保参保人数约为 0.23 亿人,新农保参保人数达到 4.6 亿人,可见新农保的制度覆盖面及影响力要远大于城居保,且新农保在发展过程中存在的问题也是城乡居民养老保险发展中需着重解决的问题。因此,本文仍以新农保为研究对象,探索其制度模式的优化路径,从而为城乡居民养老保险的发展提出科学合理的建议。

自我国在"七五"规划中提出了探索研究建立农村社会保障制度以来,我国农村养老保险大致经历了老农保、地方新农保和国家新农保三种制度的变革。每次变革都在努力提升养老保险的保障作用,不断探索合理的财政补贴形式,加大财政补贴的力度。老农保时期资

[①] 北大赛瑟(CCISSR)论坛·2014,北京大学,2014 年 4 月 18 日。感谢教育部人文社会科学重点研究基地重大项目(10JJD790038)、北京市哲学社会科学规划项目(11JGB089)、教育部新世纪优秀人才支持计划(NCET-11-0755)的支持。

[②] 中央财经大学中国精算研究院/保险学院教授。

[③] 中央财经大学保险学院 2013 级博士研究生。

金来源很窄,全靠个人缴费支持,没有财政补贴。地方新农保时期开始强调政府的责任,加大了财政补贴的投入,并在不同地区形成了"进口补"、"出口补"和"进出口"双补贴三种补贴形式。国家新农保是在地方新农保基础上发展而来的,更加强化了政府作用,确定了"进出口"双补贴形式以及各级政府补贴基准。《国务院关于开展新型农村社会养老保险试点的指导意见》(国发〔2009〕32号)规定:新农保基金由个人缴费、集体补助、政府补贴构成。个人缴费标准目前设为每年100元、200元、300元、400元、500元5个档次,地方可根据实际情况增设缴费档次。村集体对参保人缴费的补助标准由村民委员会召开村民会议民主确定。地方政府对参保人缴费的补贴标准不低于每人每年30元;对选择较高档次标准缴费的,可给予适当鼓励,具体标准和办法由省(区、市)人民政府确定。中央确定的基础养老金标准为每人每月55元。地方政府可以根据实际情况提高基础养老金标准,对于长期缴费的农村居民,可适当加发基础养老金,提高和加发部分的资金由地方政府支出。

但目前国家新农保还存在如下问题:大多数参保人缴费都选择最低缴费档次,集体补助和地方政府补贴水平很低,制度的激励机制不足。例如,江西省对缴费补贴统一为国家规定的最低补贴每人每年30元;吉林省长春市根据不同的缴费档次进行补贴但最高不超过50元。村集体经济由于普遍缺乏产品竞争力,随着国家产业升级与结构调整而逐步走向没落,直接导致集体补助乏力。对选择较高档次标准缴费的参保人给予的鼓励力度不够。虽然对基础养老金有加发政策,但加发力度小。如,江西省规定缴费超过15年的,每增加1年缴费,基础养老金增加1元;长春市规定参保人选300元以上缴费档次,连续缴费15年,每增加1年缴费,基础养老金增加1元。如果地方政府补贴、村集体补助对农民高档次缴费、长期缴费无显著激励效果,就不利于制度的可持续发展。因此,新农保在制度全覆盖后应增强激励机制,逐步提高筹资水平和待遇水平。

研究新农保要结合我国的具体情况。首先,新农保待遇有待提高。基础养老金每月55元,按农民人均年纯收入6977.29元计算,基础养老金替代率仅为9.5%。如果农民年缴费200元,缴满15年,替代率为17.8%;如果缴满30年,替代率为22.9%。远低于国际劳工组织建议的基本养老金替代率水平(40%~70%)。其次,尽管新农保对财政资金需求量不高,但是按目前的新农保财政责任划分来看,地方财政负担要重于中央。在地方,县级财政的负担又重于省级与地市级,并随着时间推移,县级负担将进一步加重。

Barro(1974)根据OLG模型证明了只要相邻两代人之间通过遗产相联系,社会保障制度的变化对稳定状态的资本存量就没有任何影响。Samuelson(1975)研究了生命周期增长模型中的最优社会保障,通过社会保障税来调节生产资本,使其达到修正黄金律水平。其求解最优社会保障税的方法是使市场经济的利率等于经济增长率。Blanchard和Fischer(1989)更详细地阐述了关于最优社会保障税的标准和原则,那就是帕累托最优。社会计划者通过合理分配社会资源来使社会福利最大化。虽然他们没有推导政策变量值的计算公式,但这一标准同样适用于中国的养老保险制度。Badu等(1997)用Samuelson(1975)的方法,通过税收手段来调节市场经济的定态资本劳动比,使其达到社会最优的资本劳动比,虽然他们研究的是环境与资源的问题,但他们的方法可以被借鉴来推导中国养老保险的最优政策变量值。Zhang和Zhang(1998)用一个具有各种养儿动机的内生增长OLG模型分析了传统的社会保障对经济增长和人口增长率等变量的影响。不过,这些文献都是基于发达国家经济背景研究现收现付制或者完全积累制养老保险的。

中国实行的是社会统筹与个人账户相结合的部分积累制社会养老保险，用OLG模型研究这一社会养老保险制度的文献也不少。王燕等人（2001）用可计算一般均衡模型分析了中国养老金改革的影响，比较了支付隐性养老金债务和转制成本的各种选择方案，考察了各种改革方案对养老体系可持续性和整个经济增长的影响。杨再贵（2006）用具有生存不确定性的OLG模型分析了中国的部分积累制养老保险，通过控制缴费率来调节市场经济的定态资本劳动比，使其达到社会最优的资本劳动比以实现社会福利最大化，进而寻求最优的个人缴费率和企业缴费率。康传坤（2012）在一般均衡的OLG模型框架下对比分析了城镇企业职工提高养老保险缴费率和推迟退休年龄对人均资本、个人和社会统筹账户养老金水平等的影响。但这些文献研究的都是企业职工基本养老保险，对新农保的研究很少。杨再贵（2011）用OLG模型分析了中国的新农保，考察了个人缴费率、集体补助率、地方政府补贴率和基础养老金率对农民劳动收入增长率、人口增长率、消费率、储蓄率和教育费率的影响。不过，其模型是一个内生增长模型，并且没有从社会福利最大化的角度进行讨论。

本文将建立一个外生的OLG模型，根据新农保制度的实际，不仅考虑个人缴纳养老保险费，而且将村集体补助和政府补贴都纳入模型中，即个人、集体和地方政府都缴纳养老保险费。根据农村的实际情况估计有关参数值，通过控制新农保政策变量以及人口增长率来调节市场经济的定态资本劳动比，使其达到社会最优的资本劳动比以实现社会福利最大化，进而寻求最优的政策变量及人口增长率，就提高新农保的待遇水平和减轻地方财政负担提出政策建议，并为今后城乡居民社会养老保险制度的完善提供参考。

二、模型

本文建立Diamond（1965）式两期OLG模型。在一个封闭经济中，有为数众多的个人、为数众多的自然村和一个政府。每个人的一生分为两个时期：劳动期和退休期。在第 t 期初，有 N_t 个相同的第 t 代的个人成长为劳动者。人口增长率为 $n = N_t/N_{t-1} - 1$。

（一）个人

每个人在劳动期向劳动市场无弹性地提供一单位劳动，取得劳动收入后，缴纳养老保险费，消费收入的一部分，储蓄收入的其余部分。到了退休期，将储蓄的本息、个人账户养老金、基础养老金都用于自身消费。每个人的效用来源于劳动期消费 $c_{1,t}$ 和退休期消费 $c_{2,t+1}$，个人效用最大化问题为：

$$\max_{\{s_t, c_{1,t}, c_{2,T=1}\}} U_t = \ln c_{1,t} + \theta \ln c_{2,t+1} \quad (1)$$

$$s.t. \quad c_{1,t} = (1-\tau)w_t - s_t \quad (2)$$

$$c_{2,t+1} = (1+r_{t+1})s_t + I_{t+1} + J_{t+1} \quad (3)$$

其中，$\theta \in (0, 1)$ 是个人折现因子，$\tau \in (0, 1)$ 是养老保险的个人缴费率，w_t 是劳动收入，s_t 是储蓄，r_{t+1} 是利率，I_{t+1} 是个人账户养老金，J_{t+1} 是基础养老金。该效用最大化的一阶条件为：

$$\theta(1 + r_{t+1})c_{1,t} = c_{2,t+1} \quad (4)$$

该式意味着减少一单位劳动期的消费造成的效用损失，等于增加 $(1 + r_{t+1})$ 单位退休期消费得到的效用增加。

（二）村集体

各村在竞争的市场里都生产同质的产品。用柯布-道格拉斯生产函数 $Y_t = AK_t^\alpha N_t^{1-\alpha}$ 或

$y_t = Ak_t^\alpha$ 刻画生产。其中，Y_t 是 t 期的净产出，K_t 是 t 期初的资本存量，$\alpha \in (0, 1)$ 是资本的收入份额，A 是劳动生产率，y_t 是产出劳动比，$k_t = K_t/N_t$ 是资本劳动比。

以农村居民的劳动总收入为基数，村集体按比率 $\eta \in (0, 1)$ 补助养老保险费，地方政府按比率 $\zeta (0, 1)$ 补贴养老保险费；基础养老金率为 $j \in (0, 1)$[①]。从长期看，集体补助缴费、地方政府补贴缴费以及中央和地方政府联合支付的基础养老金都来源于农民的劳动成果，即劳动所得的一部分。根据产出的分配可得：$AK_t^\alpha N_t^{1-\alpha} = r_t K_t + (1 + \eta + \zeta + j) N_t w_t$。由 Euler 定理，得：

$$r_t = \alpha A k_t^{\alpha - 1} \tag{5}$$

$$w_t = \frac{(1 - \alpha) A k_t^\alpha}{1 + \eta + \zeta + j} \tag{6}$$

（三）政府

政府把农民个人缴纳的养老保险费、集体补助缴费和地方政府补贴缴费都存入个人养老账户，累积本息用于支付农民退休后的个人账户养老金：

$$I_{t+1} = (1 + r_{t+1})(\tau + \eta + \zeta) w_t \tag{7}$$

政府基于劳动一代农民的劳动总收入，按基础养老金率支付退休一代农民的基础养老金：$N_{t-1} J_t = j N_t w_t$，简化为

$$J_t = (1 + n) j w_t \tag{8}$$

（四）资本市场

第 t 期劳动者的储蓄、个人缴纳的养老保险费、村集体补助缴费和地方政府补贴缴费之和构成第 $t + 1$ 期初的资本存量：$K_{t+1} = N_t [s_t + (\tau + \eta + \zeta) w_t]$，即

$$(1 + n) k_{t+1} = s_t + (\tau + \eta + \zeta) w_t \tag{9}$$

（五）动态均衡系统

将式（2）-（3）和（5）-（9）带入式（4）式整理，得下列差分方程所描述的动态均衡系统：

$$k_t^\alpha = \frac{(1 + \eta + \zeta + j)(1 + \theta)(1 + n)}{\theta (1 + \eta + \zeta)(1 - \alpha) A} k_{t+1} + \frac{(1 + n) j k_{t+1}^\alpha}{\theta (1 + \eta + \zeta)(1 + A \alpha k_{t+1}^{\alpha - 1})} \tag{10}$$

假设该动态均衡系统存在唯一、稳定又无振荡的定态均衡。为求稳定条件，将动态系统式（10）围绕定态（k）线性化，经推导，得

$$p(k_{t+1} - j) + q(k_t - k) = 0$$

其中，系数 p、q 是偏导数在定态处的值：

$$p = -\frac{(1 + \eta + \zeta + j)(1 + \theta)(1 + n)}{\theta (1 + \eta + \zeta)(1 - \alpha) A} - \frac{(1 + n) j \alpha k^{\alpha - 1}(1 + A k^{\alpha - 1})}{\theta (1 + \eta + \zeta)(1 + A \alpha k^{\alpha - 1})^2} < 0$$

$$q = \alpha k^{\alpha - 1} > 0$$

存在唯一、稳定又无振荡的定态均衡意味着 $0 < \frac{k_{t+1} - k}{k_t - k} = -\frac{q}{p} < 1$。所以，稳定条件为：

$$p + q < 0$$

[①] 由于各地农民的劳动收入不同，缴费额不同，故模型中将缴费额变量换成缴费率变量更合理。同理，将地方政府补贴额换成地方政府补贴率；将基础养老金额换成基础养老金率。详见杨再贵（2011）。

三、社会最优

将从今往后各世代的代表性个人的效用折现值之和定义为社会福利（Blanchard 和 Fischer，1989；Groezen 等人，2003；也这样定义社会福利函数）：

$$W = \theta \ln c_{20} + \sum_{i=0}^{\infty} \rho^i (\ln c_{1i} + \theta \ln c_{2i+1}) \tag{11}$$

其中 $\rho \in (0, 1)$ 为社会折现因子，反映社会计划者对各代人效用的重视程度。资源约束为：

$$k_i + A k_i^\alpha = (1+n) k_{i+1} + c_{1i} + \theta \frac{c_{2i}}{1+n} \tag{12}$$

初始条件 k_0 已知，终极条件为 $k_\infty = 0$。社会计划者在服从资源约束、初始条件和终极条件下使社会福利最大化。拉格朗日函数为：

$$\begin{aligned}
L = &\cdots \\
&+ \rho^{t-1}(\ln c_{1t-1} + \theta \ln c_{2t}) + \lambda_{t-1} \left[k_{t-1} + A k_{t-1}^\alpha - (1+n) k_t - c_{1t-1} - \theta \frac{c_{2t-1}}{1+n} \right] \\
&+ \rho^t (\ln c_{1t} + \theta \ln c_{2t+1}) + \lambda_t \left[k_t + A k_t^\alpha - (1+n) k_{t+1} - c_{1t} - \theta \frac{c_{2t}}{1+n} \right] \\
&+ \rho^{t+1} (\ln c_{1t+1} + \theta \ln c_{2t+2}) + \lambda_{t+1} \left[k_{t+1} + A k_{t+1}^\alpha - (1+n) k_{t+2} - c_{1t+1} - \theta \frac{c_{2t+1}}{1+n} \right] \\
&+ \cdots
\end{aligned}$$

其中，λ_t 是第 t 期资源约束的拉格朗日乘数。令 L 对 c_{1t}、c_{2t} 和 k_{t+1} 的偏导数为零，并在稳定状态（k^*, c_1^*, c_2^*）整理，得社会福利最大化问题的一阶条件：

$$(1+n) c_1^* = \rho c_2^* \tag{13}$$

$$1 + \alpha A (k^*)^{\alpha-1} = (1+n)/\rho \text{ 或 } k^* = \left(\frac{1+n-\rho}{\alpha A \rho} \right)^{\frac{1}{\alpha-1}} \tag{14}$$

上标 * 代表变量的最优定态值。满足式（14）的资本劳动比处于修正黄金律水平。为了让市场经济的稳定状态实现社会福利最大化，就应通过政策变量的调整、将市场经济稳定状态的资本劳动比调节到修正黄金律水平，即 $k_{t+1} = k_t = k^*$。将式（14）代入式（10），整理得

$$\frac{1+n-\rho}{\alpha A \rho} = \frac{(1+\eta^* + \zeta^* + j^*)(1+\theta)(1+n)}{\theta(1+\eta^* + \zeta^*)(1-\alpha) A} + \frac{(1+n) j^* - \rho j^*}{\theta \alpha A (1+\eta^* + \zeta^*)} \tag{15}$$

可见，政策变量的最优组合取决于个人折现因子 θ、社会折现因子 ρ、资本的收入份额 α 和人口增长率 n。给定任意两个政策变量的最优值，就可求出第三个政策变量的最优值。

四、数值实验

（一）参数设定

由于 OLG 模型通常假定一期的时间跨度在 25 年至 30 年之间，本模型将一期的时间跨度设定为 28 年。类似于 Pecchenino 和 Pollard（2002），本文将个人退休期消费带来效用的每年的折现率设为 0.985，那么一期的折现率为 $\theta = 0.985^{28}$。

发达国家通常取资本的收入份额为 0.3（如 Barro 和 Sala – I – Martin，2004；Zhang et al.，2001）。相对于发达国家，中国劳动力相对便宜，因而劳动的收入份额相对较低，资本的收入份额相对较高，故在中国资本的收入份额 α 可取 0.35。由于本文将考察个人缴费率等五个外生变量对资本劳动比、人均消费和养老金的影响及影响程度，所以可将常数 A 正规化为 1。

人口的统计口径有多种。由于中国城乡的社会保障制度差别明显，本文考察的是农村养老保险制度，故选择"乡村就业人口"作为统计口径。根据 2013 年《中国统计年鉴》，可算出 1984 年至 2012 年期间的就业人口增长率为 $n = 39602/35968 - 1 \approx 10.103\%$。

为估计政策变量的最优组合，必须先估计社会折现因子。由于它反映社会计划者对各代人效用的关注程度，即社会计划者给各代人效用的权重，因此，要通过政策规定来估计。根据国发〔2009〕32 号文件，地方政府对参保人缴费的补贴标准不低于每人每年 30 元；村集体对参保人缴费的补助标准由村民会议民主确定。由于各地政府补贴力度不同而且缺少权威数据，因此假设地方政府每年人均补贴 45 元，则地方政府补贴率 $\zeta^* = 45/6977.29$。集体补助会低于地方政府补贴，因此假设每年人均补助 30 元，则集体补助率 $\eta^* = 30/6977.29$。目前，我国新农保参保人每年人均缴费 183 元，退休农民人均每月领取养老金 82 元（高帆，2013）。按农村居民人均年纯收入 6977.29 元计算，个人缴费率 $\tau = 183/6977.29$，由人均年领养老金 $J = 12 \times 82$ 元和式（8）得基础养老金率 $j^* = J/[(1+n)w] \approx 12.809\%$。以上数值为各外生变量的基准值。将以上基准值代入式（15）反复试算直至等式成立，得 $\rho \approx 0.389672$。

（二）政策变量的优化

由式（10）、（15）可见，η 和 ζ 的作用相同，以上推导中也发现 η 和 ζ 在模型中的功能以及对其他政策变量的反应也一致，并且在其他变量不变的情况下 η 和 ζ 为互补关系，提升 η 会降低 ζ，同样提升 ζ 会降低 η，因此我们将 η 与 ζ 合并为缴费补贴率 δ 进行模拟，$\delta^* = \eta^* + \zeta^* = 1.075\%$。

对政策变量最优组合的模拟测算分两步进行：首先，n 保持基准值不变，分别考察 j^* 提高、不变以及降低三种情况下对应的 δ^*；然后进一步考察当 n 增加和下降时，相应的三组 j^*、δ^* 的对应值。结果如表 1 所示。

表 1　　　　　　　　　　　政策变量的最优组合

n	10.200%			10.103%			10.000%		
j^*	12.850%	12.809%	12.750%	12.850%	12.809%	12.750%	12.850%	12.809%	12.750%
δ^*	1.150%	0.827%	0.363%	1.400%	1.075%	0.611%	1.670%	1.346%	0.879%

由表 1 可知，当人口增长率保持不变时，缴费补贴率与基础养老金率同向变动，且基础养老金率的小幅变动会带来缴费补贴率的大幅变动。当基础养老金率保持不变时，人口增长率小幅增加会大幅降低缴费补贴率；反之，人口增长率小幅下降会大幅增加缴费补贴率。

五、结论

本文用一般均衡的 OLG 模型分析了中国新型农村社会养老保险制度，从社会福利最大化的角度出发，通过政策变量的调整、将市场经济稳定状态的资本劳动比调节到修正黄金律水平，求解了政策变量的最优组合公式。根据新农保实施情况估计模型中有关参数，分析了某些政策变量之间的相互关系，模拟了政策变量具体的最优组合值。主要结果如下：村集体补助率与地方政府补贴率为互补关系，当人口增长率保持不变时，缴费补贴率与基础养老金率同向变动，且缴费补贴率相对基础养老金率变动幅度更大。当基础养老金率保持不变时，人口增长率小幅增加会大幅降低缴费补贴率；反之，人口增长率小幅下降会大幅增加缴费补贴率。

要增强新农保的吸引力，必须强化其激励机制，这就需要从新农保的入口和出口着手，也就是要想方设法加强入口的补助和提高出口的养老金待遇，即提高缴费补贴率、基础养老金率，降低人口增长率。要减轻地方财政负担，就必须控制基础养老金增幅，缓慢降低人口增长率，同时必须加强中央财政的作用，改善当前的财政支出结构。结合我国实际以及新农保实施情况，综合考量外生变量相互之间的影响程度，可提出一个很有意义的政策建议：以调整财政支出结构的形式提高缴费补贴率，使基础养老金率只是略有提升，控制人口增长，确保人口平稳缓慢地下降。

由（8）式可知，基础养老金率与人口增长率及农村居民年人均纯收入有关，因此，中央可根据人口增长率与农村居民年人均纯收入建立基础养老金最低标准正常调整机制，确保基础养老金率小幅增加。要提高缴费补贴额，同时减轻地方财政负担，可通过调整现行财政支出结构来实现。首先，地方政府加发的基础养老金可降低增速甚至暂时不调增，节约的资金相应地用于增加对个人缴费的补贴，也就是将部分对新农保制度出口的补贴转变为对进口的补贴。其次，有条件的村集体经济组织应当对参保人缴费给予补助，可以拓宽筹资渠道，如通过其他社会经济组织、公益慈善组织、个人为参保人缴费提供资助，村集体补助增加便可减少地方政府补贴，减轻地方政府负担。再次，由于对基础养老金增幅要求很低，中央政府可将计划调增的基础养老金额转移划拨给地方政府，提高地方政府补贴额。通过以上几点当农村居民看见政府增加了对参保人缴费的补贴，个人缴费越多政府补贴也越多，参保人就能体会到自身利益的增长，并增加对未来养老金的信心，从而自觉提高缴费档次，实现个人缴费率的提高。

当基础养老金率不变时，人口增长率的增加会降低缴费补贴率，从而弱化地方政府的补贴力度，降低居民参保积极性，不利于制度的可持续发展；人口增长率降低会增加缴费补贴率，提高居民养老保险的待遇水平，促进参保率的提高，但人口增长率下降过快会急剧增加财政负担，特别是地方政府财政负担。根据《中国统计年鉴》显示，自1997年以来，我国农村就业人口逐年下降，已从1997年的49039万人，下降至2012年的39602万人，且降幅呈增加趋势，这会引起地方政府补贴的大幅增加，使地方政府面临过重的支付负担。但随着人口政策的适度放开，如单独二孩政策的逐步执行，必然会缓解人口下降趋势，从而一定程度地缓解地方财政压力，推进新农保制度持续发展。因此要控制人口增长的同时，避免人口快速减少，确保人口平稳缓慢下降。

参考文献

1. Badu, R. G., K. S. KaviKumar and N. S. Murthy, 1997, "An overlapping generations model with exhaustible resources and stock pollution", *Ecological Economics* 21, 35–43.

2. Barro R. J., 1974, "Are government bonds net wealth?", *Journal of Political Economy* 82, 1095 – 1117.

3. Blanchard O. J. and Fischer S., 1989, *Lectures on Macroeconomics*, London: MIT Press.

4. Barro R. J. and Sala – I – Martin X., 2004, *Economic Growth*, Cambridge: MIT Press.

5. Pecchenino R., and Pollard P., 2002 "Dependent children and aged parents: funding education and social security in an aging economy", *Journal of Macroeconomics* 24, 145 – 169.

6. Groezen, B., T. Leers and L Meijdam, 2003, "Social security and endogenous fertility: pensions and child allowances as siamese twins", *Journal of Public Economics* 87, 233 – 251.

7. Samuelson, P. A., 1975, "Optimum social security in a life – cycle growth model". *International Economic Review* 16, 539 – 544.

8. Zhang J. and Zhang J., 1998, "Social security, intergenerational transfers, and endogenous growth", *The Canadian Journal of Economics* 31, 1225 – 1241.

9. Zhang J., Zhang J., and Lee R., 2001, "Mortality Decline and Long – Run Economic Growth", *Journal of Public Economics* 80: 485 – 507.

10. 高帆."新型农村和城镇居民社会养老保险基本情况",城乡居民社会养老保险制度研讨会,2013.

11. 康传坤."提高缴费率还是推迟退休",《统计研究》,2012(12):59 – 68 页.

12. 王燕、徐滇庆、王直、翟凡."中国养老金隐性债务、转轨成本、改革方式及其影响",《经济研究》,2001(5):3 – 12 页.

13. 杨再贵."人口增长率、平均预期寿命与养老保险最优费率",中国社会保障论坛 2006 年会.和谐社会与社会保障.中国劳动社会保障出版社,2006.9:753 – 759 页.

14. 杨再贵."新农保、农民收入与内生增长",《十二五·新挑战:经济社会综合风险管理——北大赛瑟(CCISSR)论坛文集》,2011(4):356 – 369 页.

15. 杨再贵,公共养老金的 OLG 模型分析:原理和应用.北京:光明日报出版社,2010.

养老保险缴费率与个人账户实账率的优化[①]

高 彦[②] 杨再贵[③]

中央财经大学中国精算研究院/保险学院

【摘要】 本文用一般均衡的 OLG 模型分析我国企业职工基本养老保险制度，通过考察政策变量对内生变量的影响并基于社会福利最大化标准，求解政策变量的最优组合，考察劳动人口增长率对最优的个人账户实账率的影响。综合这些影响和经济目标，采取提高个人账户实账率、降低企业缴费率和提高个人缴费率的措施，能够提高企业退休人员养老金和扩大内需。若最优的个人缴费率取 10%，最优的企业缴费率取 18%，那么最优的个人账户实账率约为 83%。最优的个人账户实账率与劳动人口增长率同方向变化。

【关键词】 养老保险；缴费率；个人账户实账率；最优化

一、引言

《国务院关于完善企业职工基本养老保险制度的决定》（国发〔2005〕38号）明确提出：为与做实个人账户相衔接，从 2006 年 1 月 1 日起，个人账户的规模统一由职工缴费工资的 11% 调整为 8%，全部由个人缴费形成，单位缴费不再划入个人账户。该文件发布以来全国有十几个省份进行了做实个人账户试点，人力资源和社会保障部也组织科研力量进行了基本养老保险个人账户做实及其基金运营管理的专项研究，但个人账户资产不实的问题（常被称为空账运行）依然严重。中国社会科学院发布的《中国养老金发展报告 2012》显示：2011 年底，全国企业职工基本养老保险个人账户为 2.5 万亿元，但个人账户实有资金 2703 亿元，空账金额达 2.2 万亿元。意味着个人缴纳的社会养老保险费进入个人账户的比例仅为 10.8%，可称之为个人账户实账率。广东省是养老保险基金结余最多的省份，但是其个人账户实账率也只有 75.8%，离做实个人账户还有不小差距。

人力资源和社会保障部 2013 年第三季度新闻发布会上传出了主管部门的声音：我国统账结合的基本养老保险制度模式还要坚持，要继续做实个人账户。推进个人账户做实会对养老金待遇、居民消费和资本积累等产生什么影响以及影响程度如何？这关系到企业退休人员的切身利益，关系到人口老龄化高峰期养老金支付的巨大压力，也关系到后金融危机时代国民经济平稳、持续、健康发展。首先，企业退休人员的养老金水平低于机关事业单位退休人

[①] 北大赛瑟（CCISSR）论坛·2014，北京大学，2014 年 4 月 18 日。感谢教育部人文社会科学重点研究基地重大项目（10JJD790038）、北京市哲学社会科学规划项目（11JGB089）、教育部新世纪优秀人才支持计划（NCET-11-0755）的支持。

[②] 中央财经大学保险学院 2013 级博士生。

[③] 中央财经大学中国精算研究院/保险学院教授。

员的养老金水平。近十年来,中国政府每年都在增加企业退休人员养老金。这方面虽然取得了明显的进步,但离企业职工的期望仍有不小差距。进一步缩小企业退休人员与机关事业单位退休人员养老金水平的差距是今后努力的方向。其次,国际金融危机后世界经济增长乏力,复苏缓慢。中国经济受其影响,近两年的增长率也明显回落。虽然经济发展的质量和效率受到空前重视,但发展速度也必须重视,因为它关系到劳动就业和社会稳定。为保持我国经济平稳持续健康发展,在后金融危机时代主要得靠扩大内需,包括消费需求和投资需求。

国外用 OLG 模型 (overlapping – generations model) 研究社会养老保险与养老金水平、居民消费和资本积累的文献不胜枚举,如 Diamond (1965)[1], Barro (1974)[2], Feldstein (1974)[3], Blanchard 和 Fischer (1989)[4], Fuster (2000)[5]等等。这些研究都是基于发达国家的经济背景和公共养老金制度,包括现收现付制和完全积累制养老金。它们的一个共同特点是模型中只有个人缴纳养老保险费、没有企业缴费。Yang (2009)[6]研究了中国的社会统筹与个人账户相结合的部分积累制公共养老金,而且考虑了个人和企业都缴纳养老保险费,但是模型中没有考虑个人账户做实的问题。

国内也有不少用 OLG 模型研究社会养老保险的文献,如,王燕等人 (2001),杨再贵 (2009, 2011)[7][8],等等。这些研究虽然没有考察做实个人账户问题,但对本文的研究很有启发。田银华和龙朝阳 (2008)[9]用内生增长模型分析了公共养老保险计划对个人消费和储蓄的影响。但他们分析的是现收现付制养老保险,不同于中国的部分积累制养老保险。杨再贵 (2010)[10]研究了企业缴费和个人缴费分别进入社会统筹账户和个人账户的比例与缴费率的最优组合,但其模型是建立在《国务院关于建立统一的企业职工基本养老保险制度的决定》(国发 [1997] 26 号) 的基础上。本文将以《国务院关于完善企业职工基本养老保险制度的决定》(国发 [2005] 38 号) 为依据来建立模型,符合正在施行的基本养老保险制度。

Samuelson (1975)[11]通过社会保障税调节资本劳动比,使其达到修正黄金律水平 (modified golden rule level),以求解最优的社会保障税。Blanchard 和 Fischer (1989) 详细阐述了 Samuelson (1975) 关于最优社会保障税的求解方法,即社会计划者通过合理分配社会资源使社会福利最大。该方法可用来研究中国基本养老保险政策变量的最优组合,求解政策变量的最优值。

正视个人账户资产不实的现状,本文用 OLG 模型分析中国的企业职工基本养老保险制度。基于社会福利最大化标准求解政策变量的最优组合,寻求个人账户实账率的优化并考察个人账户实账率随劳动人口增长率的变化。本文与以往研究的明显不同,是基于国发 [2005] 38 号文件规定的部分积累制养老保险,显性引入做实个人账户的因素。

二、模型

在一个封闭经济中,有为数众多的个人、企业和一个政府。每个人的寿命都是有限的,都经历了工作期和退休期 (通常假设一期为 25~30 年,本文设定每期 28 年)。本文采用 Diamond (1965) 两期 OLG 模型。在第 t 期初有 N_t 个相同的第 t 世代的个人成长为劳动者。劳动者增长率为 $n = \frac{N_t}{N_{t-1}} - 1$。

（一）个人

每个人都生存两个时期：工作期和退休期。在工作期，每个人向劳动市场无弹性地提供一单位劳动，取得工资收入，缴纳养老保险费，消费可支配收入的一部分，储蓄其余部分。到了退休期，每个人将其工作期储蓄的本息、得到的个人账户养老金和社会统筹养老金都用于消费。每个人都从其工作期消费 c_{1t} 和 $c_{2,t+1}$ 退休期消费中得到满足，用相对风险厌恶恒定的效用函数（constant relative risk aversion utility function）来反映效用水平。个人选择储蓄和两期消费使效用最大，因此，个人的效用最大化问题为：

$$\max_{\{c_{1t},c_{2,t+1},s_t\}} U_t = \frac{c_{1,t}^{1-\sigma}}{1-\sigma} + \theta \frac{c_{2,t+1}^{1-\sigma}}{1-\sigma}, \sigma > 0, \sigma \neq 1 \quad (1)$$

$$s.t. \quad c_{1,t} = (1-\tau)w_t - s_t \quad (2)$$

$$c_{2,t+1} = (1+r_{t+1})s_t + I_{t+1} + P_{t+1} \quad (3)$$

其中 $\theta \in (0,1)$ 是折现因子，σ 是相对风险厌恶系数，τ 是养老保险个人缴费率，w_t 是工资，s_t 是储蓄，r_{t+1} 是利率，I_{t+1} 是个人账户养老金，P_{t+1} 是社会统筹养老金。该效用最大化问题的一阶条件为：

$$[\theta(1+r_{t+1})]^{\frac{1}{\sigma}} c_{1t} = c_{2t+1} \quad (4)$$

该式意味着减少一单位工作期的消费造成的效用损失，等于增加 $(1+r_{t+1})$ 单位退休期消费得到的效用增加。

（二）企业

各企业在竞争的市场里都生产同质的产品，用柯布－道格拉斯生产函数 $Y_t = AK_t^\alpha N_t^{1-\alpha}$ 或 $y_t = Ak_t^\alpha$ 来描述生产。其中 Y_t 是第 t 期的净产出，K_t 是第 t 期初的资本存量，y_t 是产出劳动比，$k_t = \frac{K_t}{N_t}$ 是资本劳动比。

各企业基于工资总额按费率 $\eta \in (0,1)$ 缴纳养老保险费。由净产出的分配可得：$AK_t^\alpha N_t^{1-\alpha} = r_t K_t + (1+\eta)w_t N_t$。企业在市场中竞争地运作，根据 Euler 定理，得：

$$r_t = \alpha A k_t^{\alpha-1} \quad (5)$$

$$w_t = \frac{(1-\alpha)Ak_t^\alpha}{1+\eta} \quad (6)$$

（三）政府

由于个人账户被统筹账户透支用于支付当期退休人员的养老金，因此只有个人缴费的一部分进入了个人账户。假设个人缴费进入个人账户的比例即个人账户实账率为 $v \in (0,1)$，则：

$$I_{t+1} = (1+r_{t+1})v\tau w_t \quad (7)$$

全部企业缴费和大部分个人缴费都用于支付当期退休人员的养老金：$N_{t-1}P_t = N_t[(1-v)\tau+\eta]w_t$，简化为

$$P_t = (1+n)[(1-v)\tau+\eta]w_t \quad (8)$$

（四）资本市场

第 t 期劳动者的储蓄和进入个人账户的个人缴费构成第 $t+1$ 期初的资本存量：

$$s_t + v\tau w_t = (1+n)k_{t+1} \quad (9)$$

（五）动态均衡系统

该经济的一个竞争均衡是在已知初始条件（k_0）和政策参数 τ、η 和 υ 的情况下，各期变量都满足式（1）-（9）的数列 $\{c_{1t}, c_{2t+1}, s_t, w_t, r_t, I_{t+1}, P_t, k_{t+1}\}_{t=0}^{\infty}$。

将式（2）、（3）和式（6）-（9）代入式（4），得下列差分方程所描写的动态均衡系统：

$$[\theta(1+\alpha A k_{t+1}^{\alpha-1})]^{\frac{1}{\sigma}} \left[(1-\tau+\upsilon\tau)\frac{(1-\alpha)A k_t^{\alpha}}{1+\eta} - (1+n)k_{t+1}\right]$$

$$= (1+\alpha A k_{t+1}^{\alpha-1})(1+n)k_{t+1} + (1+n)\frac{(1-\upsilon)\tau+\eta}{1+\eta}(1-\alpha)A k_{t+1}^{\alpha} \quad (10)$$

假设该动态均衡系统存在唯一、稳定又无振荡的定态均衡。这意味着微分 dk_{t+1}/dk_t 在定态（k）处的值大于0而小于1。为求该系统的稳定条件，将式（10）对 k_{t+1} 和 k_t 微分，得：

$$i dk_{t+1} + j dk_t = 0 \quad (11)$$

其中，系数 i、j 是偏导数在定态处的值：

$$i = \frac{1}{\sigma}[\theta(1+\alpha A K^{\alpha-1})]^{\frac{1-\sigma}{\sigma}} \times \theta A \alpha(\alpha-1)k^{\alpha-2} \times \left[(1-\tau+\upsilon\tau)\frac{(1-\alpha)A k^{\alpha}}{1+\eta} - (1+n)k\right]$$

$$- [\theta(1+\alpha A K^{\alpha-1})]^{\frac{1}{\sigma}}(1+n) - (1+n)(1+\alpha^2 A k^{\alpha-1}) - (1+n)(1-\alpha)\alpha A k^{\alpha-1}\frac{\tau-\upsilon\tau+\eta}{1+\eta}$$

$$j = [\theta(1+\alpha A K^{\alpha-1})]^{\frac{1}{\sigma}}(1-\tau+\upsilon\tau)\frac{(1-\alpha)A\alpha}{1+\eta}k^{\alpha-1} > 0$$

因为 $0 < dk_{t+1}/dk_t = -j/i < 1$，所以该动态均衡系统的稳定条件为 $i+j<0$。

三、帕累托最优

在均衡系统式（10）收敛于定态后，考察企业缴费率、个人缴费率和个人账户实账率对资本劳动比等内生变量的影响。可得：提高个人账户实账率会增加资本劳动比、人均消费和养老金；提高企业缴费率和个人缴费率都会减少资本劳动比和人均消费、增加养老金。所以通过调节政策变量可将资本劳动比调整到修正黄金律水平使社会福利达到最大。

（一）社会福利最大化

政策变量会影响资本劳动比就会影响其他内生变量，所以通过调节政策变量可将资本劳动比调整到修正黄金律水平使社会福利达到最大。将从今往后各世代的代表性个人的效用折现值之和定义为社会福利（Blanchard 和 Fischer，1989；Groezen 等人，2003；也这样定义社会福利函数）：

$$W = \theta \frac{c_{2,0}^{1-\sigma}}{1-\sigma} + \sum_{i=0}^{\infty} \rho^i \left(\frac{c_{1,i}^{1-\sigma}}{1-\sigma} + \theta \frac{c_{2,i+1}^{1-\sigma}}{1-\sigma}\right) \quad (12)$$

其中 $\rho \in (0,1)$ 是社会折现因子，反映社会计划者对各代人效用的关注和重视的程度。资源约束为

$$k_i + A k_i^{\alpha} = (1+n)k_{i+1} + c_{1i} + c_{2i}/(1+n) \quad (13)$$

初始条件 k_0 已知，终极条件为 $k_{\infty}=0$。社会计划者在服从资源约束、初始条件和终极条件的情况下使社会福利最大。构造相应的 Lagrange 函数：

$$L = \cdots$$

$$+ \rho^{t-1}\left(\frac{c_{1t-1}^{1-\sigma}}{1-\sigma} + \theta\frac{c_{2t}^{1-\sigma}}{1-\sigma}\right) + \lambda_{t-1}\left[k_{t-1} + Ak_{t-1}^{\alpha} - (1+n)k_t - c_{1t-1} - \frac{c_{2t-1}}{1+n}\right]$$

$$+ \rho^{t}\left(\frac{c_{1t}^{1-\sigma}}{1-\sigma} + \theta\frac{c_{2t+1}^{1-\sigma}}{1-\sigma}\right) + \lambda_{t}\left[k_{t} + Ak_{t}^{\alpha} - (1+n)k_{t+1} - c_{1t} - \frac{c_{2t}}{1+n}\right]$$

$$+ \rho^{t+1}\left(\frac{c_{1t+1}^{1-\sigma}}{1-\sigma} + \theta\frac{c_{2t+2}^{1-\sigma}}{1-\sigma}\right) + \lambda_{t+1}\left[k_{t+1} + Ak_{t+1}^{\alpha} - (1+n)k_{t+2} - c_{1t+1} - \frac{c_{2t+1}}{1+n}\right]$$

$$+ \cdots$$

其中，λ_t 是第 t 期资源约束的拉格朗日乘数。令 L 对 c_{1t}、c_{2t} 和 k_{t+1} 的偏导数为零，并在稳定状态（k^*, c_1^*, c_2^*）整理，得社会福利最大化问题的一阶条件：

$$(1+n)\theta c_1^{*\sigma} = \rho c_2^{*\sigma} \tag{14}$$

$$1 + \alpha A(k^*)^{\alpha-1} = \frac{1+n}{\rho} \quad \text{或者} \quad k^* = \left(\frac{1+n-\rho}{\rho\alpha A}\right)^{\frac{1}{\alpha-1}} \tag{15}$$

上标 * 代表变量的最优定态值。满足式（15）的资本劳动比处于修正黄金律水平。为了让市场经济的稳定状态实现社会福利最大化，就应通过政策变量的调整、将市场经济稳定状态的资本劳动比调节到修正黄金律水平，即 $k_{t+1} = k_t = k = k^*$。将式（15）代入式（10），整理得

$$\frac{\varphi(1 - \tau^* + v^*\tau^*) - (1+n)(\tau^* - v^*\tau^* + \eta^*)}{1 + \eta^*} = \frac{\alpha(1+n)(1+n+\rho\varphi)}{(1-\alpha)(1+n-\rho)} \tag{16}$$

其中 $\varphi = \left[\theta\frac{1+n}{\rho}\right]^{\frac{1}{\sigma}}$。可见，政策变量的最优组合取决于个人折现因子 θ、社会折现因子 ρ、资本的收入份额 α 和人口增长率 n。给定任意两个政策变量的最优值，就可求出第三个政策变量的最优值。

（二）政策变量的优化

先设定参数。发达国家通常取资本的收入份额为 0.3（如 Barro 和 Sala-I-Martin，2004[12]；Zhang[13] 等人，2001；等等）。中国的劳动力相对便宜，因而劳动的收入份额相对较低，资本的收入份额比发达国家的高。因此在中国，资本的收入份额 α 取 0.35 比较合适。

关于人口的统计口径有多种，由于中国的社会保障制度是城乡分割的，本文考察的是城镇职工实行的养老保险制度，所以选择《中国统计年鉴》"城镇就业人口"这一统计口径。由于 OLG 模型通常假定一期的时间跨度在 25 年至 30 年之间，故本模型设定 28 年为一期。根据《中国统计年鉴》中 1982 年全国第三次人口普查和 2010 年全国第六次人口普查中城镇就业人员数，计算出 28 年间城镇就业人员的增长率 $n = \frac{346870000}{114280000} - 1 = 2.03526$。

根据 Pecchenino 和 Pollard（2002）[14]，将个人效用每年的折现因子设为 0.98，那么一期的折现因子为 $\theta = 0.98^{28} = 0.567976$。根据 Blanchard 和 Fischer（1989）和 Miyazato（2010）[15]，σ 取值为 2。由于这里希望看到的是资本劳动比、人均消费和养老金等内生变量随政策变量如何相对变动，所以可将常数 A 正规化为 1。

根据 2005 年 12 月出台的《国务院关于完善企业职工基本养老保险制度的决定》，确定我国企业缴费率 $\eta = 20\%$，个人缴费率 $\tau = 8\%$。根据中国社会科学院发布的《中国养老金发展报告 2012》：2011 年底，全国城镇职工基本养老保险个人账户为 2.5 万亿元，但是个人

账户实有资金 2703 亿元。可估计出个人账户实账率 $v \approx 10.812\%$。

由于社会折现因子反映社会计划者对各代人效用的关注程度，即社会计划者给各代人效用的权重，因此要通过政策规定来估计。由《国务院关于完善企业职工基本养老保险制度的决定》和《国务院关于完善企业职工基本养老保险制度的决定》可知社会计划者认为的政策变量最优值：$\tau^* = 8\%$，$\eta^* = 20\%$，$v^* = 100\%$。将以上参数基准值代入式（16）反复试算直至等式成立，得 $\rho \approx 0.18193$。以上取值为参数的基准值。

其他参数取基准值，将 τ^* 由 9% 提高到 10%，分别模拟 η^* 由 19% 下降到 18% 时对应的 v^*，结果如表1所示。当最优的个人缴费率上升、最优的企业缴费率下降时，最优的个人账户实账率会降低。若最优的个人缴费率取 10%，最优的企业缴费率取 18%，那么最优的个人账户实账率为 83%。原因在于两个缴费率对后者的影响程度不同，v^* 对 η^* 的弹性远远大于 v^* 对 τ^* 的弹性，说明最优企业缴费率对最优个人账户实账率的影响远远大于最优个人缴费率的影响。必须指出，即使在提高最优个人缴费率、降低最优企业缴费率时，最优个人账户实账率会降低，但其数值也远远高于目前实际的约 10.8% 的个人账户实账率。

表1　政策变量的最优组合

τ^*	η^*	v^*	v^* 对 η^* 的弹性	v^* 对 τ^* 的弹性
9%	19%	91%	198%	—
9%	18%	81%	—	10%
10%	19%	92%	178%	—
10%	18%	83%	—	21%

劳动人口增长率对最优的个人账户实账率也有影响。为考察该影响，求 v^* 对 n 的偏导。可以证明该偏导数的正负取决于有关参数值的大小，故通过模拟来检验。城镇劳动人口目前还呈下降趋势，假设每期的劳动人口增长率从 2.06 按间隔 0.03 逐渐降到 1.94，τ^* 取 10%，η^* 取 18%，其他参数取基准值，模拟结果如表2所示。可见，最优的个人账户实账率与劳动人口增长率同方向变化。在城镇劳动人口增长率下降的情况下，最优的个人账户实账率可低于 83%。若劳动人口增长率超过现期 2.03 的水平，最优的个人账户实账率则应高于 83%。

表2　不同人口增长率对应的 v^*

n	2.06	2.03	2.00	1.97	1.94
τ^*	85%	83%	81%	80%	78%

六、结论与政策建议

针对我国企业职工基本养老保险中个人账户资产不实的情况，本文用 OLG 模型分析了这一统账结合的部分积累制养老保险。通过考察企业缴费率、个人缴费率和个人账户实账率对资本劳动比、人均消费和养老金的影响，求解了政策变量的最优组合，考察了劳动人口增长率对最优的个人账户实账率的影响。本文明确引入个人账户做实的因素，突出反映通过提高个人账户实账率来增加企业退休人员养老金。

结果如下：提高个人账户实账率会增加资本劳动比、人均消费和养老金；提高企业缴费率和个人缴费率都会减少资本劳动比和人均消费、增加养老金。因此，要增加退休人员养老金，就有必要提高个人缴费率、个人账户实账率和企业缴费率；要增加消费需求，就有必要降低企业缴费率和个人缴费率，提高个人账户实账率；要增加投资需求，也有必要降低企业缴费率和个人缴费率，提高个人账户实账率。

中国政府表示要继续提高企业退休人员养老金，进一步缩小其与机关事业单位退休人员养老金水平的差距。受国际金融危机拖累，中国经济还存在下行风险，为保持我国经济平稳健康持续发展，需要扩大内需。由上述结果可见，采取提高个人账户实账率、降低企业缴费率和提高个人缴费率的政策措施，能够增加养老金、消费和投资，有利于提高企业退休人员养老金和国内需求。降低企业缴费率对养老金的负面影响可被提高个人账户实账率的正面影响所覆盖，况且提高个人缴费率对养老金的正面影响比个人账户实账率的更大，因而提高个人账户实账率、降低企业缴费率和提高个人缴费率三者的总效果是大大增加养老金。提高个人缴费率对消费和投资的负面影响又远不及降低企业缴费率的正面影响，另外还有提高个人账户实账率的正面影响，因而提高个人账户实账率、降低企业缴费率和提高个人缴费率总体上会大大增加消费和投资。

政策变量的最优组合取决于个人折现因子、社会折现因子、资本的收入份额和就业人口增长率。当最优的个人缴费率上升、最优的企业缴费率下降时，最优的个人账户实账率会降低。若最优的个人缴费率取 10%，最优的企业缴费率取 18%，那么最优的个人账户实账率为 83%。劳动人口增长率对最优的个人账户实账率也有影响。最优的个人账户实账率与劳动人口增长率同方向变化。在劳动人口增长率下降的情况下，最优的个人账户实账率可低于 83%，意味着个人账户可不急于马上完全做实。当夫妇一方为独生子女可生第二胎的政策起作用、出现城镇劳动人口增长率反弹时，最优的个人账户实账率也应递增。若劳动人口增长率超过现期的水平，最优的个人账户实账率则应高于 83%。如果劳动人口增长率继续上升、一旦需要个人账户实账率超过 100%，那么超出个人缴费的资金就应由财政给予补贴。从做实个人账户的试点来看，财政补贴是必不可少的。

参考文献：

1. Diamond, P. A., 1965, "National debt in a neoclassical growth model", *American Economic Review* 55: 1126–1150.

2. Barro, R. J., 1974, "Are government bonds net wealth?" *Journal of Political Economy* 82: 1095–1117.

3. Feldstein, M., 1974, "Social security, induced retirement, and aggregate capital accumulation", *Journal of Political Economy* 82: 905–926.

4. Blanchard, O. J. and S. Fischer, 1989, *Lectures on Macroeconomics*, London: MIT Press.

5. Fuster, L., 2000, "Capital accumulation in an economy with dynasties and uncertain lifetimes", *Review of Economic Dynamics* 3: 650–674.

6. Yang, Z., 2009, "Urban public pension, replacement rates and population growth rate in China", *Insurance: Mathematics and Economics* 45 (2): 230–235.

7. 王燕、徐滇庆、王直、翟凡. 中国养老金隐性债务、转轨成本、改革方式及其影响, 经济研究, 第5期, 3–12页, 2001.

8. 杨再贵. 城镇社会养老保险、人口出生率与内生增长, 统计研究, 第26卷第5期, 77–81页, 2009.

9. 杨再贵. 不定寿命条件下城镇公共养老金最优替代率的理论与实证研究, 管理评论, 第23卷第2期, 28–32页, 2011.

10. 田银华、龙朝阳. 论公共养老金计划对个人消费和储蓄的影响, 消费经济, 第24卷第1期, 35–38页, 2008.

11. 杨再贵. 公共养老金的OLG模型分析：原理和应用. 北京：光明日报出版社, 2010.

12. Samuelson, P. A., (1975), "Optimum social security in a life-cyclegrowth model", *International Economic Review* 16: 539–544.

13. Barro, R. J., X. Sala-I-Martin. *Economic Growth*. Cambridge: MIT Press, 2004.

14. Zhang, J., J. Zhang, and R. Lee. 2001, "Mortality Decline and Long-Run Economic Growth", *Journal of Public Economics*, 80: 485–507.

15. Pecchenino, R. and P. Pollard, 2002, "Dependent children and agedparents: funding education and social security in an aging economy", *Journal ofMacroeconomics* 24: 145–169.

16. Miyazato, N., (2010), "The optimal size of Japan's public pensions: An analysis considering the risks of longevity and volatility of return on assets", *Japan and the World Economy* 22: 31–39.

保险告知义务规则的最新发展及其启示[①]

张 虹[②]

【摘要】 保险告知义务的传统规则的两大特征是投保人的自动申告义务和对于违反告知义务的"全赔或全不赔"救济原则。当代最新保险立法确立的书面询问主义的立法原则,以及比例原则等补偿性救济方法,有利于在保险人和被保险人之间达成一种公平的利益均衡,既维护了保险人的合法利益而不施加不必要的限制,又确保保险能达到潜在消费者的合理预期,进而增强对保险业的信任。

【关键词】 保险告知义务;自动申告;书面询问;全赔或全不赔原则;补偿性救济方法

投保人的告知义务,特别是在缔结保险合同时的告知义务,一直是保险法发展中的一个重要问题,在各国最新保险立法中仍保持着重要的地位。关于保险告知义务的制度内容一般涉及告知义务主体、告知义务内容、告知义务的时间、告知义务违反之构成以及违反这一义务的法律后果等方面。在这些方面,各国由于政治、经济、历史文化以及法律传统的不同,相关规范有很大的差异。有关告知义务的规则,与保险合同法的其他许多重大问题一样,近年来有不少国家出现了相当多的立法活动,特别值得注意的是,在欧盟层面上,为了建立内部统一的保险市场的需要,由"欧洲保险合同法重述"项目组起草了"欧洲保险合同法原则"(Principles of European Insurance Contract Law,简称PEICL),[③] 作为欧洲立法机构的保险合同示范法。虽然PEICL并不具有强制约束力,其性质是可供保险合同当事人选择的文件,但它代表协调保险合同法的最新进展,其规定也反映了欧洲最新保险立法发展趋势。鉴于欧盟法律体制的特殊性,其立法精神和原则必将对各成员国国内立法产生深刻影响。事实上,从英国法律委员会2009年提出的《消费者保险法(先合同披露与不实告知)》的立法报告[④]中就可以看到这一文件的鲜明影响。

本文拟以此为中心,就有关保险告知义务及其违反后果的规则在传统立法与当代最新立法之间进行对比研究,着眼于其间的差异,剖析其中的法理,从而得出启示,以期对中国保险立法的进一步完善与保险业的发展有所裨益。

一、从投保人的自动申告到保险人的书面询问

各国保险法一般都规定投保人在订立保险合同时负有告知义务,并规定了违反这一义务

[①] 此文为作者参加北京市金融服务法学研究会2014年年会"市场化、法治化背景下金融服务法创新与发展研讨会"所提交的论文。

[②] 中央财经大学保险学院副教授。

[③] "欧洲保险合同法原则"(PEICL)于2007年12月首次出版并提交欧盟委员会,2009年8月再版。

[④] Consumer Insurance Law: Pre-contract Disclosure and Misrepresentation, Law Com. No. 319, December 2009.

的后果。从法理上讲,保险告知义务的依据在于最大诚信原则。① 由于保险合同是一种特殊类型的合同,投保人与保险人订立合同的目的在于将其财产或人身所面临的危险转移至保险人,保险人向投保人收取的保险费的多少,取决于保险人对其承保的危险的正确估计;保险人是否愿意承保危险,同样也取决于其对危险发生程度的正确估计;即使保险人同意承保风险,仍然有必要在保险单承保的风险范围内,能够依照其对风险的判断采取控制风险发生的措施。② 因此,在保险合同订立前,投保人应当如实告知有关标的危险的重要事实。如果投保人没有适当履行告知义务,致使保险人在没能对风险有正确评估的情况下缔结保险合同,实质上就是双方订约时意思表示有瑕疵,投保人依法要承担相应的不利法律后果。

关于保险告知义务的传统制度的首要规则是对投保人施加自动申告风险特征的义务。依此义务,投保人对重要事实的告知不以保险人所询问的范围为限,在询问范围之外,投保人所知或应知的重要事实也应当自动披露和告知。在保险事业发展初期,囿于通讯、交通、检测技术等收集信息手段的落后状况,各国保险法不得已采自动申告主义的立法政策,实属无奈之举。③ 采取这种立法政策的典型代表为英国。在英国,通常认为,"投保单所列的任何问题被推定为具有重要性,但不能做出相反的推定,即投保单未提及的事项不具有重要性,因此,无论保险人在投保单中是否插入问题,保险人均受告知义务立法意旨的保护"。④ 后来,随着技术手段的发达,这一自动申告的制度被认为给投保人施加了一种不合理的负担,因为投保人几乎总是风险评估问题的门外汉。在许多法律制度中,这个规则逐渐为一种"询问表"制度所取代。即由保险人书面提出一系列询问,要求投保人如实准确回答。正如我国台湾保险法学者江朝国先生所说,"重大事项之判断困难性亦众所皆知。尤其对要保人而言,身为外行人,如何善尽诚信原则,倾其所知,知无不言,实比登天还难。因此,立法技术之演进即由'自动申告主义'转为'书面询问主义',以限制要保人之告知说明范围"。⑤

书面询问主义立法例以德国保险合同法和中国台湾地区保险法为代表。⑥ 书面询问主义在立法技术上的进步体现在以下三个方面:首先,在实体法上,通过书面询问形式解决和明确了投保人告知义务的范围,使其有所遵从,不致陷入不测损害,其立法技术特征是列出的问题推定具有重要性,反之,未列出的问题推定不具有重要性。其次,在诉讼法意义上,书面证据的保全功能避免了当事人之间因举证困难而陷入的麻烦。最后,要求保险人加强危险管理和提高注意程度,最大限度地将凡是影响其承保危险估计的一切因素纳入其规划和设计问题的范围。⑦

关于告知义务的内容,根据 PEICL 第 2∶101 条的规定:(1) 订立合同时,投保人应当告知保险人其知道的或应当知道的情况,以及保险人清晰而准确地问到的情况。(2) 第 1

---

① 关于最大诚信原则与告知义务规定的逻辑关系,详见李庭鹏:《保险合同告知义务研究》,法律出版社 2006 年版,第 8—9 页。
② See John F. Dobby, Insurance Law, West Publishing Co., 1981, p. 144.
③ 李庭鹏. 保险合同告知义务研究,北京:法律出版社,2006 年版,第 20 页。
④ See Merkin. R, "Uberrima Fidea Strikes Again" (1976) 39 MLR 478, in Ray Hodgin, Insurance Law, London: Cavendish Publishing Ltd., 1998, pp. 216 – 217.
⑤ 江朝国. 保险法论文集(一). 台湾瑞兴图书股份有限公司,1993 年版,第 162 页。
⑥ 李庭鹏. 保险合同告知义务研究,北京:法律出版社,2006 年版,第 22 页。
⑦ 李庭鹏. 保险合同告知义务研究,北京:法律出版社,2006 年版,第 22 页。

段的情况包括被保险人知道或本应知道的情况。据此，告知内容还应包括被保险人所知道或应知道的情形。这是基于保险告知义务制度设计的初衷是为了保险人正确评估风险，进而做出承保决定以及承保条件，包括费率及其他条件，如限制责任、规定免赔等。我国保险法第16条第1款规定也规定，订立保险合同，保险人就保险标的或者被保险人的有关情况提出询问的，投保人应当如实告知。据此，投保人仅在保险人询问的情况下才承担告知义务，由此可认定我国现行立法采用的是询问告知主义。在实践中多以保险人提供风险询问表的形式出现。①

至于在投保人与被保险人不是同一人的情况下，被保险人是否也负有告知义务，在理论界和实务界都存在着争议。各国基于不同立法政策，也有不同规定，我国亦如此。如我国《保险法》中只规定投保人负有告知义务，而在我国《海商法》中则规定被保险人负有告知义务②。从理论上说，告知义务制度的立法目的在于使保险人能够获取危险信息进而正确评估风险，而被保险人是财产或人身受保险合同保障的利害关系人，亦即是危险事故的本体，其对保险标的危险情况的了解较投保人更为透彻，要求其承担告知义务亦不为过。③ 虽然我国《保险法》第 16 条规定的是投保人的如实告知义务，但是就其内容而言，将被保险人的有关情况也作为告知义务的内容，在司法实践中，推定被保险人的危险状况为投保人知道或应当知道的范围。这样，既具有理论上的依据，又维护了保险人的利益，与立法初衷不相违背。④

二、从不告知下的"全赔或全不赔"原则到新的补偿性救济方法

（一）告知义务之违反与"全赔或全不赔"原则

告知义务之违反，通常有两种情形：一为告知不确实，即为不实告知（Misrepresentation）；一为应告知而不告知，即为隐瞒（Concealment），系指投保人对已知或可得而知之事实，应告知而不为告知；或仅为一部分之告知，并未说明全部事实，这些都足以影响保险人对危险之测定，故任何隐瞒的事项，不论它是由于意外、过失、疏忽或错误，如属重要事项，与故意与欺诈相同，对保险契约有同样的重大影响。因此，隐瞒与告知不实之法律效果相同，保险人皆可据为解除契约之理由。⑤ 英国法律规定，保险人应知之每一具体事实，投保人必须尽量告知之，否则不论其为过失或故意，保险人皆可解除契约。美国各州法律，大部分对此限制稍宽，隐瞒并不能使保险人解除契约，除非保险人能证明隐瞒事实之重要性，并出于投保人有诈欺之意图。⑥

关于保险告知义务的传统制度的第二个特征是在违反告知义务的法律后果上采用"全赔或全不赔"原则（the All - or - Nothing Principle，亦译为"全有或全无原则"）。根据这一原则，违反义务将导致丧失全部保险金，即使这个过失是很小的，并且即使未告知的情况

---

① 奚晓明主编.《中华人民共和国保险法》保险合同章条文理解与适用. 中国法制出版社, 2010, 第 87 页.
② 我国《海商法》第 222 条的规定，合同订立前，被保险人应当将其知道的或在通常业务中应当知道的有关影响保险人据以确定保险费率或者确定是否同意承保的重要情况，如实告知保险人。
③ 覃有土主编. 保险法概论. 北京：北京大学出版社, 2001, 第 153 页.
④ 张海棠主编. 保险合同纠纷. 北京：法律出版社, 2010, 第 178 页.
⑤ 袁宗蔚. 保险学.（增订三十四版）, 北京：首都经济贸易大学出版社, 2000, 第 257 页.
⑥ See Mehr, R. I. and Cammack, E., Principles of Insurance, 7th ed., 1980, p. 113.

与保险事故之间毫无关系。

关于违反告知义务的制裁,最严重的见于英国、爱尔兰、瑞士。被保险人失去一切保单保障,即使不告知是无辜的,或者未告知的情况与保险事故无关系。① 对于不实告知,不管是欺诈、过失,还是无辜的,保险人都可以宣告合同无效。这种宣告通常要求双方返还已从对方取得的东西,使双方回到订约前状态;保险人可以对索赔予以拒绝或者收回已赔款,保单持有人大多数时候可以要求返还保险费,只是在欺诈性陈述时保险人可扣留保险费。

在这种全赔或全不赔的救济方法之下,只要保险人表明,要是知道真实情况,就会修改合同,哪怕是很细微的修改,甚至与所争议的索赔毫无关联,都可以拒付。从保险人的角度看,不拒付,就得全部赔,放弃全部抗辩权。除此之外,再没有中间路线可走。

应该说这种做法是一种过于激烈的方法,它使得保险人能够在发现风险已证实是一种现实的坏风险之后,而不是在此之前,拒绝承担责任。但是这样做,会使被保险人完全失去他以为通过缔约并且支付保费而本应获得的保护。所以这一过于绝对的做法必须有所缓和。

当然,在实践中,大多数相关案件都是通过和解来解决的。保险人声称存在不实告知的情况,被保险人一方则否认有关事实的重要性。考虑到双方的声明要得到确证,并不是很容易的事情,因此经过讨价还价,最终往往会达成和解。在这样的实践之下,代表保险人一方的理论观点出于维护自身利益的考虑,认为如果修改传统的全赔或全不赔的做法,代之以比例赔付——对此下文对此会加以详细论述——的救济方法,那么在谈判中就可能处于一个比较不利的地位。换言之,保险人不再能够以"我们可以完全不赔"作为初始的谈判立场,在经过讨价还价之后,最终赔了一半,而是以"我们只能赔 1/3 作为初始的谈判报价,但经过讨价还价之后,可能最终会赔 2/3"。

保险人对这一问题的担心不无道理。的确,大多数案件即使是在当事人之间通过谈判以和解的方式予以解决,但是谈判所达成的方案往往是在法律规则的影响之下形成的。但问题在于,保险人一方的这种担心,只反映了自身的利益诉求。而同样的问题在被保险人一方同样存在。传统的全赔或全不赔规则,在事实上给保险人提供了一种可用来打压被保险人的利益诉求的武器,在实践中也会降低最终和解方案的金额。所以对这一做法的合理性仍然必须予以反思。

(二)过失的不实告知下的比例原则

与违反告知义务情况下采取"全赔或全不赔"的做法不同,也有一些欧洲国家,根据违反告知义务的性质,选择一种按比例扣减保险金的方法。这就是所谓的比例原则。这一原则得名于保险人在实际赔付时按照实付保费与应付保费之间的比例,相应扣减保险金额的一种赔付保险金的办法。这一原则在保险法中早已存在,各国保险法对人寿保险中被保险人的年龄误报问题,除非被保险人年龄超过承保范围,无论故意或过失,保险人均不解除合同,而是依照精算出来的"年龄费率表",或要求投保人补交保险费,或者依照比例减少保险金的给付。早期的比例原则对于投保人或被保险人年龄误报时合同效力的维持起着重要重要,但其仅限于年龄误报。② 我国保险法第 32 条第 2 款对于人身保险合同中年龄误述情况下保险人的救济方法作出了特别的比例赔偿规定。根据该款规定,投保人申报的被保险人年龄不

---

① See Principles of European Insurance Contract Law PEICL, Art. 2:102, note 1.
② 肖和保. 保险法诚实信用原则研究. 北京:法律出版社,2007. 第 192 – 193 页。

真实，致使投保人支付的保险费少于应付保险费的，保险人有权更正并要求投保人补交保险费，或者在给付保险金时按照实付保险费与应付保险费的比例支付。

在法国法上，比例原则得到了长期运用。根据法国法的有关规定，如果在损失发生后发现不实告知（有过失的情况），按比例扣减赔偿金。这一比例为在风险得到如实和全面披露的情况下应付保险费率与实付保险费率之间的比例。① 根据这一做法，如果未披露导致保单持有人实际只支付应付保费的一半，那么就只有一半的请求赔偿额会得以支付。

作为对比例原则的一种极端运用，澳大利亚法更加严格。在澳大利亚，对寿险和非寿险实行区别对待，寿险可以适用比例原则，非寿险则适用一种极端做法。根据澳大利亚《1984年保险合同法》，在非寿险领域，对于非欺诈情形，保险人应有权根据合同措施请求损害赔偿。该法第28（3）条规定，"保险人对于一项请求的责任减至它在没有发生未告知或误述情况下本应处的地位时的金额"。不过，在确定损害赔偿方法上，区分三种情况：一是要求赔偿与支付的保险金相同的金额，条件是在得知真实情况后本不会承保，实际的效果就是没有赔偿；二是损害赔偿额，相当于应付保费与实付保费之间的比例——有人认为这是比例原则的变异；三是如果按不同条件承保，即赔偿额为保险人依约要赔的（要不是因为法定的有权减少赔付的权利就得赔）与如果当初按不同条件承保时该付的金额之间的差额。②

关于违反告知义务的后果，当代最新保险立法还注重区分保险事故发生之前与之后的情形，以便保险人能够终止合同或调整基于错误的风险披露而订立的合同的条件，使之与正确的风险评估相适应。此外，还区分无辜、有过失和欺诈的投保人，对于欺诈者不值得任何保护，不给予比例模式的保护，而对于有过失的投保人，至少给予按比例减少后的保险保障。这种扣减模式可见于欧盟理事会关于保险合同法指令建议修正案的第3条3（c），以及比利时、丹麦、法国、芬兰、希腊、意大利、卢森堡、荷兰、葡萄牙和西班牙的法律。荷兰民法典限制了扣减模式的适用范围，规定如果未披露或正确披露的事实对于风险评估不是重要的，保险人必须全额支付保险金。更灵活的形式是瑞典新保险法，消费者保险金不是严格按比例扣减，而是合理扣减，根据有关事实原本对于保险人风险评估的重要程度来做出判断，不管这种忽视是有意还是过失。③

在传统保险合同法制度框架之下，违反告知义务在性质上被理解为是影响合同双方合意是否存在的一个缺陷，从而是影响合同效力的一个重大瑕疵，其导致的结果是合同无效。④ 这种把告知义务的违反，与合同有效与否问题联系起来的做法，解释了为什么对于未能充分准确告知风险的制裁方法是合同无效。但问题是，这样的做法也过于绝对。因为否认合同效力导致双方的缔约的基本目的都被完全否认，这并不是一种有效率的解决问题的方法。

基于这一考虑，最近一些立法放弃了把违反告知义务的问题与"合同效力"判断挂钩起来的做法，代之以另一种更加有效率、更加经济的方法，也就是基于实际风险与保险价格

---

① See Article L1139 of the Code des Assurances. CP No. 182, p. 106.
② See Robert Merkin, Reforming Insurance Law: Is There a Case for Reverse Transportation? available at http://www.lawcom.gov.uk/docs/merkin_report.pdf, p. 36.
③ See Principles of European Insurance Contract Law PEICL, Art. 2: 102, note 2.
④ See Herman Cousy, The Principles of European Insurance Contract Law: the Duty of Disclosure and the Aggravation of Risk, published online, ERA, 2008.

金额（保费）之间的均衡的考虑，除了故意欺诈之外，告知义务的违反，不会导致合同关系的取消，而是尽可能使合同关系持续，伴之以根据双方之间新的协议对保险费进行调整。

值得注意的是，虽然英国保险法与其他国家保险法立场上的鲜明差别，但在保险实践上并无太大差异。因为在英国法上，普通法的严厉立场，至少对于消费者合同来说，在很大程度上被一些实务惯例规则所软化，如英国保险人协会发布的《一般保险惯例陈述》（the Statements of Insurance Practice）、金融服务局的规则以及金融监察机构的指引。[1] 而且，在此基础上，2009年英国法律委员会针对消费者保险提出的法律草案中建议，如果消费者投保人因过失作出了不实告知，保险人有权获得一种补偿性救济，这种补偿性救济的基本原理很简单，就是看保险人在当初如果知道真实情况时会如何做。具体而言：（1）如果保险人会排除特定类型的索赔，保险人就不必支付属于该排除范围内的索赔，而对于不属排除范围的索赔，则予以赔付；（2）如果保险人会拒保，那么就可以拒绝赔偿请求，但必须退还保险费；（3）如果保险人会增加保费，那么应当对索赔金额按与少付部分成比例地减少。英国法律委员会所提出的法律草案的意图在于使保险人回复到当初如果知道全部事实后会处于的那种地位。[2] 通过引入一种补偿性救济方法，细化在过失的不实告知情况下可能出现的种种情形，可以克服比例原则的不足，更加切实地保护保险消费者的利益。根据投保人的过错程度给予了非常详尽的规定，这是为了针对不同的情形实现最大程度的正义。此外，通过详细规定各种情形下的法律后果，也会强有力地推动消费者提供更加准确的信息。

（三）一种更广泛的补偿性救济方法的运用

就其本质而言，比例原则属于一种补偿性救济方法，用以解决保险人在非欺诈性情况下不得撤销合同，但又必须对投保人违反告知义务有所惩罚（比较过失）时平衡双方利益的一种方法。采用这种方法时，是根据投保方的过错程度或者义务违反与保险事故之间的关系密切程度来确定保险人的保险金赔付责任，而非全部免除。比例原则的引进能够克服全赔或全不赔原则的缺陷，有利于保护被保险人的利益，但是对比例原则的应用仍存在一些质疑。

首先，比例原则对那些被保险人如实告知后将导致保险人拒绝承保的情况出现时如何处理没有规定；其次，比例原则对被保险人履行如实告知义务将导致保险人以提高保险费以外的方式承保（如将风险作为免责事由）如何处理缺乏规定；再次，如何确定"应当收取的保险费"，这也是一个比较难解决的问题。[3] 为了解决这些缺陷，有必要适用一种更广泛的补偿性救济方法，在适当的情况下采取比例方法，而在另一些情况下则采取使消费者所要求的赔偿与保险人所受损害之间更紧密一致的补偿方法。

为了充分实现这种补偿性救济方法的效果，有必要全面考虑各种情形可能产生的影响。这主要包括以下方面：

（1）排除特定情况。保险人比较常见的说法是，如果他们知道被保险人的健康问题，他们会将特定情况排除在保障范围之外。那么问题就是，这种排除会对现实已经提出的索赔

---

[1] See Insurance Contract Law: Misrepresentation, Non-Disclosure and Breach of Warranty by the Insured, The Law Commission Consultation Paper No 182, ix, 2007. Http://www.lawcom.gov.uk/insurance_contract.htm.

[2] See Consumer Insurance Law: Pre-contract Disclosure and Misrepresentation, Law Com. No. 319, December 2009, pp. 77-78.

[3] See Hamwi and Ruegger, The Good, the Bad, and Propotionality, Society of Chartered Property and Casualty Underwriters CPCU Journal, Vol. 51, 1998, pp. 188-191.

产生什么影响？在有些时候，这种排除不影响索赔。如存在听力问题，后来因为白血病死亡。保险人如果知道听力问题就会将听力有关问题排除在保单之外，而白血病与此无关，故判令保险人全额支付因白血病死亡的保险金。同样的，未提及怀孕后背部疼痛，后来得了与之无关的乳腺癌。保险人必须复原保单将背部问题排除在外，但必须支付癌症的保险金。而在另一些情况下，索赔可能正好属于排除范围。如投保人未告知即将转诊眼睛，后来得了严重的眼病。法院指令保险公司恢复保单，但将眼部问题排除在外，故不赔。在有些情况下，这个结果对于一时失去判断力从而失去一大笔赔偿的保单持有人来说，看来很严酷。但从保险人角度看是公平的结果。并且从被保险人的角度看，这种做法比起不管有关无关，全都不赔相对公平。

（2）保证事项和免赔额。从理论上，保险人在得知真实情况后也可能会额外增加一项保证事项或免赔额。法院应该问如果保险人重新订保单将新的条件加入，后果会怎样。如果索赔满足新的条件，则应赔付保险金。

（3）增加保费。按比例方法在有明显证据表明保费会是多少时最有效。在有些情况下可能证据有争议，精确也不可能。而法官必须确定在现有可得证据下合理的保费会是多少。有评论指出，在许多情况下法院也不能给出准确的扣减比例，只能做出多少有些武断的判决。① 但是它仍是恢复当事人之间的平衡（这种平衡因为不实告知而被破坏了）的最好方法。合理的观点应该是这样的：宁可允许法官不精确地瞄准正确的数字，也好过准确地适用坏的数字（如同在仅仅因为会略微增加点保费就完全解除合同的情况下）。在许多时候，法院被迫对损害赔偿额做出武断的决定，特别是在人身伤害的损害赔偿案件中。在这方面不精确程度似乎在可接受的限度内。②

（4）拒保。如果保险人会完全拒绝风险，起点就肯定是保险人不应赔偿。从理论上，要求保险人遵守其在知晓真实情况后也会缔结的合同，这是对的，但不应强迫它们遵守其本不会同意缔结的合同。理性的保险人由于担心实际发生的损失而会拒绝风险，这是公平的。但是，也可能产生一些复杂情形。一种情形是，某一个保险人可能拒绝，而其他保险人可能会接受，条件是增加保费。很难知道在这样的情况下应怎么办。另一种情形是，当损失与这种风险无关时也可能产生不公平：投保人未告知高血压而在工作中因为一次意外事故而死亡。在法国，法官首先可能确定在这些情况下的一个公平的扣减，作为一个事实问题和自由裁量问题。那么，法院是否应有权缓和在某些情况下解除合同的严酷后果呢？这种自由裁量权应该可以应用于投保人过失极轻微，以及保险人没有遭受重大损失，或者虽然损失较大，但可以通过减少赔偿而得到适当弥补的场合。

（5）对未来保障的效力。上面的讨论集中于已经提出的索赔请求。但还必须考虑保险人是否还应继续承保的问题。总的来看，如果没有不实告知保险人会完全拒保，则保险人应仍有权解除保单，并有权拒绝索赔请求。在其他情况下，保险人应提议以它本来会提出的条件继续保单。如果会收取更高保费，就可以按比例额外收取保费以继续后面合同。保单持有人有权选择接受这些新的条件或者取消保单。

最后，应予注意的是，这种补偿性救济方法不仅仅只是出于公平合理的考虑，补偿性救

---

① See Insurance Contract Law, Issues Paper 1, Misrepresentation and Non Disclosure, September 2006, p. 64.
② Ibid., p. 65.

济方法的目的在于使保险人处于它在消费者履行义务后原本会处的那个地位。因此，这种方法考查的是给保险人带来的损失，而不是被保险人的过失程度。它也不考虑不实告知与索赔请求之间有无因果关系。如果保险人会增补一项除外责任，补偿性救济方法的效果可能类似于一种因果关系测试。例如，保险人要是得知听力损伤的情况就会从重大疾病保单中排除听力问题，但它仍有义务赔偿其他的请求，如关于其他与听力无关的疾病。但是，如果保险人仅仅是增加保费，消费者将只能得到一部分赔偿，即使它与不实告知无关。如果保险人能够证明它本来不会订立合同的，则它可以拒绝全部索赔并只返还保险费。[1]

三、保险告知义务规则的最新发展对中国的启示

保险合同是一种特殊类型的合同，交易双方必须遵循最大诚信原则，否则交易双方利益都无法得到保障。关于保险告知义务的立法改革的出发点是，法律应在保险人和保单持有人利益之间达成一种公平的均衡，应在保护保险人的合法利益而不施加不适当的成本或不必要的限制同时，确保保险能够满足潜在保单持有人的合理预期，从而给予潜在保单持有人对保险的信任。

现代规则对传统规则第一大突破是偏重对于保险消费者的保护。在欧美保险立法的最新趋势中，实行区别立法，对于以自然人身份获得保险保障者，法律更偏重保护，当事人不得通过约定背离法律，作对保险消费者不利的规定；而对于从事职业或商业活动的保单持有人，则允许当事人通过约定背离法律的规定。此一立法精神体现对保险消费者的加重保护，而对于职业性或商业性投保人则要求实行自我保护。

如《荷兰民法典》第 7 章第 928 条规定保单持有人在缔结保险合同时的披露义务，第 929、930 条规定违反义务的后果。这些条款是强制性规定。这意味着，背离这些规定对保单持有人或者有权获得保险金的人（被保险人或受益人）不利是不允许的，如果保单持有人是作为一个自然人缔结合同而不是从事某项职业或商业活动。[2] 相反，如果保单持有人不是以自然人的身份而是从事某项职业或商业活动中缔约的，背离法律的规定是允许的（荷民第 943 条），即使这会对保单持有人或有权获得保险金的人不利。又如英国的消费者保险法草案，旨在将消费者保险与商业保险相区别，不允许保险人通过约定排除该法有关条款的适用而对保险消费者不利。[3]

现代规则对传统规则突破的另一个重要方面在于，区分欺诈性违反告知义务和非欺诈性违反告知义务。对于欺诈者的严重制裁（有关举证责任应由保险人承担），对于非欺诈的情形不适用，这样可以间接保护非欺诈的保险消费者。对于非欺诈性情形，放弃全赔或全不赔，而根据具体情形，适用比例赔付或依相应条件承担责任。这种做法让保险消费者能够获得相应的保障，因为一旦被拒绝，可能得不到任何保障，在未来的投保也会遭到拒保。通过要求保险人在非欺诈情形下区分具体情况进行赔偿或不赔偿，从而可以促使保险人在事先进行认真审核，做好事前的风险评估。相比之下，传统规则及其激进的制裁对保单持有人的确

---

[1] See Consumer Insurance Law, Law Com no. 316, Appendix B, pp. 178 – 183.
[2] See Yvonne Delfos‐Roy, The PEICL and the Duty of Disclosure, European Review of Private Law, 1 – 2011, p. 73.
[3] See Consumer Insurance Law: Pre‐contract Disclosure and Misrepresentation, Law Com. No. 319, December 2009, p. 87.

过于严苛,只要投保人没有告知,不管是否故意过失一律免责,这样做对投保人和被保险人来说不公平,太过苛刻。通过引入现代规则,不允许一律拒赔,就会迫使保险人在事先(投保阶段)进行风险评估,而不是等到索赔时再核查风险。

现代规则对传统规则突破的第三方面体现在,在消费者保险领域,对于过失的不实告知的救济方法。传统的全赔或全不赔原则,给予保险人撤销整个保单的权利,这通常超出了对保险人保护的必要程度。因为撤销是一种严厉的救济方法。例如,这会使保险人能够仅仅因为未被告知听力损伤就拒绝因癌症死亡的索赔,即使它当初知道这种听力损伤后只是会将听力索赔从保单排除。而一种补偿性的方法,即按比例标准的方法,以及使对消费者所要求的赔偿与保险人所受损害之间更紧密一致的补偿方法更符合立法精神。比例原则已经为一些国家立法所认可,其本质上是一种对保险人的补偿性救济方法。这种补偿性救济方法不仅仅只是出于公平合理的考虑,其更着眼于使保险人处于它在消费者履行义务后原本会处的那个地位。因此,这种方法考查的是给保险人带来的损失,而不是被保险人的过失程度,它更有利于保护保险消费者的利益。

我国保险法第16条对于告知义务及违反这一义务的后果作出了一般性的规定。根据其第1款的规定,订立保险合同,保险人就保险标的或者被保险人的有关情况提出询问的,投保人应当如实告知。由此可知,就告知义务的形式而言,我国保险法采取了询问主义原则,但从法律条文来看并未明确规定"书面"询问。如前所述,相较专业的保险人来说,投保人通常认识与评估风险能力有限,由保险人以书面形式详细列明投保人需要告知的事项与情况,既有利于保险人充分了解与衡量风险,也有利于投保人正确地履行告知义务。而且在保险实践中保险人多是通过提供风险询问表的形式来了解保险标的或被保险人的有关情况的。[1] 故我国保险立法今后有必要在法律上确立书面询问原则,明确投保人的告知义务以保险人的书面询问为限,这样既可以将法律与实践统一起来,也可以更好地维护双方的合法利益。

对于违反告知义务的后果,我国保险法第16条进一步规定,投保人故意或者因重大过失未履行如实告知义务,足以影响保险人决定是否同意承保或者提高保险费率的,保险人有权解除合同。投保人故意不履行如实告知义务的,保险人对于合同解除前发生的保险事故,不承担赔偿或者给付保险金的责任,并不退还保险费。投保人因重大过失未履行如实告知义务,对保险事故的发生有严重影响的,保险人对于合同解除前发生的保险事故,不承担赔偿或者给付保险金的责任,但应当退还保险费。由此可见,我国保险法设置了赋予保险人解除合同权利和拒绝赔偿两种法律后果。从表面上看,该条使用了"故意或重大过失"的表述,在投保人有故意或重大过失未履行如实告知义务时,保险人均可免除赔偿责任,在一定意义上可以说采用的是全赔或全不赔的原则。[2] 如前文所述,这种全赔或全不赔的做法,对保险消费者明显保护不力,所以,我国保险法有必要借鉴国际上最新的立法经验和做法。如对于投保人的故意或欺诈的不实告知,保险人可以免除赔偿责任;而对于过失的不实告知,则适

---

[1] 奚晓明主编.《中华人民共和国保险法》保险合同章条文理解与适用.北京:中国法制出版社.2010,第87页。
[2] 王战涛.中德保险法中的消费者保护比较研究.保险研究.2010年第10期,第116页。但是,严格说来,对投保人因重大过失未履行如实告知义务,要求未告知事项"对保险事故的发生有严重影响",保险人对于合同解除前发生的保险事故,不承担赔付责任;反之,如对保险事故发生没有严重影响,则保险人仍应承担赔付责任。

用比例原则等补偿性救济方法，公平合理地确定保险人的责任。

四、结论

保险告知义务的传统规则的两大特征是投保人的自动申告义务和对于违反告知义务的"全赔或全不赔"救济原则。当代最新保险立法确立了书面询问主义的立法原则，以取代自动申告主义，确立比例原则等补偿性救济方法，以取代全赔或全不赔的救济原则。为了促进中国保险业的进一步发展，培育保险消费者的信心，有必要根据保险告知义务的最新发展对中国保险法的相关规定进行进一步的完善。即使不修改当下条文的具体表述，也可以根据上述发展中所体现出来的理念来指导相关的法律解释以及司法实践活动。

Delaying Retirement Strategy with Longevity Risk and Social Welfare Maximization in China[1]

Qiang Cui[2]

Abstract: Pressure on the public pension system by longevity risk have received more and more attention in recent years, many countries have begun to take measures to alleviate this pressure, such as the implementation of delaying retirement strategy. This paper analyzes the influence of delaying retirement by employing an exogenous growth OLG model (Overlapping generations model) with lifetime uncertainty factor. Then we combine the Pareto optimal method to work out the formula of the optimal delay retirement coefficient. According to the situation of China, we estimate the parameter values and simulate to obtain the optimal delay retirement coefficient under different survival probabilities and population growth rates. Through these analyses, we can get the direction of survival probability and population growth rate influence on the optimal delay retirement coefficient. The optimal delay retirement coefficient increases as the survival probability goes up; and decreases as the population growth rate goes down. However, the impact of the survival probability on the delay retirement coefficient is much stronger than that of the population growth rate. In order to guarantee social welfare maximization under longevity risk and falling population growth rate, it is necessary to delay the retirement age.

Keywords: OLG Model, Delay Retirement, Longevity Risk, Social Welfare Maximization

1. Introduction

With the development of economy and society, the progress of medicine, the changes of people's life style and the enhancement of people's health consciousness, the improvement of average life has become a worldwide phenomenon. In 2012, Chinese Ministry of Civil Affairs issued the "Social service development statistical communique in 2012", this document shows that, in 2012, 193.9 million people in China aged no less than 60 years old. The population of this group covered 14.3% of the overall population, which was 3.97% higher than the year of 2000. Among them, the population aged 65 or more were 127.14 million, which covered 9.4% of the total. The improvement of average life brought us an aging population and a series of social problems, while aging pop-

---

[1] 18th Asia – Pacific Risk and Insurance Association Annual Conference, Moscow, 2014.
[2] Postgraduate, School of Insurance, Central University of Finance and Economics, Beijing, China.

ulation enjoy the benefits of longevity, they also facing some longevity risk.

To different subjects, the longevity risks are different. For individuals, longevity means that people can enjoy more years of life, but their savings in their working period are often insufficient to cover the longer spending. Moreover, a longer life brings a lot of medical expense. Currently, China's social pension insurance system is not perfect; a lot of public still rely on family pension. However, because of the family planning policy, China's population growth rate is declining year after year and the family size is getting smaller and smaller, rely solely on the children's alimony, their children will face great economic burden. So, in the face of the benefits of longevity, old people are also facing the risk of longevity, and this kind of risk is a system risk of the whole society. For society, the aging of population causes a substantial increase in public pensions, which will bring a heavy burden on the government, while in the partially funded pension system, with the aging phenomenon intensifies, social pool fund will face a great gap, and this gap will bring adverse effect on the development of social security. In addition, population aging will also affect the amount of future labor force, and may have an impact on economic development. Pressure on the public pension system by longevity risk have received more and more attention in recent years, many countries have begun to take measures to alleviate this pressure, such as the implementation of delaying retirement strategy. This paper analyzes the influence of delaying retirement by employing an exogenous growth OLG model (Overlapping generations model) with lifetime uncertainty factor. Through this model we can find out that in order to guarantee social welfare maximization under longevity risk and falling population growth rate, it is necessary to delay the retirement age. In China, the proposals of the delay retirement came out and immediately aroused wide discussion. But comparing to other countries, the current domestic retirement system is indeed a more lenient way. For long – term consideration of social development, it is necessary to conduct an in – depth study of China's delaying retirement strategy.

Literatures which used the OLG model to study the public pension can be divided into three categories: First is pay – as – you – go (PAYG) public pension system research. Second is fully funded pension system research, and third is study on both. Blanchard and Fischer (1989) summarize the results of previous studies, systematically exposit how to use the OLG model to investigate PAYG system public pension and fully funded system public pension.

Blanchard (1985) summarized the results of previous studies, established an overlapping generations model (OLG), the newborn birth in his model is continuous. Fuster, L. (2000) studied the effect of the accumulation of capital on economic growth under the condition to lifetime uncertainty. Introduction of lifetime uncertainty is one of the most popular abroad used methods to reflect the longevity risk.

There are also a lot of literatures with OLG model to analyze the social pension problems in China. Professor Yang Zaigui (2010) explained how to use the OLG model to study the basic issues of public pensions in his book OLG Model Analysis on Public Pension: Principles and Applications. Hu Shiqiang and Xu Jinliang (2011) used OLG model to explore the relationship between longevity risk and capital accumulation. They consider that under China's current pension system, the increasing of longevity risk will promote capital accumulation.

Currently, the Chinese government and academic circles are studying and thinking how to improve China's pension system to deal with the problem of appearing longevity risk. Zheng Bingwen, the director of the world social security research center at the Chinese academy of social sciences and GongSen, the vice minister of social development research at the state council development research center consider that it should appropriately raise the retirement age to ease the longevity risk and the pressure of population aging.

Based on the principle of Social Welfare Maximization, this paper analyzes the influence of delaying retirement by employing an exogenous growth OLG model (Overlapping generations model) with lifetime uncertainty factor. In order to achieve quantitative research on the issue of delay retirement, we added the delay retirement coefficient in the model. Then we combine the Pareto optimal method to work out the formula of the optimal delay retirement coefficient. According to the situation of China, we estimate the parameter values and simulate to obtain the optimal delay retirement coefficient under different survival probabilities and population growth rates. Through these analyses, we can get the direction of survival probability and population growth rate influence on the optimal delay retirement coefficient. Based on this direction, we can combine the actual situation of China to make appropriate delaying retirement strategy.

The rest of this paper is organized as follows: section 2 presents the basic model. Section 3 makes the Pareto optimal analysis. Section 4 makes some simulations according to the situation of China. The last section concludes the paper and makes some policy advices.

2. The Model

There is a closed economy composed of numerous individuals, firms, and a government. Each individuals lives at most three periods divided into childhood, working period, and retirement period. We assume that in the childhood, individuals do not make consumer decision and the consumer decision only be made in the working period and the retirement period. Depending on above circumstances and the objective of this study, we just focus on the working period and the retirement period in our model. Each individual goes through the childhood and working period, however, in the retirement period, whether she/he will survive is uncertain. Suppose the probability of survival in the retirement period is $p \in (0,1)$. At the beginning of period t, L_t identical individuals of generation t enter the workforce. The population growth rate $n = L_t/L_{t-1} - 1$.

2.1 Individuals

In the working period, each individual has one unit labor to invest in the labor market to earn wage. They use the income to make pension contributions, save apart of income to support consumption in their retirement period, and consume the rest. In order to describe the situation of delaying retirement, we divide the retirement period into two stages, stage θ and stage $1 - \theta$. Where $\theta \in [0, 1]$ denotes the delay retirement coefficient. It means, in the retirement period, people's working time is $\theta\%$ and retirement time is $(1 - \theta)\%$. If individuals survive in the retirement period, they can get their savings with accrued interest, individual account benefits, social pool benefits and their wage in the delaying retirement period, all these incomes are used for their consumption and do not leave intentional heritage to their children. If they die at the beginning of the retirement period, their savings with accrued interest and individual account benefit are inherited equally by their children as bequests. Obviously, people who died at the beginning of their retirement period cannot get the social pool benefits. As a kind of incentive for the delay retirement, wages during the delay retirement will not be withheld annuity based on individual contribution rate.

Each individual derives utility from their working – period consumption $C_{1,t}$, and retirement – period consumption $C_{2,t+1}$ (if possible). The utility can be described by an additively separable logarithmic function. So, the utility maximization problem is:

$$max_{\{s_t\}} U_t = \ln C_{1,t} + \beta p \ln C_{2,t+1} \quad (1)$$

$$s.t. \quad C_{1,t} = (1-\tau)W_t + (1-p)B_t - S_t \quad (2)$$

$$C_{2,t+1} = (1+r_{t+1})S_t + \theta W_{t+1} + (1-\theta)P_{t+1} + I^*_{t+1} \quad (3)$$

$$(1+n)B_{t+1} = (1+r_{t+1})S_t + I_{t+1} \quad (4)$$

where $\beta \in (0,1)$ denotes the individual discount rate, W_t denotes the wage, B_t the involuntary bequests from their parents for children in generation t, S_t the savings, τ the individual contribution rate, r the interest rate, I^*_{t+1} the individual account benefits after people delay their retirement time, I_{t+1} the individual account benefits, P_{t+1} the social pool benefits.

Substituting equations (2) and (4) into equation (1), and letting the partial derivatives of equation (1) with respect to S_t be zero gives the first – order conditions for the utility maximization.

$$\beta p(1 + r_{t+1})C_{1,t} = C_{2,t+1} \quad (5)$$

Equation (5) implies that the utility loss from reducing one unit of working – period consumption is equal to the utility gain with the probability p from increasing $(1 + r_{t+1})$ units of retirement – period consumption discounted by β.

2.2 Firms

Firms produce homogeneous commodity in competitive markets. The production can be described by Cobb – Douglas function $Y_t = AK_t^\alpha (L_t + p\theta L_{t-1})^{1-\alpha}$ or $y_t = A(\frac{1+n}{1+n+p\theta})^\alpha k_t^\alpha$, where Y_t is the output in period t, K_t the physical capital stock at the beginning of period t, the total labor population in periods t are $L_t + p\theta L_{t-1}$, $A > 0$ the productivity of physical capital production, y_t the output per unit of labor, $k_t = K_t / L_t$ the physical capital – labor ratio, $\alpha \in (0,1)$ the physical capital share of income.

Firms make pension contributions at the rate of $\eta \in (0,1)$ on their payroll. According to the product distribution, one can get $AK_t^\alpha (L_t + p\theta L_{t-1})^{1-\alpha} = r_t K_t + (1+\eta)W_t(L_t + p\theta L_{t-1})$. The first – order conditions for the profit maximization are:

$$r_t = \alpha A (\frac{1+n+p\theta}{1+n})^{1-\alpha} k_t^{\alpha-1}$$

$$W_t = \frac{(1-\alpha)(\frac{1+n+p\theta}{1+n})^{-\alpha} A k_t^\alpha}{1+\eta}$$

Letting $\frac{1+n+p\theta}{1+n}$ be G and arranging above equations can get:

$$r_t = \alpha A G^{1-\alpha} k_t^{\alpha-1} \tag{6}$$

$$W_t = \frac{(1-\alpha)AG^{-\alpha}k_t^{\alpha}}{1+\eta} \tag{7}$$

2.3 The Government

The old-age insurance premiums paid by the workers were put into the individual account, used to pay the individual when she/he retires as funded pension benefits.

$$T_{t+1} = (1 + r_{t+1})\tau W_t \tag{8}$$

As a kind of incentive for the delay retirement, wages during the delay retirement will not be withheld annuity based on individual contribution rate and after workers retires, they can also get the benefit during the delay retirement period:

$$I_{t+1}^* = T_{t+1} + \theta(1 + r_{t+1})\tau W_{t+1} \tag{9}$$

Firm pension contributions are credited into the social pool account. The social pool fund is paid to the retirees in the current period as PAYG pension benefits, $p(1-\theta)P_{t+1}L_t = L_{t+1}\eta W_{t+1} + \theta p\eta L_t W_{t+1}$, or

$$P_{t+1} = \frac{(1+n)\eta W_{t+1} + \theta p\eta W_{t+1}}{p(1-\theta)} \tag{10}$$

2.4 Physical Capital Market

The savings and the individual pension contributions in generation t generate the physical capital stock in period $t+1$: $(S_t + \tau W_t)L_t = L_{t+1}k_{t+1}$. Arrange it:

$$S_t = \tau W_t = (1+n)k_{t+1} \tag{11}$$

2.5 Dynamic Equilibrium System

A competitive equilibrium for this market economy is a sequence as $\{C_{1,t}, C_{2,t+1}, S_t, W_t, r_{t+1}, I_{t+1}, P_{t+1}, B_t, k_{t+1}\}_{t=0}^{\infty}$ that satisfies equations (1) – (11) for all t, at the given initial conditions (k_0,) and the parameter values of η and τ.

Substituting equations (2) – (4) and (6) – (11) into (5) and rearranging yields:

$$\beta p(1 + \alpha A G^{1-\alpha}k_{t+1}^{\alpha-1})\left[\frac{(1-\alpha)G^{-\alpha}Ak_t^{\alpha}}{1+\eta} + (1-p)(k_t + \alpha A G^{1-\alpha}k_t^{\alpha}) - (1+n)k_{t+1}\right]$$
$$= (1+n)(k_{t+1} + \alpha A G^{1-\alpha}k_{t+1}^{\alpha}) + \left[\theta + \frac{(1+n)\eta}{p} + \theta\eta + \theta\tau(1 + \alpha A G^{1-\alpha}k_{t+1}^{\alpha-1})\right]\frac{(1-\alpha)AG^{-\alpha}k_{t+1}^{\alpha}}{1+\eta} \tag{12}$$

Equation (12) is the dynamic equilibrium system to describe the economy.

Assume that the dynamic equilibrium system has unique and stable equilibrium without oscillation, and that means dk_{t+1}/dk_t is great than 0 and less than 1 at the steady state.

Differentiating (12) with respect to k, gives:

$$edk_{t+1} + fdk_t = 0 \tag{13}$$

The coefficients of partial derivatives are:

$$\beta p\alpha(\alpha-1)AG^{1-\alpha}k^{\alpha-2}\left[\frac{1-\alpha}{1+\eta}AG^{-\alpha}k^{\alpha} + (1-p)(k + \alpha A G^{1-\alpha}k^{\alpha}) - (1+n)k\right]$$

$$e = -\beta p(1+n)(1+\alpha AG^{1-\alpha}k^{\alpha-1}) - (1-n)(1+\alpha^2 AG^{1-\alpha}k^{\alpha-1})$$
$$- \frac{\alpha(1-\alpha)AG^{-\alpha}k^{\alpha-1}}{1+\eta}\left[\theta + \frac{(1+n)\eta}{p} + \theta\eta + \theta\tau + (2\alpha-1)\theta\tau AG^{1-\alpha}k^{\alpha-1}\right] \quad (14)$$

$$f = \beta p(1+\alpha AG^{1-\alpha}k^{\alpha-1})\left[\frac{(1-\alpha)\alpha AG^{-\alpha}k^{\alpha-1}}{1+\eta} + (1-p)(1+\alpha^2 AG^{1-\alpha}k^{\alpha-1})\right] > 0 \quad (15)$$

Since $0 < \frac{dk_{t+1}}{dk_t} = -\frac{f}{e} < 1$, obviously, the stability condition of the system is:

$$e + f < 0$$

3. Pareto Optimality

Define the social welfare function as the discounted sum of personal utility from each generation, thus

$$E = \beta p \ln C_{2,0} + \sum_{\varepsilon=0}^{\infty} \rho^{\varepsilon}(\ln C_{1,\varepsilon} + \beta p \ln C_{2,\varepsilon+1}) \quad (16)$$

where ρ denotes the social discount rate. It reflects the degree of social planner paying attention to the utility of each generation.

The resource constraint is:

$$k_{\varepsilon} + AG^{-\alpha}k_{\varepsilon}^{\alpha} = (1+n)k_{\varepsilon+1} + C_{1,\varepsilon} + p\frac{C_{2,\varepsilon}}{1+n} \quad (17)$$

The initial condition k_0 is known.

Social planners maximize social welfare under the condition of the resource constraint and the initial condition. The Lagrangian function corresponding to the social welfare maximization problem is:

$$L = L$$
$$+ \rho^{t-1}(\ln C_{1,t-1} + \beta p \ln C_{2,t}) + \lambda_{t-1}\left[k_{t-1} + AG^{-\alpha}k_{t-1}^{\alpha} - (1+n)k_t - C_{1,t-1} - p\frac{C_{2,t-1}}{1+n}\right]$$
$$+ \rho^{t}(\ln C_{1,t} + \beta p \ln C_{2,t+1}) + \lambda_{t}\left[k_{t} + AG^{-\alpha}k_{t}^{\alpha} - (1+n)k_{t+1} - C_{1,t} - p\frac{C_{2,t}}{1+n}\right]$$
$$+ \rho^{t+1}(\ln C_{1,t+1} + \beta p \ln C_{2,t+2}) + \lambda_{t+1}\left[k_{t+1} + AG^{-\alpha}k_{t+1}^{\alpha} - (1+n)k_{t+2} - C_{1,t+1} - p\frac{C_{2,t+1}}{1+n}\right] + L$$
$$(18)$$

where λ_t is the Lagrange multiplier of resource constraint at generation t. Partially differentiating L with respect to $C_{1,t}, C_{2,t}$ and k_{t+1} gives

$$\frac{\rho^t}{C_{1,t}} - \lambda_t = 0$$

$$\frac{\rho^{t-1}\beta p}{C_{2,t}} - \frac{\lambda_t p}{1+n} = 0$$

$$-\lambda_t(1+n) + \lambda_{t+1}(1+\alpha AG^{-\alpha}k_{t+1}^{\alpha-1}) = 0$$

Arranging these three equations at the optimal state k^*, C_1^*, C_2^* gives

$$\beta(1+n)C_1^* = \rho C_2^* \tag{19}$$

$$1 + \alpha A G^{-\alpha}(k^*)^{\alpha-1} = \frac{1+n}{\rho} \ or \ k^* = G^{\frac{\alpha}{\alpha-1}}\left(\frac{1+n-\rho}{\rho\alpha A}\right)^{\frac{1}{\alpha-1}} \tag{20}$$

The capital – labor ratio in equation (20) meets the modified golden rule level. At this point, the social welfare reaches the maximum level. Enable to let the market economy achieves to the optimal steady state, we should adjust policy parameters so as to get the capital – labor ratio reached the optimal steady state level, namely $k_t = k_{t+1} = k = k^*$. Substituting equations (20) into (12) yields:

$$\beta p \left(1 + G \cdot \frac{1+n-\rho}{\rho}\right)$$

$$\left[\frac{(1-\alpha)A\left(G\cdot\frac{1+n-\rho}{\rho\alpha A}\right)^{\frac{\alpha}{\alpha-1}}}{1+\eta} + (1-p)\alpha A G^{\frac{2\alpha-1}{\alpha-1}}\left(\frac{1+n-\rho}{\rho\alpha A}\right)^{\frac{\alpha}{\alpha-1}} - (p+n)G^{\frac{\alpha}{\alpha-1}}\left(\frac{1+n-\rho}{\rho\alpha A}\right)^{\frac{1}{\alpha-1}}\right]$$

$$= (1+n)\left[G^{\frac{\alpha}{\alpha-1}}\left(\frac{1+n-\rho}{\rho\alpha A}\right)^{\frac{1}{\alpha-1}} + \alpha A G^{\frac{2\alpha-1}{\alpha-1}}\left(\frac{1+n-\rho}{\rho\alpha A}\right)^{\frac{\alpha}{\alpha-1}}\right]$$

$$+ \left[\theta + \frac{(1+n)\eta}{p} + \theta\eta + \theta\tau\left(1 + G \cdot \frac{1+n-\rho}{\rho}\right)\right]\frac{(1-\alpha)A\left(G \cdot \frac{1+n-\rho}{\rho\alpha A}\right)^{\frac{\alpha}{\alpha-1}}}{1+\eta}$$

(21)

In order to investigate the direction of optimal delay retirement coefficient under the increasing survival probability and declining population growth rate, partially differentiating θ with respect to p and n, we can find that the positive and negative of the result is not determinable. It means that the effect of the survival probability and population growth rate on the optimal delay retirement coefficient is ambiguous. Therefore, we test this by simulation.

4. Simulations

4.1 Estimation of Parameter Values

A period length is usually as long as 25 – 30 years in the literature on OLG model and the standard retirement age in China is 60, so this model sets a period length of 30 years. Analogous to Pecchenino and Pollard (2002), we assume that the individual discount rate per year is 0.985, hence the individual discount rate per period is. Since what we want to see is the effect of the survival probability and population growth rate on the optimal delay retirement coefficient, the constant A can be normalized to 1.

The capital share of income α is usually to be estimated as 0.3 in developed countries. Since China is a developing country with a large number of population, labor in China is comparatively cheaper, thus the labor share of income is lower, while the capital share of income is higher than that in developed countries. So we assume that α in China could be 0.35.

The survival probability in retirement period can be obtained from the life expectancy. According to the statistics, the life expectancy of Chinese people in 2005 is 72 years old. Since one period length is 30 years, the life – span from birth to the end of working – period is 60 years. The life – span from birth to the end of retirement period is 90 years. According to the concept of life expectancy, we can get $(1-p) \times 60 + p \times 90 = 72$, so $p = 40\%$.

This study is on urban public pension system, so we select the "urban population" as the statistical caliber. According to the data in China Statistical Yearbook population and composition table, we can figure out the population growth rate in the period 1974~2004 is $n = 2.481$.

Based on the Chinese State Council Document 26 of 1997 and the Chinese State Council Document 38 of 2005, we can know that in 2005, Chinese State Council Document released the standard pension contribution rate. The firm contribution rate is $\eta = 20\%$, and the individual contribution rate is $\tau = 8\%$.

The delay retirement coefficient cannot be observed directly. The retirement age now in China is 60 years old. So the delay retirement coefficient θ can be regarded as zero. Substituting relative baseline parameter values into the equation (21) and calculate gives: $\rho = 0.2621$

The estimated values above are the baseline parameter values as shown in Table 1.

Table 1　　　　　　　　　　　　Baseline parameter values

β	α	n	η	τ	p	ρ	A
0.6355	0.35	2.481	20%	8%	40%	0.2621	1

4.2 Effect of Exogenous Variables

According to the World Population Prospects (2010 Revision): the life expectancy of Chinese people in 2010 and 2015 are 72.71 and 73.76 years old. Hence, the survival probability in retirement period can be worked out as 42.37% and 45.87%. With other parameters constant, letting the survival probability be 40% 42.37% and 45.87% respectively, and substituting these parameters into the equation (21) we can get the result as in Table 2. The increase in the survival probability leads to the increase in the delay retirement coefficient, the individual account and the social pool fund and decrease in the physical capital – labor ratio. Therefore, under other conditions remain unchanged; with the improvement of survival probability, the optimal decision of the individual is to delay retirement.

Table 2　　　　　　　　　　　Effect of survival probability

p	40%	42.37%	45.87%
k	0.00420	0.00416	0.00409
θ	0	0.15038	0.36448
I*	0.07834	0.09782	0.11772
P	0.13880	0.15558	0.19399

And then, let us see the effect of population growth rate. Hold other parameters constant, letting the survival probability be 45.87%, the population growth rate be 2.481, 2.425 and 2.369 respectively, run the simulation process and get the result as in Table 3: A decline of the population growth rate decreases the delay retirement coefficient, the individual account and the social pool fund, while increases the physical capital – labor ratio. So, as the decline of the population growth rate, people will choose to reduce delay retirement.

Table 3	Effect of population growth rate		
n	2.481	2.425	2.369
k	0.00409	0.00420	0.00432
θ	0.36448	0.36074	0.35693
I*	0.11772	0.11664	0.11552
P	0.19399	0.19216	0.18983

In order to observe the influence degree of the survival probability and population growth rate to the delay retirement coefficient and other endogenous variables, we can calculate the elasticity of the endogenous variables with respect to p and n, which is shown in Table 4. They reflect the sensitivities of the endogenous variables with respect to the exogenous variables. From Table 4, we can see that the optimal delay retirement coefficient increases as the survival probability goes up; and decreases as the population growth rate goes down, but the effects of population growth rate to the delay retirement compared to the effects of survival probability is much smaller. Therefore, we may get the conclusions that, delay retirement decisions are mainly affected by longevity risk. In addition, in order to deal with longevity risk, relieve the influence of the population growth rate decline to delay retirement, we can improve the rate of population increasing appropriately.

Table 4	Elasticity of endogenous variables with respect to p and n	
	p	n
k	-20.37%	-119.15%
θ	1723.52%	45.46%
I*	246.27%	40.65%
P	298.87%	41.79%

5. Conclusions and Policy Suggestions

This paper analyzes the influence of delaying retirement by employing an exogenous growth OLG model (Overlapping generations model) with lifetime uncertainty factor. Then we combine the Pareto optimal method to work out the formula of the optimal delay retirement coefficient. According to the situation of China, we estimate the parameter values and simulate to obtain the optimal delay retirement coefficient under different survival probabilities and population growth rates. Through these analyses, we can get the direction of survival probability and population growth rate influence on the optimal delay retirement coefficient.

Based on the above works, we obtain the following results: The increase in the survival probability leads to the increase in the delay retirement coefficient, the individual account and the social pool fund and decrease in the physical capital – labor ratio. The decline of the population growth rate decreases the delay retirement coefficient, the individual account and the social pool fund, but it also increases the physical capital – labor ratio. In addition, the effect of population growth rate to the delay retirement coefficient, the individual account and the social pool fund compared to the effects of survival probability is much smaller. So under the influence of longevity risk, in order to gain more utility, rational individuals will choose to delay retirement plan.

According to the above results, we can put forward corresponding policy recommendations combining with the situation in China. In order to ease the longevity risk, guarantee social welfare maximization in China, it is necessary to implement retirement delay policy. In addition, consider the negative effect of population growth rate on the delay retirement, the individual account and the social pool fund, we can loosen the family planning policy to improve population growth rate appropriately.

References

1. Blanchard, O. J. and S. Fischer, (1989) Lectures on Macroeconomics, London: MIT Press.

2. Yang, Zaigui, (2010) OLG Model Analysis on Public Pension: Principles and Applications, Guangming Daily Press.

3. Fuster, L., (2000) "Capital accumulation in an economy with dynasties and uncertain lifetimes", Review of Economic Dynamics 3, 650 – 674

4. Sheshinski, E. and Y. Weiss, (1981) "Uncertainty and optimal social security systems", Quarterly Journal of Economics 96, 189 – 206

5. Pecchenino, R., and K. Utendorf, (1999) "Social security, social welfare and the aging population", Journal of Population Economics 12, 607 – 623

6. Zhang, J. S., Zhang, J., and Lee, R., (2001). Mortality Decline and Long – run Economic Growth, Journal of Public Economics, Vol. 80, No. 3: 485 – 07

7. Diamond, P. A., (1965). National Debt in a Neoclassical Growth Model, The American Economic Review, 55, No. 5, 1126 – 1150

8. Pecchenino, R. A., and Pollard, P. S., (2002). Dependent Children and Aged Parents: Funding Education and Social Security in an Aging Economy, Journal of Macroeconomics, Vol. 24, No. 2:145 – 169

9. Zeng Yan, Guo Yanfeng and Zhang Ling, (2013). "Delaying Retirement Strategy Based on Longevity Risk and OLG Model", Journal of Finance and Economics, Vol28, No4: 83 – 93

10. Jin Gang, (2010) "The Analysis on the Status and Problems of China's Retiring Age and the Necessity of Extending Retiring Age", Social Security Studies, 2010,02: 33 – 39

Comparison of Two kinds of Bonus – Malus Systems in Environmental Impairment Liability Insurance[①]

Dan Yao[②], Sujin Zheng[③]

Abstract: Environmental Impairment liability Insurance was introduced to China since 1990s, but this type of insurance was not accepted by the market. Until 2007, Environmental Protection Agency and China Insurance Regulation Commission published the "Guidelines on Environmental Impairment liability Insurance work", and started to promote the development of Environmental Impairment liability Insurance. As of 2013, pilot work has been carried out for six years. During this time, the high price of this insurance product has always been a problem. To improve this situation, Bonus – Malus system starts to be used in this type of insurance. Bonus – Malus System is a kind of premium adjustment procedure, often used in non – life insurance, especially in automobile insurance. In market practice, there exists two kinds of BMS; one is based on the number of claims while another is based on loss ratio. In this paper, we want to give a comparison between the existing BMS. We choose "The Relative Stationary Average Premium Level, (RSAL)", "The coefficient of variation of the insured premium, (CV)", "The efficiency of BMS", and "Implicit punishment for new policyholders" to compare the Systems. Through calculation these analysis index, we want to define an "Index of toughness" to figure out the system which is more suitable to Environmental Impairment liability Insurance and give some recommendations for improvement.

Keywords: Bonus – malus System; Environmental Impairment Liability Insurance

1. Background

1.1 Development of China's Environmental Impairment Liability Insurance

China's economy has experienced 30 years of extensive development. During this period, we achieved brilliant achievements but our environment has been seriously polluted. In recent years, environmental issues has been widespread concerned, yet the status doesn't improve. On the one hand, small factories lack of pollution treatment equipment; on the other hand, because of the increasing compensation costs of environmental impairment accident and poor status of the small factories, this responsibility was often delivered to government eventually. In this background, environ-

---

① 18th Asia – Pacific Risk and Insurance Association Annual Conference, Moscow, 2014.
② Dan Yao, Insurance School, Central University of Finance and Economics, China. yaodancufe@hotmail.com.
③ Sujin Zheng, Associate Professor, Insurance School, Central University of Finance and Economics, China.

mental impairment liability (EIL) insurance gains much attention as important risk transfer and control equipment.

China's Environmental impairment Liability insurance started a pilot in the 1990s, but due to the low level of insurance loss ratio and high premium, the sales declined until withdrawn from the market. Until 2007, Environmental Protection Agency and China Insurance Regulation Commission published the "Guidelines on Environmental impairment liability Insurance work", and started to promote the development of EIL Insurance. After a six – year pilot project, Environmental Protection Agency and China Insurance Regulation Commission jointly issued "Guidance on conducting environmental impairment liability insurance mandatory pilot work". EIL insurance ushered in a new round of development opportunities. 6 – year pilot project has accumulated much experience, but it also exposed many problems.

During this time, the high price of EIL insurance has always been a problem and the EIL Insurance has not been universally recognized. The reason of this high premium level can be divided into two parts, one is lack of data and the other is the low level of sum assured. Since the EIL insurance introduced to China's market, there have been only about twenty years and the real survival time is less than ten years. The poor experience makes insurance company to be more cautious about pricing, while the high level of premium makes insured unwilling to purchase insurance product.

1.2 Bonus – malus System

To alleviate the problem of premium, some scholars have proposed to introduce Bonus – malus system (BMS) into EIL insurance. Limited by poor experience, to rationalize the premium in pricing procedure is unlikely in a short time. But for a specific insured, adjust the premium to a reasonable level during the insurance period is feasible. Wang Shunqing (2010) thought we should introduce a severe BMS into EIL insurance in the early stages of development.

Bonus – malus System is a rate adjustment system, mainly used in non – life Insurance practice. The system can adjust the premium level of next year according to the claim status of policyholder. For the insured that with no claims occurred during last year, the renewal premium can be reduced by discount. While for the insured that had some claims last year, the renewal premium should be increased. The renewal premium of an insured is depending on the current premium level and claim status. Through this procedure the insurer can distinguish the insured from different levels of risks and encourage the insured to bear small loss of their own, reducing the company's costs.

BMS is most common in automobile insurance. The BMS is also called No Claim Discount System (NCD) in China. It means that if the insured don't have any claim last year, they can get a discount, but if they do have claims, they will not be punished. The research about BMS is mainly focus on two aspects: one is system design and the other is system evaluation. Dionne G (2005) assessed the empirical impact of BMS on road safety in Tunisia; Venter G G (1991) compared the BMS in 13 different countries; Chang Shasha (2011) compared the BMS in China under a limited time. The research is very rich but most of them are associated with automobile insurance. This paper wants to talk about the BMS in EIL insurance in China and give some advice.

1.3 BMS in Environmental Impairment liability insurance in China

In my opinion, it's practicable to add a BMS into EIL insurance for the following reasons:

1. The current premium of EIL insurance is relatively high according to the low loss ratio, so introducing the BMS into premium adjustment procedure is affordable for the insurance company. And this action will not affect the solvency of insurer.

2. On China's current market, EIL insurance only covers accidental environmental pollution accidents, and it is difficult to regard progressive environmental risks as an insurance risk in a short term. The risk characteristic of accidental environmental pollution accident is suitable for BMS.

3. For EIL insurance, the risk of insured is really different. Although the insurer could conduct a risk assessment of the insured before signing a policy, the risk status of insured cannot be fully considerate. The BMS gives insurer a chance to use the posteriori information to adjust their premium.

4. The high premium has already been a problem in the promotion of EIL insurance. Introducing the BMS into premium adjustment procedure gives insured a chance to reduce their costs and encourage them to purchase EIL insurance.

For all reasons above, add BMS into EIL insurance is feasible, so that the low risk insured can achieve lower premiums, while the high risk insured will be punished by higher premium. This act can encourage more insured to enhance risk management and reduce environmental pollution accidents. Although most of the policies have not introduced the Bonus-malus system into premium adjustment, there have been a few of environmental liability policies containing BMS rate adjustment mechanism.

2. Two Types of Bonus-malus systems

Currently, Bonus-malus system on the market can be broadly divided into two types, namely the renewal premium is adjusted according to the number of claims or loss ratio. The number of claim is a traditional factor of BMS. Because automobile insurance may have several claims in a year and often has a low amount of loss. So the number of claims is a suitable factor and there is no need to considering other factors when taking the cost into account. But when talking about the BMS in EIL insurance, the situation may be totally different. A factory has two environmental accident in a year is almost impossible. So some insurers introduced the loss ratio into the BMS.

2.1 Based on number of claims

Premiums are divided into seven levels, the corresponding adjustment factors of each level are 0.7, 0.8, 0.9, 1, 1.1, 1.2, 1.3, policyholders' premiums equal to the basic premium multiple adjustment factor.

The initial premium of each policyholder is level four, that first year premium adjustment factor is 1. If a claim happened in this year, the adjustment factor for the next year raised one level; if the insured event did not occur for two consecutive years, and then adjust factor decline one level. The adjustment factor is limited by the minimum and maximum level.

2.2 Based on Loss ratio

Premiums were divided into four levels, the corresponding adjustment factors of each level are 0.9, 1, 1.1, 1.3, policyholders' premiums equal to the basic premium multiple adjustment factor.

The initial premium of each policyholder is level two, that first year premium adjustment factor is 1. If yearly loss ratio does not exceed 30%, adjustment factor declines one level; If yearly loss ratio is greater than 30% but does not exceed 60%, it remains original level; If yearly loss ratio is greater than 60% but does not exceed 120%, then the adjustment factor raised one level; If yearly loss ratio is greater than 120%, then adjustment factor up by two levels. The adjustment factor is limited by the minimum and maximum level.

2.3 The Transfer matrix and Steady – state level premium of the BMS

With the development of environmental Impairment liability insurance, academics pay more attention on this kind of insurance. Scholars and researchers have analyzed the loss features of this insurance. You Guiyun (2009) analysis the environmental pollution accidents occurred in 2004 to 2006. He assumes there is a deductible of CNY 100,000 and fits the distribution of claim frequency and amounts. According to his conclusion, the claims assumptions in this paper are as follows:

(1) The insurance company's deductible per policy is CNY 100000 and compensation limit is CNY 2 million;

(2) Claim frequency follows N (0, 1) distribution. The probability of one claim occurs is 0.00282694;

(3) Claim amount follows a truncated exponential distribution with a parameter of 73.5 (Unit: 10 thousand CNY). The distribution function is:

$$F_X(x) = \begin{cases} 1 - e^{-\frac{1}{73.5}x}, 0 < x < 190 \\ 1, x \geq 190 \end{cases}$$

(4) Total claims amount is a compound distribution of N and X. N is claim frequency and X is claim amount.

$$S = \begin{cases} X, N = 1 \\ 0, N = 0 \end{cases}$$

(5) The safe factor of premium is 40%.

This paper will analysis the BMS of EIL insurance based on the conclusion above. Through calculation, we got that:

The average claim amount is (Unit: 10 thousand CNY):

$$E(X) = \int_0^{190} x \frac{1}{73.5} e^{-\frac{x}{73.5}} dx + 190 e^{-\frac{190}{73.5}} = 67.95857664$$

The pure premium of an EIL policy is (Unit: 10 thousand CNY):

$$P = E(S) = E(X)P(N=1) + 0 = 67.95857663 \times 0.00282694 = 0.19211482$$

The gross premium of an EIL policy is (Unit: 10 thousand CNY):

$$G = P(1 + c) = 0.19211482 \times (1 + 40\%) = 0.26896075$$

Therefore, in the analysis below, the gross premium of an EIL policy is CNY 2689.6.

Comparison of Two kinds of Bonus – Malus Systems in Environmental Impairment Liability Insurance

Set p_{ij} as the probability of an insured with premium level i transfer to level i in next year. So that the $Q = (p_{ij})$ can represent the transfer matrix of the BMS. This matrix represents that the transfer probability of each insured with all kinds of premium level. We can get the steady – state distribution with $Q = (p_{ij})$.

BMS based on number of claims

Claim frequency follows N (0, 1) distribution. The probability of one claim occurs (p) is 0.00282694.

If a claim occurred in current year, the premium level will transfer above a grade. The corresponding probability is 0.00282694.

If there is no claim occurred in current year, we need to considerate the claim status last year. If there is also no claim occurred last year, the premium level can be down one grade, the corresponding probability is $(1 - 0.00282694) \times (1 - 0.00282694) = 0.9943541116$; and if there is a claim occurred last year, the premium level should stay the same, the corresponding probability is $0.00282694 \times (1 - 0.00282694) = 0.0028189484$.

We can get the transfer matrix of this Bonus – malus system as below:

$$Q = \begin{pmatrix} 0.99717306 & 0.00282694 & 0 & 0 & 0 & 0 & 0 \\ 0.99435411 & 0.00281895 & 0.00282694 & 0 & 0 & 0 & 0 \\ 0 & 0.99435411 & 0.00281895 & 0.00282694 & 0 & 0 & 0 \\ 0 & 0 & 0.99435411 & 0.00281895 & 0.00282694 & 0 & 0 \\ 0 & 0 & 0 & 0.99435411 & 0.00281895 & 0.00282694 & 0 \\ 0 & 0 & 0 & 0 & 0.99435411 & 0.00281895 & 0.00282694 \\ 0 & 0 & 0 & 0 & 0 & 0.99435411 & 0.00564589 \end{pmatrix}$$

Through calculation, the steady – state distribution is:

$\pi = (0.99715701 \quad 0.00283491 \quad 0.00000806 \quad 0.00000002 \quad 0.00000000 \quad 0.00000000 \quad 0.00000000)$

BMS based on loss ratio

Define the loss ratio as $\eta = \dfrac{S}{G}$, where G is the base premium and S is claim amount.

When the adjustment factor is 1, if yearly loss ratio is less than 30%, namely:

$$\frac{S}{G} \leq 30\% \Rightarrow S \leq 0.3G = 0.08068822$$

Then the premium level will down one grade, the corresponding probability is:

$$p_{21} = P(N = 0) + P(N = 1)F_X(0.08068822)$$

Through calculation, we can know that $p_{21} = 0.99717616$.

If yearly loss ratio is greater than 30 % but does not exceed 60%, namely:

$$30\% < \frac{S}{G} \leq 60\% \Rightarrow 0.08068822 < S \leq 0.16137645$$

Then the premium should stay the same, the corresponding probability is:

$$p_{22} = P(N = 1)(F_X(0.16137645) - F_X(0.08068822))$$

Through calculation, we can know that $p_{22} = 0.00000310$.

If yearly loss ratio is greater than 60 % but does not exceed 120%, namely:

$$60\% < \frac{S}{G} \leq 120\% \Rightarrow 0.16137645 < S \leq 0.32275290$$

Then the premium will raise a grade, the corresponding probability is:

$$p_{23} = P(N = 1)(F_X(0.32275290) - F_X(0.16137645))$$

Through calculation, we know that $p_{23} = 0.00000619$.

If yearly loss ratio is greater than 120%, namely:

$$\frac{S}{G} > 120\% \Rightarrow S > 0.32275290$$

Then the premium will raise two grades, the corresponding probability is:

$$p_{24} = P(N = 1)(1 - F_X(0.32275290))$$

Through calculation, we know that $p_{24} = 0.00281455$.

In the same way, we can get all p_{ij}.

The transfer matrix of this Bonus – malus system is:

$$Q = \begin{pmatrix} 0.99717926 & 0.00000619 & 0.00281455 & 0 \\ 0.99717616 & 0.00000310 & 0.00000619 & 0.00281455 \\ 0 & 0.99717616 & 0.00000310 & 0.00282074 \\ 0 & 0 & 0.99717616 & 0.00282384 \end{pmatrix}$$

Through calculation, the steady – state distribution is:

$$\pi = (0.99435678 \quad 0.00281276 \quad 0.00281455 \quad 0.00001590)$$

3. Analysis to the two kinds of Bonus – malus systems

In order to compare the two systems, we choose "The Relative Stationary Average Premium Level, (RSAL)", "The coefficient of variation of the insured premium, (CV)", "The efficiency of Bonus – malus system (Eff_{Loi})", "Implicit punishment for new policyholders" and "Index of toughness" five indicators.

3.1 The Relative Stationary Average Premium Level

The Relative Stationary Average Premium Level (RSAL) measures the when the BMS reached steady state, the degree of aggregation in the lower level of premium, namely the general location of the insured. If the relative stationary average premium level is low (less than 50%), we can say that most of insured are aggregated in the favorable rating and the BMS is moderate. On the contrary, the BMS is severe. Chang Shasha (2011) said the ideal relative stationary average premium level is 50%.

The relative stationary average premium level is defined as:

$$RSAL = \frac{\text{Average premium in steady state} / \text{Minimum premium level}}{\text{Maximum premium level} / \text{Minimum premium level}}$$

The average premium in steady state is the weighted average of each premium level with steady state distribution.

BMS based on number of claims

Through calculation, the average premium in the steady state is CNY 1.8834921 thousand.

The maximum premium level is CNY 3.4964897 thousand and the minimum premium level is CNY 1.8827252 thousand.

$$RSAL = 0.00047518 = 0.0005$$

BMS based on loss ratio

Through calculation, the average premium in the steady state is CNY 2.4229344 thousand. The maximum premium level is CNY 3.4964897 thousand and the minimum premium level is CNY 2.4206467 thousand.

$$RSAL = 0.00212637 = 0.0021$$

According to the result, we can say that two Bonus – malus systems are all very moderate, and the RSAL are far away from the 50%. It means that most insured finally stay in the lower level of premium. This phenomenon is closely linked with the low occurrence probability of environmental pollution accident. Comparing these two systems, the BMS based on loss ratio is relatively severe than the BMS based on number of claims.

3.2 The coefficient of variation of the insured premium

The coefficient of variation (CV) of the insured premium measures the insured's annual premium volatility. This volatility is for the premium of insured. If an owner of factory didn't buy EIL insurance, then the premium he needs to pay is zero and the volatility is zero. If an owner of factory did buy EIL insurance but there isn't a BMS is embedded in the policy, his volatility is zero too. The coefficient of variation of the insured premium is defined as:

$$CV = \frac{Tie\ standard\ deviation\ of\ steady\ state\ average\ premium}{Tie\ expectation\ of\ steady\ state\ average\ premium}$$

BMS based on number of claims

The standard deviation of steady state premium is 0.00143818.

$$CV = 0.00763571 = 0.0076$$

BMS based on loss ratio

The standard deviation of steady state premium is 0.00321102.

$$CV = 0.01325260 = 0.0133$$

It is obvious that the CV of BMS based on number of claims is less that the CV of BMS based on loss ratio. According to the rules of premium adjustment, the BMS based on number of claims has a broader adjustment range. So we know that under the BMS based on loss ratio, the volatility is larger. The BMS based on loss ratio is relatively severe.

3.3 The efficiency of Bonus – malus system

The efficiency of BMS is defined as the elasticity. Elasticity of the Bonus – malus system measures the sensitive degree of the systems to number of claims or loss ratio. When designing the Bonus – malus system, we assume that when loss ratio or loss frequency become larger, the premium that insured has to pay become more. The speed of premium increases along with loss ratio or frequency can be weighted by Elasticity. In this paper, we choose the Loimaranta Elasticity based on the gross premium and steady – state distribution.

BMS based on number of claims

Claim frequency follows N (0, 1) distribution. The probability of one claim occurs is p. Define $\bar{r}(p)$ as the steady state premium. The Loimaranta Elasticity can be represented as:

$$Eff_{Loi}(p) = \frac{\frac{d\bar{r}(p)}{\bar{r}(p)}}{\frac{dp}{p}} = \frac{d\bar{r}(p)}{dp} \times \frac{p}{\bar{r}(p)}$$

The steady-state distribution can be represented by p as follow:

$$\pi_1 = \frac{(1-p)^{12}p - (1-p)^{14}}{p^7 - (1-p)^{14}} = \frac{1}{p^7 - (1-p)^{14}}[(1-p)^{12}p - (1-p)^{14}] = f(p)g_1(p)$$

$$\pi_2 = \frac{(1-p)^{10}p^2 - (1-p)^{12}p}{p^7 - (1-p)^{14}} = \frac{1}{p^7 - (1-p)^{14}}[(1-p)^{10}p^2 - (1-p)^{12}p] = f(p)g_2(p)$$

$$\pi_3 = \frac{(1-p)^{8}p^3 - (1-p)^{10}p^2}{p^7 - (1-p)^{14}} = \frac{1}{p^7 - (1-p)^{14}}[(1-p)^{8}p^3 - (1-p)^{10}p^2] = f(p)g_3(p)$$

$$\pi_4 = \frac{(1-p)^{6}p^4 - (1-p)^{8}p^3}{p^7 - (1-p)^{14}} = \frac{1}{p^7 - (1-p)^{14}}[(1-p)^{6}p^4 - (1-p)^{8}p^3] = f(p)g_4(p)$$

$$\pi_5 = \frac{(1-p)^{4}p^5 - (1-p)^{6}p^4}{p^7 - (1-p)^{14}} = \frac{1}{p^7 - (1-p)^{14}}[(1-p)^{4}p^5 - (1-p)^{6}p^4] = f(p)g_5(p)$$

$$\pi_6 = \frac{(1-p)^{2}p^6 - (1-p)^{4}p^5}{p^7 - (1-p)^{14}} = \frac{1}{p^7 - (1-p)^{14}}[(1-p)^{2}p^6 - (1-p)^{4}p^5] = f(p)g_6(p)$$

$$\pi_7 = \frac{p^7 - (1-p)^{2}p^6}{p^7 - (1-p)^{14}} = \frac{1}{p^7 - (1-p)^{14}}[p^7 - (1-p)^{2}p^6] = f(p)g_7(p)$$

So the steady state premium is:

$$\bar{r}(p) = (0.7, 0.8, 0.9, 1, 1.1, 1.2, 1.3)(\pi_1, \pi_2, \pi_3, \pi_4, \pi_5, \pi_6, \pi_7)^T \times G$$
$$= f(p)(0.7g_1(p) + 0.8g_2(p) + 0.9g_3(p) + g_4(p) + 1.1g_5(p) + 1.2g_6(p) + 1.3g_7(p)) \times G$$

The deviation of steady state premium for p can be obtained:

$$\frac{d\bar{r}(p)}{dp} = [f'(p)(0.7g_1(p) + 0.8g_2(p) + 0.9g_3(p) + g_4(p) + 1.1g_5(p) + 1.2g_6(p)$$
$$+ 1.3g_7(p)) + f(p)(0.7g'_1(p) + 0.8g'_2(p) + 0.9g'_3(p) + g'_4(p)$$
$$+ 1.1g'_5(p) + 1.2g'_6(p) + 1.3g'_7(p))] \times G$$

Through calculation, we got that the Loimaranta Elasticity.

$$Eff_{Loi}(p) = 0.02065247 = 0.0207$$

BMS based on loss ratio

The Loimaranta Elasticity can be defined as:

$$Eff_{Loi}(E\eta) = \frac{\frac{d\bar{r}(E\eta)}{\bar{r}(E\eta)}}{\frac{dE\eta}{E\eta}} = \frac{d\bar{r}(E\eta)}{dE\eta} \times \frac{E\eta}{\bar{r}(E\eta)}$$

Among this formula, $E\eta$ is the expectation of loss ratio, $E\eta = E\left(\frac{S}{G}\right) = \frac{E(S)}{G} = \frac{pE(X)}{G}$;

$$E(X) = \int_0^{190} x \frac{1}{\theta} e^{-\frac{x}{\theta}} dx + 190 e^{-\frac{190}{\theta}} = \theta \times (1 - e^{-\frac{190}{\theta}})$$

θ is the parameter of exponential distribution and G is a constant. So $E\eta$ can be represented by p and θ, namely $E\eta = E\left(\dfrac{S}{G}\right) = \dfrac{E(S)}{G} = \dfrac{p\theta(1-e^{-\frac{190}{\theta}})}{G}$.

$\bar{r}(E\eta)$ is the steady state premium:

$\bar{r}(E\eta) = 0.9G\pi_1 + G\pi_2 + 1.1G\pi_3 + 1.3G\pi_4 = (0.9\pi_1 + \pi_2 + 1.1\pi_3 + 1.3\pi_4)G$

Because the transfer probability is a function on p and θ. and the gross premium is a constant, so the steady state premium is the function on p and θ.

The transfer matrix can be represented by p and θ as:

$$\begin{pmatrix} 1 - pe^{-\frac{0.6G}{\theta}} & p(e^{-\frac{0.6G}{\theta}} - e^{-\frac{1.2G}{\theta}}) & pe^{-\frac{1.2G}{\theta}} & 0 \\ 1 - pe^{-\frac{0.3G}{\theta}} & p(e^{-\frac{0.3G}{\theta}} - e^{-\frac{0.6G}{\theta}}) & p(e^{-\frac{0.6G}{\theta}} - e^{-\frac{1.2G}{\theta}}) & pe^{-\frac{1.2G}{\theta}} \\ 0 & 1 - pe^{-\frac{0.3G}{\theta}} & p(e^{-\frac{0.3G}{\theta}} - e^{-\frac{0.6G}{\theta}}) & pe^{-\frac{0.6G}{\theta}} \\ 0 & 0 & 1 - pe^{-\frac{0.3G}{\theta}} & pe^{-\frac{0.3G}{\theta}} \end{pmatrix}$$

Among this matrix, p is the occurrence probability of environmental pollution accident.

Define $x = e^{-\frac{0.3G}{\theta}}$.

So the steady-state distribution can be represented by c as follow:

$\pi_1 = \dfrac{(1-px)^3}{1 - 3px + (3p^2+p)x^2 - (p^3+2p^2)x^3 + (p^3+p^2+p)x^4 - (p^3+2p^2)x^5 + (2p^3+2p^2)x^6 - 2p^3x^7} \cdot \dfrac{g_1(p,\theta)}{f(p,\theta)}$

$\pi_2 = \dfrac{px^2 - 2p^2x^3 + p^3x^4}{1 - 3px + (3p^2+p)x^2 - (p^3+2p^2)x^3 + (p^3+p^2+p)x^4 - (p^3+2p^2)x^5 + (2p^3+2p^2)x^6 - 2p^3x^7} \cdot \dfrac{g_2(p,\theta)}{f(p,\theta)}$

$\pi_3 = \dfrac{(p^2+p)x^4 - (p^3+2p^2)x^5 + p^3x^6}{1 - 3px + (3p^2+p)x^2 - (p^3+2p^2)x^3 + (p^3+p^2+p)x^4 - (p^3+2p^2)x^5 + (2p^3+2p^2)x^6 - 2p^3x^7} \cdot \dfrac{g_3(p,\theta)}{f(p,\theta)}$

$\pi_4 = \dfrac{(p^3+2p^2)x^6 - 2p^3x^7}{1 - 3px + (3p^2+p)x^2 - (p^3+2p^2)x^3 + (p^3+p^2+p)x^4 - (p^3+2p^2)x^5 + (2p^3+2p^2)x^6 - 2p^3x^7} \cdot \dfrac{g_4(p,\theta)}{f(p,\theta)}$

From the information above, we can know that, there is no direct expression between $E\eta$ and $\bar{r}(E\eta)$. And both of $E\eta$ and $\bar{r}(E\eta)$ can represented by p and θ, it means that there are two influence factors. So we cannot get the Elasticity directly.

Define ε_p and ε_θ as the elastic based on p and θ. Hold one influence factor (p or θ) as a constant, we can get the elastic based on the other.

$$\varepsilon_p = \dfrac{d\bar{r}(E\eta)}{dE\eta} = \dfrac{\dfrac{d\bar{r}(E\eta)}{dp}}{\dfrac{dE\eta}{dp}}, \varepsilon_\theta = \dfrac{d\bar{r}(E\eta)}{dE\eta} = \dfrac{\dfrac{d\bar{r}(E\eta)}{d\theta}}{\dfrac{dE\eta}{d\theta}}$$

It means that we can get two elastics in this part.

$$\dfrac{d\bar{r}(E\eta)}{dp} = G\left(0.9\dfrac{d\pi_1}{dp} + \dfrac{d\pi_2}{dp} + 1.1\dfrac{d\pi_3}{dp} + 1.3\dfrac{d\pi_4}{dp}\right),$$

$$\dfrac{d\bar{r}(E\eta)}{d\theta} = G\left(0.9\dfrac{d\pi_1}{d\theta} + \dfrac{d\pi_2}{d\theta} + 1.1\dfrac{d\pi_3}{d\theta} + 1.3\dfrac{d\pi_4}{d\theta}\right)$$

Among this expression:

$$\dfrac{d\pi_i}{dp} = \dfrac{g'_i(p)f(p) - g_i(p)f'(p)}{[f(p)]^2}, \quad i = 1,2,3,4$$

$$\frac{d\pi_i}{d\theta} = \frac{d\pi_i}{dx} \cdot \frac{dx}{d\theta}, \quad i = 1,2,3,4$$

$$\frac{d\pi_i}{dx} = \frac{g'_i(x)f(x) - g_i(x)f'(x)}{[f(x)]^2}, \quad i = 1,2,3,4$$

$$\frac{dx}{d\theta} = \frac{d}{d\theta}(e^{-\frac{0.3G}{\theta}}) = \frac{0.3G}{\theta^2}e^{-\frac{0.3G}{\theta}}$$

Through calculation we know that:

$$\varepsilon_p = 0.0094, \quad \varepsilon_\theta = 0.00000321$$

According to the results above, we know that under the BMS based on number of claims, $Eff_{Loi}(p) = 0.0207$. It means that if the frequency raises 1%, the premium of insured in next period increases 0.0207%. As of the BMS based on loss ratio, $\varepsilon_p = 0.0094$ and $\varepsilon_\theta = 0.00000321$, namely if the loss ratio raises 1% because of the change of occurrence probability p, the premium of insured in next period increases 0.0094% and if the loss ratio raised 1% because of the change of θ, the premium of insured in next period increased 0.00000321%. The premium increases along with frequency or loss ratio raises. Such result is in line with our expectation. And the Elasticity in BMS based on claim number is higher, and this situation might be related to the broader adjustment range. As to the BMS based on loss ratio, ε_θ is much less. It means that although we add the claim amount into BMS through loss ratio, the effect of this factor is not ideal.

3.4 Implicit punishment for new policyholders

Implicit punishment for new policyholders (IPN) measures the gap between the premium level of new insured and stability premium level. Because for a new insured, the adjustment factor is 1 and cannot get any price decreases. Therefor the paid premium that more than steady state premium can be seen as the punishment for new policyholders.

$$IPN = \frac{Tie\ premium\ for\ new\ policylolder\ I\ Average\ premium\ in\ steady\ state}{Average\ premium\ in\ steady\ state}$$

BMS based on number of claims

Through calculation, the IPN is 0.4280.

BMS based on loss ratio

Through calculation, the IPN is 0.1101.

The index of BMS based on number of claims is higher. In both BMS, the insured finally generated in lower discount level, but the lowest level for BMS based on number of claims is 0.7 and for BMS based on loss ratio is 0.9. The level for new policyholder is 1 in both systems. Considering that the BMS based on number of claims has a broader discount range, the main reason for this result might be the discount range other than BMS basis.

3.5 Index of toughness

These four indicators mentioned above are relevant. In Bonus – malus system evaluation, we usually use principle component analysis to formulate a comprehensive index. Limited by information, there are only two systems discussed in this paper. If we use only two sets of indicators to do principle component analysis, the accuracy of results will be very poor. Therefore we abandon the principle component analysis. We range these four indicators according to its importance, and give each indicator a weight to build the index of toughness (T) and evaluate the Bonus-malus system.

The Relative Stationary Average Premium Level (RSAL) represents the average premium level of insured when reaching the steady state and is a core indicator in evaluation of BMS. The coefficient of variation (CV) of the insured premium reflects the degree of fluctuation in premiums paid by the insured. This indicator is related with the transfer rules and discount range. The efficiency of BMS, namely the Elasticity measures the reflection of premium to frequency or loss ratio. Implicit punishment for new policyholders (IPN) measures the gap between the premium level of new insured and stability premium level.

To evaluate a toughness of a Bonus-malus system, we give a certain weights to each indicator according to importance. The importance range of these indicators is: RSAL > Eff_{Loi} > CV > IPN. Their weights are 40%, 30%, 20%, 10%. Before building the index of toughness, we need to standardize these indicators to avoid the impact of magnitude differences. The adjustment method is as follow:

$$Standardized\ Indicator\ Under\ BMS1 = \frac{Indicator\ under\ BMS1}{Indicator\ under\ BMS1 + Indicator\ under\ BMS2}$$

$$Standardized\ Indicator\ Under\ BMS2 = \frac{Indicator\ under\ BMS2}{Indicator\ under\ BMS1 + Indicator\ under\ BMS2}$$

Since the BMS based on loss ratio has two Eff_{Loi}, we choose the average of these standardized Elastics as the final indicator.

BMS based on number of claims

$$T = RSAL^* \times 40\% + Eff_{Loi}^* \times 30\% + CV^* \times 20\% + IPN^* \times 10\% = 0.4789$$

BMS based on loss ratio

$$T = RSAL^* \times 40\% + Eff_{Loi}^* \times 30\% + CV^* \times 20\% + IPN^* \times 10\% = 0.5211$$

Through this indicator, the BMS based on loss ratio is more severe than the BMS based on number of claims. The toughness does not mean better or worse. It means that the degree of separation between different levels.

4. The Comparison of the Bonus-malus systems.

Based on analysis above, the comparing result can be displayed as follow:

Table 1   **Summary of index**

Name of Index	BMS based on loss ratio (1)	BMS based on number of claims (2)	The one more severe
RSAL	0.0021	0.0005	(1)
CV	0.0133	0.0076	(1)
IPN	0.1101	0.4280	(2)
Eff_{Loi}	$\varepsilon_p = 0.0094$, $\varepsilon_\theta = 0.00000321$	0.0207	(2)
T	0.5211	0.4789	(1)

According to the four indicators and the Index of toughness, we can say that the BMS based on loss ratio is the more severe one. The RSAL, CV, T of BMS based on loss ratio are obvious larger the other. As for the IPN and Eff_{Loi}, the main reason for this result might be the discount range other than BMS basis.

To discuss the BMS basis and get rid of the impact of other reasons, we redesign the discount range of BMS based on number of claims. Set the discount range as 0.9 to 1.3, the gap between each level and transfer rule as the same. Therefore, the discount ranges of two systems become the same. Recalculate the indicators of BMS based on number of claims with the same method and get the following results.

Table 2 Summary of index after revised

Name of Index	BMS based on loss ratio (1)	BMS based on number of claims (2)	The one more severe
RSAL	0.0021	0.0007	(1)
CV	0.0133	0.0059	(1)
IPN	0.1101	0.1107	(2)
Eff_{Loi}	$\varepsilon_p = 0.0094$, $\varepsilon_\theta = 0.00000321$	0.00032	-
T	0.4875	0.2125	(1)

In this table, the larger one of RSAL, CV and T is BMS based on loss ratio; IPN indicator is almost the same; and the Eff_{Loi} of BMS based on number of claims is larger than ε_θ and smaller than ε_p. We can judge that loss ratio as a basis of BMS is more severe than number of claims.

Through these indicators, we know that the relative stationary average premium level based on loss ratio is a little higher than based on number of claims. But both of them stay in a low level. This is because the occurrence probability of environmental pollution accident is very small, finally most insured will stay close to the lowest discount level. This fact reflects to IPN indicator too. The maximum IPN is $(1-0.9)/0.9 = 0.1111$. In this situation, all insured stay in the lowest premium level in steady state. We can see that the actual IPN is very close to this level. The premium volatility of BMS based on loss ratio is almost twice of BMS based on number of claims, means that loss ratio is a more sensitive BMS basis. The Eff_{Loi} of both systems stay in a low level, indicating that in fact there is no obvious punishment and the system is moderate. Venter (1991) believes that for a Bonus - malus system, the perfect efficiency should be 1.

5. Conclusion and Recommendation

Loss ratio as a basis of Bonus - malus system is more severe than number of claims, and has higher risk discrimination ability. In my opinion, for Environmental Impairment Liability insurance, choosing loss ratio as the basis of Bonus - malus system is more appropriate. On the one hand, these two existing systems are all moderate, in order to distinguish the risk of insured, we should select a more severe one; On the other hand, considering the characteristics of EIL insurance, loss amount is a very important factor, while the number of claims become less sensitive. For automobile insurance, the claim frequency is high and loss amount is often low, so the number of claims can represent the risk situation of insured. But EIL insurance is completely different, the loss amount can be very large, so take this factor into account is necessary. Choosing loss ratio as the basis of BMS is a useful attempt.

Under the two Bonus – malus systems discussed in this paper, when the insured reached steady state, most of them will stay in the lower premium level, close to the minimum. Apart of risk distinguish; the Bonus – malus system plays a role in promoting the rationalization of premium. So an insurer should be cautious when designing the minimum premium level, so as not to endanger the solvency of company.

On China's current market, EIL insurance only covers accidental environmental pollution accidents. And because of the limitation of experience data, the premium of EIL insurance is relatively high. So introduce a Bonus – malus system into EIL insurance is feasible. But due to the low frequency of environmental pollution accident, only take the accident factor into Bonus – malus system will easily lead to the result that most insured aggregated in lower premium level and the lower risk discrimination. To solve this problem, we can try to link the regular examination result of the Environmental Protection Agency (EPA) to premium discount level. So that, the premium adjustment system can truly reflect the insured's risk management level and urge the insured to improve their ability of risk control. The introduction of this rule needs cooperation of insurance company and the EPA.

Hope the improvement of Bonus – malus system can facilitate premium rationalization of EIL insurance and promote the environmental risk management of insured.

References

1. You Guiyun. Insurance mode choice and Pricing analysis of Environmental Impairement Liability Insurance [D]. Qingdao: Ocean University of China, 2009.

2. Zhong Zhen, Xiao Yugu, Meng Shengwang. Evaluation of China's automobile insurance Bonus – malus system [J]. Statistics and Decision, 2007 (02).

3. Chang Shasha. Comparison of China's automobile insurance Bonus – malus system under limited time[D]. Zhengzhou: Henan University of Technology, 2011.

4. Xia Dong, Xiao Yugu, Meng Shengwang. China's current insurance Bonus – malus system[J]. Statistics and Decision, 2008 (15).

5. Dionne G, Ghali O. The (1992) Bonus - Malus System in Tunisia: An Empirical Evaluation[J]. Journal of Risk and Insurance, 2005, 72(4): 609 – 633.

6. Venter G G. A Comparative Analysis of Most European and Japanese Bonus – Malus Systems: Extension[J]. Journal of Risk and Insurance, 1991, 58(3): 542 – 547.

Collective Credit and Behavior Restriction: the Analysis and Improvement of the Credit Village Assessment for Risk Control in Liuyang, China[1]

Lanfeng Li[2]　Duo Fang[3]　Yuling Wu[4]

Abstract: Purpose – Presenting a comprehensive analysis on the mechanism of the Credit Village Assessment, the purpose of this paper is to introduce the Chinese experience on risk control in the development of rural credit. Furthermore, the paper pointed out the mechanism's advantage relative to the traditional mechanism as well as its improvement direction by considering the game between peasants and financial institutions.

Design/methodology/approach – The paper is developed as an introduction to the Credit Village Assessment based on the existing literature and fieldwork in Hunan Province. Besides, it builds game models from an evolutionary perspective and emulate through Matlab to compare the Credit Village Assessment with the traditional personal credit assessment.

Findings – The paper shows that the Credit Village Assessment is suitable for credit risk control by using the collective credit and behavior restriction considering that the Chinese rural society has some characteristics. And under this mechanism, those who are relatively bad types will be distinguished by the financial institution and excluded out of the credit market more quickly, especially when the village cadre works harder.

Research limitations/implications – Even if the fieldwork and some literatures gave us an intuition on the efficiency of the Credit Village Assessment in China, this mechanism still has some potential shortcomings may result in the invalidation of some assumptions in our model. And because we analyze from an evolutionary perspective, we simplify the peasants' decision which makes us unable to get a Nash equilibrium like the classical game theory.

Practical implication – The discussion in the paper provides a theoretical basis for the operation of the Credit Village Assessment and shows how this mechanism operates, which is necessary for the proposal of the improvement. The paper ends by pointing out the direction for improvement which is helpful for the research on this mechanism in the future.

---

[1]　3th International Agricultural Risk, Finance, andInsurance Conference, Zurich, 2014. The first two authors contributed equally to this work.
[2]　School of Insurance, Central University of Finance and Economics, Beijing, China.
[3]　School of Finance, Central University of Finance and Economics, Beijing, China
[4]　School of Economics, Central University of Finance and Economics, Beijing, China

Collective Credit and Behavior Restriction: the Analysis and Improvement of the Credit Village Assessment for Risk Control in Liuyang, China

Originality/value – The Credit Village Assessment is a particular experience for rural credit risk control in China. Combining the fieldwork with the theoretical model, the paper is the first one to probe and perfect this mechanism simultaneously.

Keywords: Collective credit, Behavior restriction, Associated responsibility, Information asymmetry, Game model

Introduction

In the last ten years, Chinese government has attached increasingly great importance to the rural financial reform, which is one of the core elements to promote the development of the Agriculture, Rural Area and Farmers. And in 2014, the No. 1 Central Document issued by central government laid stress on the innovation of the rural financial system especially the intensification of the financial institutions' responsibility to serve the agriculture, rural area and farmers.

In fact, when it comes to rural finance, it's naturally related to the higher uncertainty of the peasants' household income and agricultural production, which seems so hard for the rural financial institution to control. And just improving the interest rate to compensate the higher risk would cause adverse selection and moral hazard, which is also bad for the rural financial institution (Hoff, Stiglitz, 1990). With these prerequisites, the financial institution always tend to absorb deposits from rural area and lend money to urban area (Turvey, 2013), which the data released from the Chinese central government has also proved. In order to guide the capital back to the development of the rural economy, China has made many attempts for risk control, especially when the mortgage is inaccessible for most peasants due to the ambiguity of the rural land property nowadays.

The chief way for rural credit risk control is guarantee, to lower the information asymmetry and improve the assessment of the expected profit of the loan (Chan Y, G. Kanatas, 1985), where China has made continuous efforts to reform. In China, the peasants who want to apply for a guaranteed loan from the financial institution have to ask someone trustworthy or some institutions to guarantee his credit. Or he could choose to join a borrower group, like the Grameen solidarity lending in Bangladesh. Besides, the micro – credit insurance is another important way, which is to some extent like the guaranteed loan but the guarantor is the insurance company. However, in practice, guarantee has met some problems which impede its function to support the rural credit. For instance, the availability of guarantor is limited by the peasants' circle of friends as well as their income which means it's difficult for most peasants to find institution even civilians whose income is stable and willing to guarantee for him though many farmers seek employment in cities currently. Thus, the one they could ask for help is always another peasant who is in the same village, like the village cadres. But this type of guarantor couldn't get enough trust from the financial institutions. And to join a borrower group also faces difficulties, for that the peasant has to find another two or four peasants without kinship who also need to borrow money from the financial institution. Because they have to take associated responsibility to repay the other borrower's loan if he defaults, the peasants tend to choose peasants with similar financial position as his group member (Zhao, He, 2007). And when the rich form the alliance, the financial institution tends to lend money to them for safety. But in practice the poor peasants have to face problems that it's hard for them to find cooperative peasants because the poor peasants have relatively low demand for loan. Even if they assemble a borrower group, the financial institution still tends to control their line of credit (He, 2002). And when some of the member defaults intentionally, the other peasants may be unwilling or unable to help him repay his loan if their household situation is not good enough which may even bring about interlocking default in large scale. As for the micro - credit insurance, which has also been designed for risk control by transferring it to the insurance company and piloted in some rural areas in China, it comes to a standstill because of the limited scope of application as well as the red tape which is hard for the peasants to suffer. As a consequence of all these above, it's difficult to develop the rural credit only by guarantee, the most traditional risk control mechanism, which couldn't meet the demand of both the financial institution and the peasants.

Fortunately, in addition to the guarantee, there are some other mechanisms for credit risk control in China. One of them is the Credit Village Assessment, a particular experience in China, which has been conducted in some provinces and proved successful to some extent. It takes advantage of the characteristics of rural society in China and performs efficiently for credit risk control. However, very few researches have been carried out to analyze the rationality and effectiveness of this mechanism, leaving a huge blank remained to be filled. Based on the fieldwork in Liuyang, Hunan province, we believe that it is a valuable mechanism to recommend to the whole country even to other countries and our research on this issue is of vital significance.

This article is developed as a comprehensive analysis on the Credit Village Assessment, combining the theoretical research with the fieldwork experience. Furthermore, compared with the traditional personal credit assessment, it builds models and emulates the game between the peasants and the finance institution from an evolutionary perspective after adding the village cadre's information under the Credit Village Assessment. What it found proves the advantage of this mechanism and provides the direction for further improvement in the future.

Fieldwork experience

The reason why we wrote this paper is to some extent attributed to the fieldwork about rural credit in Liuyang at the beginning of 2014. As a county - level city in Hunan province, Liuyang has experienced a phenomenal growth in the last 8 years, and its economic strength ranking has risen from just ascending the top 100 counties in the national economy in 2006 to the forty - seventh in 2014. And the per capita disposable income of rural residents in Liuyang rose by 12.9 percent to 21,035 yuan, which is much higher than the national average level and even exceeds the average level of some eastern developed cities, like Shanghai and Beijing. In fact, what contributes to this continuous and fleeting development in economy is not only Liuyang's traditional fireworks industry, but also the financial industry, especially its advanced rural finance. In 2012, the profit of banking financial institutions in Liuyang rose by 25.39 percent to 1.12 billion yuan, with a loan balance of 22.86 billion yuan, among of which the agriculture related loan was 13.48 billion yuan. While the

Collective Credit and Behavior Restriction: the Analysis and Improvement of the Credit Village Assessment for Risk Control in Liuyang, China

balance of the agricultural related loan is running at record levels, the balance of nonperforming loans and its proportion in total loans has been continuously decreasing, which were only 0.12 billion yuan and 0.5 percent in 2012. Considering such a high proportion of its agricultural related loan, the banking financial institutions' achievement in Liuyang is a miracle in China. When interviewing with relevant personnel in the Rural Commercial bank of Liuyang, we learnt that such an achievement is largely based on the local financial institutions' various forms on credit risk control, especially the mechanism of the Credit Village Assessment cooperated with the administration. This situation interests us and we decide to conduct further in-depth studies on this mechanism.

Before making a comprehensive analysis on this mechanism, it's necessary to introduce some valuable finding we found about the rural society during our investigation in Liuyang, which is similar to some other counties in Hunan province we visited before.

1) Middle and old aged peasants are willing to return their village, regarding employment in cities just as their means of livelihood.

2) Peasants attach great importance to their villager identity and care about their reputation in the village which strongly influence not just themselves but also their family.

3) If someone harms the interest of the village, no matter who he is, the villagers will despise him even his family whenever they gossip about his behavior.

4) Peasants tend to live in concentrated communities, and the villagers intermingle more often with each other rather than with those from outside.

5) Rural credit has high market demand nowadays but the financial institutions' service can't sufficiently satisfy the peasants' requirement.

These situations mentioned above are the key points to help us understand the efficiency of the Credit Village Assessment. Following are some key measures of the mechanism described in detail which is necessary for us to distinguish it from the mechanism of the solidarity loan in Bangladesh and to discuss the game relationship later.

1) Villages are re-tested every year, and the loan repayment rate in the evaluative year is the key part of the mechanism, which is the reference for financial institution to decide whether to improve or lower the credit line of the whole village. And this rate is one of the most crucial indicators for the financial institutions' profit.

2) The financial institution cooperates with the government to commend and reward the credit village every year, and those awarded village can receive different preferential policies in services or credit interest rates.

3) The village cadre plays an important role in the credit rating of the villager, such as helping the financial institution assess the credit status of the villagers, and call in loans from the villagers, which will be awarded if he finishes the performance appraisal indicator. And he will receive subsidies in the form of a percentage of non-performing loans which he helps the financial institution call back.

4) Those who default the loans will be noticed publicly. And when the default rate up reaches a certain level, the reputation of the Credit Village already gained would be withdrawn.

Based on these fieldwork experience above, the paper would analyses the Credit Village Assessment thoroughly next, combining with the literature. And the analysis would give us a better understanding on why this mechanism can perform efficiently for risk control in Chinese rural society. Furthermore, using the idea of evolutionary game the paper builds models to analyze the traditional personal credit assessment as well as the Credit Village Assessment, providing direction for the improvement of the innovative mechanism.

Fundamental Analysis

Despite the communication between the village and outside nowadays has changed drastically, and the relationship has become more closely, there still exists the asymmetry in the exchange of information between villagers and outside parties in China (Zhang, Deng, 2003). To some extent, information is the basis to make human behavior under supervision (Zhang, 2001). However, rural financial institution, the loan provider and supervisor, can't fully acquire valid information to make a proper judgment whether they should lend money to the peasants whose risk – bearing capacity is lower, especially in the absence of enough trustworthy guarantee and realizable collaterals. Due to the market incentives, rural financial institution tends to lend to lower cost and safer non – farm business which causes further income inequality (Turvey, 2013). Even if the financial institution lend under the pressure of the policy, the loan would always accompany with additional constraints, and a higher interest rate would be priced in order to compensate the higher risk, which still fails to decrease the relatively high default rate in rural credit. Therefore, one of the most important keys to unlock the development of rural credit is to break the predicament of information asymmetry. And the Credit Village Assessment is designed to solve this problem in China.

The core of the Credit Village Assessment is collective credit and behavior restriction. What collective credit means is that rural financial institutions assess the credit status of the whole village and grant a blanket credit limit based on this assessment rather than rate and grant credit limit on the individual peasant. Behavior restriction is about the supervision from other peasants due to the associated responsibility and the village cadre who is committed by the financial institution to help call for loan. Considering that the village's credit limit will be adjusted according to the repayment rate of the whole village every year, it's apparent that every peasant's decision on loan repayment is related to the interest of the whole village, in other words, to the benefits of other peasants, which may incur incentives for strict behavior restriction from other villagers. Such a mechanism is similar to the BaoJia system[①] in ancient China to some extent, utilizing the relatively high degree of internal information sharing and devising an incentive structure by means of those with high local knowledge and associated responsibility doing the monitoring (Zhang, Deng, 2003). Obviously, the Credit Village Assessment mechanism is involved with three parties, that is, the peasant, the village cadre

---

① The Bao – Jia system was an invention of Wang Anshi of the Song Dynasty, who created this community – based system of law enforcement and civil control that was included in his large reform of Chinese government from 1069 – 1076. It took "household" (family) as a basic unit of the social organization, and formatted a pyramid type of management style.

Collective Credit and Behavior Restriction: the Analysis and Improvement of the Credit Village Assessment for Risk Control in Liuyang, China

and the rural financial institution. Before further study, it is necessary to analyze the fundamental thoroughly combining with the core elements, collective credit and behavior restriction, in order to grasp an in-depth understanding of this mechanism.

Under such a mechanism, the relationship between peasants in the same village has changed from separate individuals into a joint liability group without taking direct loss like the Grameen solidarity lending due to someone's default. But the rural financial institution still exerts collective punishment on the village such as deductions of the total credit limit or withdrawal of the already gained reputation, "the Credit Village", if the repayment rate can't reach a certain level. The penalty is not so heavy as to cause a collective concealment but has a considerable impact on the peasants for that it will not only make the credit loan in short supply more inaccessibly but also harm the reputation of the whole village which the peasants tend to cherish a lot. On the contrary, if the villagers perform well with a low enough delinquency on loan, the village would be awarded as "Credit Village", accompanied with a corresponding increase in credit limit, even with some favorable policies about interest rate or approval procedure. These incentive and penal systems take advantage of low cost and validity of information acquisition and monitoring inside the village relative to the traditional credit rating on individual outside. When personal information can't be completely observed and supervised, collective punishment is proved to be an effective measure (Zhang, Deng, 2003), in which way it efficiently uses the reward and punishment mechanism, and exploits the informational advantage and the associated responsibility of the peasants within the village, to grant them the right and the incentive to exercise the supervisory power. Apparently, the welfare of each peasant is closely related not only to his own repayment rate, but also to the default risk of others within the village. As the list of defaulters will be published regularly in the village, the defaulters would disburse enormous social costs as they would be considered as the black sheep and despised by others. Therefore, the peasants who can't tolerate a set of negative consequences brought by a bad reputation among the village will prudently weigh pros and cons before he makes the decision to default, which imposes strict and effective behavior restriction on the peasants (Stiglitz, 1990).

One of the biggest innovations in this mechanism is the incorporation of the village cadre, whose obligation is similar to the BaoJiaZhang (the one who was responsible for crime reporting, taxation, labor mobilization, inspection thieves and moral education etc. within his jurisdiction, and undertook joint and several liability) in the BaoJia system. Specialization in monitoring plus reliance on a residual claimant status will reduce shirking of the team members in a classical firm (A. Alchian, H. Demsetz, 1972), similarly, specialized monitor in the village is helpful to reduce the default of peasants. Because of the deterrent force from his original administrative status, as well as his greater amount of information compared with ordinary villagers, it's rather appropriate for the village cadre to work as the specialized monitor. In this mechanism, the village cadre serves as the internal regulator that is responsible for assessing the credit status of the villagers, maintaining the authenticity and transparency during the credit process, and urging the timely repayment of the peasants. Well-informed about the more detailed personal information of the peasants, the village cadre's audit responsibility provides a guarantee of the relatively perfect match between peasants' credit status and the loan amount they can get.

Now that the supervision of the village cadre is believed to be efficient, it's essential to make some constraints on the village cadre in case he shirks. An effective constraint can be imposed on a monitor is to give him title to the net earnings of the team, and if the monitor is agreed to receive the residual product above the prescribed amounts, he will have an added incentive not to shirk (A. Alchian, H. Demsetz, 1972). And it is exactly what the rural financial institutions promise to the village cadre because the Credit Village Assessment mechanism is essentially embodied in a kind of principal – agent relation between the rural financial institutions and the village cadre. As the agent to call loans, the village cadre is inspired by an incentive mechanism that provides him the residual claimant in the forms of pecuniary reward and the improvement of administrative achievements. For one thing, the title of "credit village" is also important to the village cadre because it is an indicator of his political achievements, which provides an incentive for the village cadre to fill the remained delinquent loans in order to maintain the reputation of the village. For another, the village cadre can receive a certain percentage of commission from rural financial institution after he calls back non – performing loans.

In this way, the direct connection between the peasants and the rural financial institutions is reduced for the village cadre works as an agent of the rural financial institutions to assess the peasants' credit status and call loans. What the financial institution should do is only to provide a credit standard for the village cadre to adjust the loan amount according to different situation of the peasants, and conduct annual inspection to redistribute total loan amount of the villages according to the total repayment rate of the borrowers in the same village. Compared to traditional personal credit assessment, the new mechanism largely shifts the loan audit within the village, and reduces information asymmetry while also enhances the ability to manage loan so as to achieve overall risk control. Taking into account the social characteristics of China's rural areas and the social attributes of the peasants, this mechanism applies internal supervision and collective rewards or punishments to the villagers, prompting them to spontaneously restrict their own behavior and in the meantime supervise others, which achieves Pareto Optimality by reducing the information cost and monitoring cost (B. Holmstrom, 1982), and helping control the default risk for the rural financial institution.

Modelling

1. General introduction

Based on the fundamental analysis above, we build models to compare the Credit Village Assessment mechanism with the traditional one. The comparison can be divided into three parts. The first part presents a basic model, describing the behavior of the financial institution and the peasants under the traditional personal credit assessment and calculates the total repayment rate. The second part shows how Credit Village Assessment mechanism works with the presence of village cadre and the change of total repayment rate. The third part provides some concluding remarks.

We assume that the line of credit can't always satisfy every peasant's demand and financial institution evaluates the line of credit of every peasant based on the information it can acquire about

Collective Credit and Behavior Restriction: the Analysis and Improvement of the Credit Village Assessment for Risk Control in Liuyang, China

the peasant's property, regular income, and the inference about the peasant's project expected return. The total loan amount provided is limited and fixed, and is allocated among the peasants in proportion according to the line of credit. At the beginning of each period, the financial institution will upgrade its inference about the peasants' project expected return roughly according to the historical information, and correspondingly adjust the allocation of loan amount.

Under the Credit Village Assessment mechanism, the village cadre possesses the information about every peasant's type about how to make their repayment decision, therefore he can estimate the probability of the repayment of every peasant based on the information provided by the financial institution. The financial institution evaluates the line of credit in the same way as in the traditional mechanism, and adds the extra information of the expected repayment probability from the village cadre as well as the total repayment rate of different villages to modify the loan amount allocation of the peasants and the villages, which reflects the main difference between the traditional and the innovative mechanism. More specifically speaking, there are two factors affecting the overall expected repayment rate: (1) each peasant's project expected return, and (2) each peasant's expected repayment probability under his actual project return rate. In the traditional mechanism, the financial institution can only obtain information about the former, but in the innovative one, the financial institution has access to both of the two factors, and weighs them to make a modification.

2. The personal credit assessment

First, we make a list and give the explanation of all the parameters that will be used in the model.

$w^*(i,t)$: The peasant i's wealth in the t period before he repays the loan;

$w_*(i,t)$: The peasant i's wealth in the t period after he repays the loan;

$inc(i,t)$: The peasant i's regular income in the t period, which subjects to uniform distribution;

$R(i,t)$: The peasant i's project return rate in the t period, which is uniformly distributed in $U(0, Rm(i))$, where $Rm(i)$ is the maximum value of peasant i's project return rate;

$k(i,t)$: The financial institution's inference about the peasant i's expected repayment in proportion to his total wealth in the t period before it lends money to the peasant;

$Mk(i,t)$: The financial institution's inference about the line of credit of peasant i in the t period;

$M(i,t)$: The loan amount peasant i receives from the financial institution in the t period;

$Pay(i,t)$: The repayment amount of peasant i at the end of the t period;

TM : The total loan amount in the rural credit market;

r : The loan interest rate;

$p(i,t)$: The repayment probability of peasant i in the t period, meet the following requirement $p(i,t) = 1 - (1+r)b_i + b_i R(i,t)$;

Under the traditional personal credit assessment, the financial institution evaluates the line of credit of each peasant after it collects information about his total wealth, regular income and the operation conditions of his project, with the belief that the peasant will take a certain proportion $k(i,t)$

of his total wealth for repayment, which will be upgraded based on his historical repayment performance. The financial institution infers that the peasant's expected repayment amount in the t period is $k(i,t)Ew^*(i,t)$, where $k(i,t)$ is the proportion mentioned above and $Ew^*(i,t)$ is the financial institution's expectation of the peasant's total wealth in the t period, which consists of the peasant's regular income and expected project return in the t period as well as his wealth in the $t-1$ period, that is $w_*(i,t-1)$. The financial institution believes that this expected repayment amount is exactly the tolerable debt burden for each peasant, that is, if the peasant is required to repay more than that amount, he won't fully repay his loan. Therefore, at the beginning of the t period, the loan amount for peasant i equals to the present value of the financial institution's expected repayment amount, which subjects to the following condition:

$$Mk(i,t)(1+r) = k(i,t)Ew^*(i,t) = k(i,t)[w_*(i,t-1) + E(inc) + Mk(i,t) \cdot E_{i,t}R]$$

We can easily get the result through some simple transformation:

$$Mk(i,t) = \frac{k(i,t)[w_*(i,t-1) + E(inc)]}{1 + r - k(i,t)E_{i,t}R} \quad (1)$$

After calculating the expected repayment amount for each peasant, the financial institution selects out the peasants who have already pay their loan in the t period, and allocates the total loan amount TM among them according to the proportion of each peasant's line of credit, so the loan amount each peasant receives is:

$$M(i,t) = \frac{Mk(i,t)}{\sum_{j \notin D} Mk(j,t)} TM \quad (2)$$

where D is the collection of peasants who haven't paid their loans yet.

However, practically, the peasants themselves don't make decisions in the way as the financial institution believes. Each period, a peasant has two kinds of repayment action, that is *fully repay or fully default*, and he randomly selects one action according to 0 - 1 two - point distribution. The probability of *fully repay* $p(i,t)$ is related to the actual project return rate $R(i,t)$ and we assume the relationship between $p(i,t)$ and $R(i,t)$ is linear for simplicity and each peasant's probability of *fully repay* equals to 1 if his project return rate $R(i,t)$ is not less than $1+r$, therefore, each peasant's probability of *fully repay* is:

$$p(i,t) = \min\{1, \max[1 - (1+r)b_i + b_i R(i,t), 0]\} \quad (3)$$

The slope b_i represents different types of the peasants, and the relationship between $p(i,t)$ and $R(i,t)$ is depicted as "return rate - repayment probability" curve of the peasants shown in the following figure:

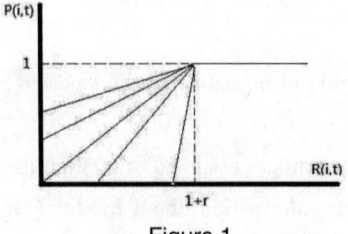

Figure 1

Collective Credit and Behavior Restriction: the Analysis and Improvement of the Credit Village Assessment for Risk Control in Liuyang, China

Peasants who get the loan in the t period invest in their own project with an uncertain project return rate which is uniformly distributed between 0 and a maximum value that is randomly generated and differs from person to person. At the end of each period, everyone's project yields an actual return rate $R(i,t)$ in accordance with its own distribution and the peasants correspondingly have a repayment probability following the formula $p(i,t) = 1 - (1+r)b_i + b_i R(i,t)$, and take repayment action according to the result of $0-1$ two-point distribution. If the result of random variable shows that the peasant decide to repay and the required repayment amount doesn't exceed his total wealth, the peasant will fully repay his loan.

The peasants can't get the loan in two cases: (1) the financial institution thinks that his wealth proportion for repayment $k(i,t)$ equals 0, and (2) the peasant hasn't paid off his previous debt. If a peasant didn't get the loan in the t period because of the second reason, then we assume that he doesn't invest in any project during this period and his $R(i,t) = 0$, which means the peasant has a probability $p(i,t) = \max(0, 1 - (1+r)b_i)$ to repay the previous unpaid debt and this $p(i,t)$ represents the intercept on the vertical axis of the peasant's "return rate – repayment probability" curve. If the intercept is larger than 0, the peasant will decide whether to repay the unpaid debt based on the repayment probability and the result of $0-1$ distribution, in which case it's possible for the peasant to pay off all his delinquent loans and regain the eligibility for a loan. If the intercept is negative, the peasant will never repay his delinquent loans and thus be permanently exclude out of the rural credit market.

After the peasants take their repayment action, the financial institution can observe their wealth and repayment amount at the end of the t period, and upgrade their inference about the proportion $k(i,t)$ as $k_{new}(i,t) = \dfrac{Pay(i,t)}{w^*(i,t)}$. Then, the financial institution calculates the arithmetic mean of all k_{new} from the first period to the t period, and regards the arithmetic mean as the inference about the repayment proportion in the $t+1$ period, that is $k(i,t+1) = \dfrac{tk(i,t) + k_{new}(i,t)}{t+1}$. In the meantime, the financial institution can estimate the project return rate using the difference between the peasant's wealth of the t period and the $t-1$ period after he repays the loan, and the rule for inference is:

$$R^e(i,t) = \frac{w_*(i,t) + Pay(i,t) - w_*(i,t-1) - E(inc)}{M(i,t)} \qquad (4)$$

The reason why the financial institution can estimate the project return rate is that the difference between the peasant's wealth of the t period and the $t-1$ period after he repays the loan mainly includes three parts: (1) the peasant's regular income during the t period, (2) the peasant's project return during the t period, and (3) the peasant's repayment amount during the t period. Considering that the regular income and the repayment amount can be observed, so the financial institution can roughly estimate the project return rate using the rule above. And the financial institution can upgrade the inference about the project expected return of each peasant:

$$E_{i,t}R = \operatorname*{mean}_{j=1:t-1}(R^e(i,t)) \qquad (5)$$

Then it turns to the next period, and the financial institution uses the upgraded $k(i,t+1)$ and

$E_{i,t}R$ to determine each peasant's loan amount.

3. The Credit Village Assessment

We make a list of added parameters as follows:

$pA(t)$: The total repayment rate of the village A in the t period;

$pB(t)$: The total repayment rate of the village B in the t period;

$TMA(t)$: The total loan amount for village A in the t period;

$TMB(t)$: The total loan amount for village B in the t period;

$E_{i,t}p$: The evaluation of peasant i's expected repayment rate in the t period based on the information from the financial institution and the village cadre;

Under the Credit Village Assessment mechanism, the total loan amount provided in the rural credit market is limited and fixed just like the traditional mechanism, but it is distributed in different villages before allocated to the peasants. For simplicity, we assume that there are only two villages with equal number of peasants. First, the financial institution determines the proportion of the total amount for each village in the t period based on its total repayment rate (the ratio of total repayment and total loan amount in the whole village) in the $t-1$ period:

$$TMA(t) = \frac{pA(t-1)}{pA(t-1)+pB(t-1)} TM, \quad TMB(t) = \frac{pB(t-1)}{pA(t-1)+pB(t-1)} TM$$

Then the total loan amount for each village is distributed among its peasants and we take village A as example. The financial institution takes action in the same way as under the traditional mechanism, using inference about the peasant's wealth, regular income, the project expected return rate and the proportion $k(i,t)$ to calculate his line of credit $Mk(i,t)$. But before allocating the total amount TMA, the financial institution takes into account the information about each peasant's type from the village cadre. The village cadre is well-informed about the detailed personal information of the peasants, so we assume that the village cadre knows the specific form of each peasant's 'return rate - repayment probability' curve, which means he knows b_i. The village cadre makes use of the expected project return rate $E_{i,t}R$ from the financial institution, and he has a belief that the peasant i's project return rate in the t period subject to the uniform distribution in $(0, 2E_{i,t}R)$, therefore he can help the financial institution to estimate the expected repayment probability of each peasant:

$$\begin{aligned} E_{i,t}p &= \frac{1}{2E_{i,t}R}\int_0^{2E_{i,t}R} \max\{0, \min[1, 1-(1+r)b_i + b_i R]\} dR \\ &= 1 - \frac{(1+r)^2 b_i^2 - I(1-(1+r)b_i)^2}{4b_i E_{i,t}R} \end{aligned} \quad (6)$$

where $I = \begin{cases} 1, 1-(1+r)b < 0 \\ 0, 1-(1+r)b \geq 0 \end{cases}$.

Subsequently, the financial institution makes use of the village cadre's information about the expected repayment probability $E_{i,t}p$ to adjust the proportion for each peasant:

$$Mk^*(i,t) = Mk(i,t)\left[\frac{E_{i,t}p}{Ep}\right]^\lambda \quad (7)$$

where λ represents the importance of the village cadre in the assessment of the peasant's line of

Collective Credit and Behavior Restriction: the Analysis and Improvement of the Credit Village Assessment for Risk Control in Liuyang, China

credit, if λ is below 0, that means the financial institution regards that the village cadre always calls white black.

In this way, given λ, the peasant with a higher expected repayment probability $E_{i,t}p$ than the average expected repayment probability of the peasants in the same village in t period will have a larger proportion $Mk^*(i,t)$ than $Mk(i,t)$, which is consistent with the peasant's relatively better character. Then, the financial institution allocates village A's total loan amount TMA among the peasants according to the proportion $Mk^*(i,t)$, therefore the loan amount for peasant i is:

$$M^*(i,t) = \frac{Mk^*(i,t)}{\sum_{j \in D} Mk^*(j,t)} TMA \tag{8}$$

And rest of the process is the same with the traditional mechanism.

4. Emulation analysis

Using the mathematical software (matlab), we simulate both of the mechanisms in 50 periods for 100 times based on our model above, and found that under the innovative mechanism, the average repayment rate of total peasants has significantly been improved ($p < 0.001$).

And we found that as the time went by, those peasants with a relatively bad character would be distinguished by the financial institution and excluded from the credit market more quickly under the Credit Village Assessment than under the traditional personal credit assessment, which has been shown in the graphs below. This also proved the innovative mechanism is better than the traditional one to some extent.

We also changed the importance of the village cadre in the assessment to further probe the village cadre's influence on the financial institution's modification of the line of credit. Here we use the b_i as the index of the peasants' type, and those who has a relatively small b_i, which in other words has a positive intercept on the vertical axis of the peasant's 'return rate – repayment probability' curve is the peasants with good type. Those who has a relatively big bi with a negative intercept or zero on the vertical axis is the peasants with bad type. The horizontal axis in the graphs below denotes the time period, and the vertical axis denotes the proportion of one type of peasants accounting for the total peasants. As we can see, if the village cadre strives to provide an effective information, the financial institution can distinguish the peasants' type and exclude the bad type. And if the financial institution attaches more importance to the village cadre's information, which means a bigger λ, this progress of separation, or we can call it as "evolution", would become more quick. If the financial institution doesn't trust the village cadre and holds a contrary view, it may make detours at first, but finally back on track.

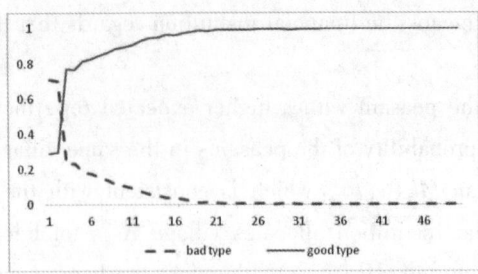

Figure 2 The fluctuation of the proportion of different types of peasants in the credit market ($\lambda = -1$)

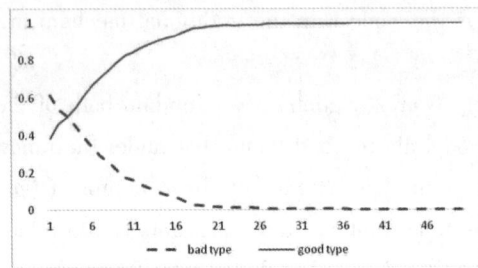

Figure3 The fluctuation of the proportion of different types of peasants in the credit market ($\lambda = 1$)

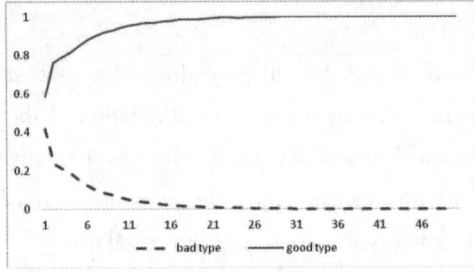

Figure 4 The fluctuation of the proportion of different types of peasants in the credit market ($\lambda = 5$)

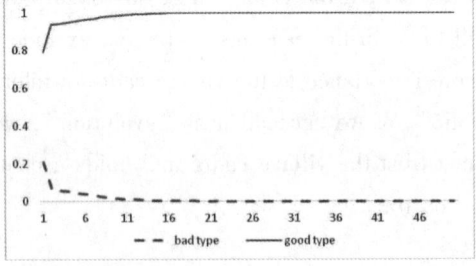

Figure 5 The fluctuation of the proportion of different types of peasants in the credit market ($\lambda = 10$)

Based on the objective of the Credit Village Assessment mechanism, in our paper, we simply focus on the importance of the village cadre's information, which is based on the estimated expected return from the financial institution. We neglect the discussion on the peasant's utility, and just cal-

Collective Credit and Behavior Restriction: the Analysis and Improvement of the Credit Village Assessment for Risk Control in Liuyang, China

culate the proportion of the relatively bad (this means the peasants whose intercept on the vertical axis is equal or less than 0) peasants in the total population who borrow money form the financial institution in multiple periods from a comparative static perspective. And the model we use in our paper as well as the emulation show an idea similar to the evolutionary game (D. Friedman, 1991). According to the more practical assumption of bounded rationality that the peasants always keep their strategic decision without learning and modifying, we can simplify their' decision and leave their types unchanged in the game process. In the innovative mechanism, the population with a relatively poor quality would be distinguished and "die out" from the system more quickly than the traditional mechanism, which also verifies the fact we got from the fieldwork. And because under the Credit Village Assessment, the individual line of credit changed violently, for instance the lowest line is 5000, the second lowest line is 10000, the third lowest line is 30000, which means the modification based on the village cadre's information may have great influence on the line of credit of each peasant, it is significant for us to probe the change of the importance of the village cadre in the assessment. And if we add in the interactive supervision of the peasants, which has already been confirmed with a positive effect for the improvement of the collective behavior like the peer monitoring (Stiglitz, 1990), the results of the game would be much better.

Improvement

Although the Credit Village Assessment has proved its effect to help the financial institution to distinguish peasants with a bad character, and finally reserve those with a good character, which is necessary for the financial institution to control its credit risk. But according to the model assumption above as well as our fieldwork experience, such a mechanism still has room to improve.

Above all, control the village cadre's power and avoid the occurrence of rent seeking behavior which has been reflected by some peasants. Because in the assessment of peasants' line of credit, the village cadre actually plays an important role to help lower the information asymmetry, his performance is important to the financial institution to control credit risk. And his intensity of effort also has an influence on the velocity of the exclusion of the peasants with bad character. About how to solve this problem which was brought by the special status of the village cadre, transparent assessment and public review would be useful for the peasants to supervise the village cadre's behavior. A rational encouragement and reward is also necessary to inspire the village cadre to work harder.

Secondly, for those who perform well, provide them some other tempting rewards, which may further encourage their repayment punctually. Besides, the financial institution had better expand the influence of these rewards, which may touch some peasants with a bad type to change their behavior. If they perform a sudden change towards good type and have been propagandized and known by other villagers, other peasants in their "population" may follow their behavior.

Finally, the financial institution had better establish a fund pool to prevent collective default even if the peasants are good types after some catastrophes shock the credit market. It can also ask the peasants who borrowed money to purchase agricultural insurance and some other insurance to cut down their loss caused by the natural and man-made calamities, so they can revive production and repay their overdraft as soon as possible if their types are good.

Acknowledgements

The authors are grateful to get the reflection from the local peasants and the manager of the Rural Commercial Bank of Liuyang. Furthermore, the authors would like to thank Associate Professor Zhou Hua from China Institute for Actuarial Science and School of Insurance, as well as Associate Professor Qiao Heng from School of Economics in Central University of Finance and Economics for contributing their expertise and helpful comments.

References

1. Alchian, A. A., & Demsetz, H. (1972). Production, information costs, and economic organization. *The American economic review*, pp. 777 – 795.

2. Chan, Y. S., & Kanatas, G. (1985). Asymmetric valuations and the role of collateral in loan agreements. *Journal of Money, Credit and Banking*, pp. 84 – 95.

3. Friedman, D. (1991). Evolutionary games in economics. *Econometrica: Journal of the Econometric Society*, 637 – 666.

4. Guangwen He. (2002). The efficiency, problem and countermeasure for the mechanism of rural micro credit. *Chinese rural credit cooperation*, Vol. 11, pp. 11 – 13.

5. Hoff, K., & Stiglitz, J. E. (1990). Introduction: Imperfect information and rural credit markets: Puzzles and policy perspectives. *The World Bank economic review*, 235 – 250.

6. Holmstrom, B. (1982). Moral hazard in teams. *The Bell Journal of Economics*, 324 – 340.

7. Stiglitz, J. E. (1990). Peer monitoring and credit markets. *The World Bank economic review*, 4(3), 351 – 366.

8. Turvey, C. G. (2013). Policy rationing in rural credit markets. *Agricultural Finance Review*, 73(2), 209 – 232.

9. Weiying Zhang, & Feng Deng. (2003). Information, incentives and associated liability. *Chinese Social Sciences*, Vol. 3, pp. 99 – 104.

10. Weiying Zhang. (2001). *Property, government and credibility*. Joint Publishing Press.

11. Yanqing Zhao & Guangwen He. (2007). The research on the validity problem of the peasants' group lending. *Journal of Financial Research*, Vol. 7, pp. 61 – 77.

12. Zhong Xu & Enjiang Chen. (2004). Interest rate policy, rural financial institution behavior and shortage of rural credit. *Journal of Financial Research*, Vol. 12, pp. 34 – 44.

Central Financial Subsidy of Agricultural Insurance in China: the Efficiency and Improvement for the Government[①]

Lanfeng Li[②]　Yaoyuan Zhang[③]

Abstract: In 2007, the Ministry of Finance in China issued a subsidy policy on agricultural insurance, selecting six provinces (autonomous regions) as the first pilot area in order to encourage peasants to purchase agricultural insurance. And from then on, more areas were included in the agricultural insurance subsidy policy until 2012, when the whole country was covered by the policy. And in 2014, the central government of China even proposed to improve the proportion of the central financial subsidy in the No. 1 Central Document, which shows the government's determination to develop the agricultural insurance. This paper mainly researches on the efficiency of the agricultural insurance subsidy policy. Our empirical analysis using DID method on provinces' data has proved the effect not only in the first year but also in the latter years. But the fieldwork in Hunan made us suspect these results and we conduct a further intuitive analysis on other provinces which wasn't included in DID. And we confirmed that there really existed some problems in the implementation of the central financial subsidy on agricultural insurance. Finally we make some speculation on the cause of the contradiction and propose our advice for the improvement of the policy efficiency.

Keywords: Central financial subsidy; Agricultural insurance; Policy efficiency; DID; Fieldwork

I. Introduction

When it comes to agricultural insurance, an important tool for securing peasants' interests and encouraging agricultural production, it always accompanies with the financial subsidy. Ahsan, Ali, Kurian(1982) pointed out the high risk of agricultural production and the weak insurance awareness of peasants, which makes the agricultural insurance market always unable to exist without the public agencies. Wright and Hewitt (1990) have come up with similar conclusions. Mishra (1996) further thought that it's not worthwhile for peasant households to purchase agricultural insurance without the

---

[①]　18th Asia – Pacific Risk and Insurance Association Annual Conference, Moscow, 2014.
[②]　School of Insurance, Central University of Finance and Economics, Beijing, China.
[③]　School of Statistics and Mathematics, Central University of Finance and Economics, Beijing, China. We would like to thank for the helpful suggestions from Associate Pro. Zhou from School of Insurance and Associate Pro. Shi from School of Public Finance. Any remaining omissions or errors are our own.

different premium rates in different areas and the financial subsidy. He considered that it's necessary to subsidize the purchase behavior which would bring welfare earnings to not only the agricultural department but also the non-agricultural department. Tuo and Zhu (2005) concluded according to their fieldwork around China that the commercial insurance company managing the agricultural insurance businesses under the direction of the government is a suitable way depending on the reality of China with a scattered small peasant economy. In fact, as a developing country with a rural population of over 500 million, China really attaches great importance to the agricultural insurance which is related to the development of the three rural issues, agriculture, rural areas and farmers. Before the central government began to subsidize crop insurance in six provinces (autonomous regions) and livestock insurance in mid-western provinces (autonomous regions) in 2007, almost all the local governments in China have ever tried to issue some financial subsidy policies on agricultural insurance based on the local finance input merely. But from the data, we could easily find that the rapid development of the agricultural insurance began after the implementation of central financial subsidy. By 2012, the central financial subsidy has been phasing to spread around the country. And at the beginning of 2014, the Chinese central government even proposed to improve the proportion of the central financial subsidy in order to support the popularization of agricultural insurance in the No. 1 Central Document.

However, even this policy costs billions of RMB from the national public finance every year, and we could find the growth of agricultural insurance premium revenue at the national level, we still doubt whether these financial subsidies from the central government can significantly promote the sales of agricultural insurance in rural market around the country in essence or the effect of our subsidy policy is just a flash in the pan. And from the reply of the state council on our fieldwork in Hunan province, we also found that our central government is also concerned about the policy of agricultural insurance. Tuo and Zhu (2005) also doubted whether the feasible operation of the financial subsidy on agricultural insurance could be solved when the central government and the local government subsidized together. If not, the financial subsidized capital couldn't be in place, or the capital couldn't play a positive role to stimulate the growth of the agricultural insurance as well as to protect the peasants' agricultural production. But by now there has barely relevant studies about this issue combining quantitative analysis with fieldwork experience in China, most of the researches on agricultural insurance subsidy especially the central financial subsidy in China mostly stayed at the theoretical and qualitative level. What Shi (2008), Feng (2004), Fei (2005) concluded representing the main existing literature about subsidy policy on agricultural insurance are the externalities, market failure and the quasi-public goods of the agricultural insurance which have already been researched for many years but referred to the policy efficiency itself less. Only Yang and Wei (2010) pointed out that the interactive subsidy which the local financial department and peasants take a certain proportion of the premium at first may cause obviously progressively reduced effect. However, we still couldn't acquire any definite information about the effect of this policy which has a critical influence on the prestige of the central and the local government as well as the development of the agricultural insurance.

So in this paper, we would use the DID (difference - in - difference) method with suitable provinces' data to conduct preliminary estimation about the efficiency of the central financial subsidy on agricultural insurance. And then through our fieldwork in Hunan province, we found that the effect of the policy in practice is to some extent contradictory with what we attain from the empirical analysis. This discovery led to our further research using an intuitive method with some other provinces' data, which made sure that the problem really existed. And finally we would make speculation on the cause of the policy inefficiency and propose our advice on the improvement of the central financial subsidy on agricultural insurance.

II. Background and Data

To estimate the effect of the central financial subsidy on agricultural insurance, we have to select valid dataset and scientific method in order to ensure the accuracy of our empirical analysis per se. In this section, we would illustrate how we select the dataset, and then based on the selection, show how to measure the effect using the sample.

Dataset selection Agricultural insurance includes crop insurance, livestock insurance, etc. And the crop insurance has long been the most important part due to its high proportion. Until 2012, the crop insurance revenue still accounts for over 75% of the total agricultural insurance premium revenue in China. So this time we mainly focus on the crop insurance, which to some extent represents the agricultural insurance.

When the six provinces (autonomous regions) - Jiangsu, Sichuan, Hunan, Jilin, Xinjiang and Inner Mongolia were announced to be the first pilot areas to receive the central financial subsidy on crop insurance in 2007, it brought a great change to the development of the agricultural insurance according to the news reports. After that more and more provinces were included until 2012, when the whole country was covered by the subsidy. Table 1 describes the progress of the crop insurance subsidy from 2007 to 2012.

During the progress of crop insurance subsidy policy, central government provides different subsidy proportion on premium to certain provinces, according to their economic conditions and the prosperity of agriculture. Generally, the central government provides 25% ~40% of the premium, while at the same time, requiring the provincial government provide 25% of the premium, the municipal and county level provide 10% of the premium. Actually, though subsidies from local government can also be regarded as the outcome of policy from the central government, since it is one of the requirements in the policy, and subsidy proportions of local governments remain constant after the policy was implemented (it will be discussed later), the subsidy on agricultural insurance from the local finance has already existed before the arrival of the central financial subsidy. The specific subsidy proportions are displayed in Table 2. We can see from the table that Jilin, Jiangsu, Hunan, Sichuan, Xinjiang and Inner Mongolia changed their subsidy proportion from 25% in 2007 to 35% in 2008; Hebei, Jilin, Heilongjiang, Anhui, Shanxi, Xinjiang, Inner Mongolia, Hunan, Sichuan, Henan and Hubei changed their subsidy proportion from 35% in 2008 to 40% in 2009. Therefore, to evaluate the pure effect of the central financial subsidy, we tick out provinces whose subsidies have changed during the progress and leave those who are subsidized with constant proportions to ensure that the increase in subsidy proportion will not interfere with our results.

Since the policy was implemented gradually in the whole country, we observe time period from three years before the certain province's implementation of subsidy to three years after the statement of the subsidy. So in our dataset, we firstly use data of all the provinces in China, ticking out those in which the proportion of subsidy changes during the observed years, and those with inadequate data, leaving 10 provinces qualified to our evaluation. Details of the provinces used are showed in Table 2.

Besides crop insurance, livestock insurance also takes a great amount of agricultural insurance that it cannot be ignored. As we know, livestock insurance in China is mainly composed of sow insurance, which always makes up over half of the total livestock insurance premium revenue. In 2007, the Ministry of Finance proposed Tentative Method on Sow Insurance Subsidy, requiring that all provinces covered by the sow insurance subsidy in order to sustain the price of the pork. Since sow insurance holds the majority of the livestock insurance and related to macro – control, both the central government and local governments provided huge proportions of premiums in subsidy, added with high odds, the subsidy soon covered almost the whole country and remained constantly (except Guangdong, Liaoning, Shandong, Zhejiang and Fujian, known as the eastern five provinces, these provinces did not receive the central financial subsidy on livestock insurance until 2013), which made us believe that this subsidy policy effect remained only in the first year of the subsidy implementation or even shorter. Consequently, in order to tick out the interference of the livestock insurance, we divide the above 10 provinces into 2 groups according to the implementation of the central financial subsidy on the livestock insurance. The first group includes the Eastern five provinces, who did not receive the central financial subsidy on the livestock insurance during our research period. And in the second group, Jiangxi, Yunnan, Gansu, Qinghai and Ningxia are included, known as the mid – western five provinces, and they have already been covered by the central financial subsidy on the livestock insurance with a constant proportion during the research period.

Measuring effectiveness of the policy To represent the implementation of the central financial subsidy on agricultural insurance, we create a dummy variable with the definition of the implementation, which equals to 1 for years after the actual implementation of the subsidy in these 10 provinces, noted as IS.

$$IS = \begin{cases} 1 & \text{implemented the subsidy} \\ 0 & \text{otherwise} \end{cases}$$

We also develop 3 dummy variables to represent the time effect, i_{th} year of implementation (i = 1, 2, 3), which equals to 1 for the i_{th} year after the implementation. And what they construct is the variables to detect long run effectiveness of the subsidy.

To evaluate the effect of the central financial subsidy, we also need to determine indicators to measure the policy outcome and explanatory variables that can also affect the agricultural insurance premium revenue.

Because the subsidy policy is to motivate the purchase of the agricultural insurance, which directly reflected on the growth of the agricultural insurance premium revenue. In this perspective, to evaluate the effectiveness of the policy, we can pay our attention to the agricultural insurance premium revenue. There are two indicators suitable for it: (1) Agricultural Insurance Premium Revenue, which is yearly premium revenue in agricultural insurance in certain district chosen by Wang Kai, Duan Sheng(2009), and it can indicate the overall development of the agricultural insurance. (2) Rate of Insurance, which is the proportion of people who purchase the insurance chosen by Li Yuhui, Wang Huichao(2012).

Considering about the accessibility to data, we use Agricultural Insurance Premium revenue as the indicator. Data can be got in the Yearbook of China's Insurance. What is more, what we concentrate on is the increase rate of the agricultural insurance premium revenue, so we take the natural logarithm of the variable, noted as *AII*.

There are other factors that have strong influence on the insurance premium revenue, which must be included in the model as explanatory variables: (1) Disposable Income, which is the yearly income per person in rural areas, noted as *DI*. It evaluates the purchase ability of the rural family, and basically, the more they earn, the more likely for them to purchase the insurance. (2) Fertilizer, which is the amount of fertilizers applied in planting, noted as *FER*. The insurance serves as something like substitute of the fertilizers, Smith and Goodwin (1996) have shown that as the rate of insurance increases, applicants tend to pay less in planting inputs, namely, fertilizers. (3) Planting Areas, noted as *PA*. Specifically, we mainly research on the subsidy on crop insurance, so the planting area is of great significance, to specify, the larger the planting area is, the more risk of loss when meeting with disaster, the more insurance that the peasants are likely to purchase. (4) Proportion of Agricultural Insurance, which is the proportion of agricultural insurance premium revenue in property insurance revenue, noted as *PAI*. Wang Kai, Duan Sheng (2009) used this variable as the reflection of the supply of agricultural insurance from the commercial insurance companies.

Summary statistics Table 4 shows the summary statistics for variables used in the analysis. Column (1) provides sample means and standard derivations for all provinces in the sample; Column (2) for provinces in Group 1, the Eastern five provinces; Column (3) for provinces in Group 2, the Mid – western five provinces. And in Table 3, we can conclude that the overall situations including economy, planting conditions and etc. of the eastern five provinces are better than those of the mid – western five provinces, so it is reasonable to divide the whole sample into two groups. Figure 1 displays the annual agricultural insurance premium revenue for these 10 provinces, and Figure 2 shows the natural logarithm of the annual agricultural insurance premium revenue for these provinces. It reveals that in the first year of policy implementation, a significant increase in agricultural insurance premium revenue is really witnessed, and the increasing rate decays gradually year by year. More details will be discussed in the modeling part.

III. Modeling

The implementation of one policy can be regarded as a "treatment", because it affects some parts of the country, leaving other parts less affected or not affected. By comparing groups affected by the policy (treatment group) and those who are less or not affected (control group), we can know about the effect of that policy.

To evaluate effectiveness of agricultural insurance subsidy, we need to estimate the following equation:

$$AII_{it} = \beta_0 + \beta_1 IS_{it} + \gamma x_{it} + u_t + \alpha_i + \varepsilon_{it} \tag{1}$$

In which IS_{it} is the dummy variable equal to 1 if the province i implemented the policy in year t, u_t is a linear trend to control for time-varying factors specific to the province i, α_i represents a fixed effect of the province i which is the permanent differences in the provinces, and x_{it} is a vector of exogenous covariates, including DI, FER, PA and PAI.

In this equation, we are interested in, the coefficient of IS, measuring the average changes in agricultural insurance premium revenue of the same province between implementation of the policy and not. In other words, β_1 represents the effect of the implementation of the policy. Specially, the error term ε_{it}, satisfies the equation:

$$E(\varepsilon_{it} \mid IS_{it}, x_{it}, u_t) = 0 \tag{2}$$

But

$$\tag{3}$$

This way, we need to use fixed effect panel data model to get the consistent estimate of β_1, and we call this estimator the difference-in-difference estimator. Actually, we use the difference-in-difference estimator to detect the treatment effect with the cross-sectional and time series differences brought by the exogenous policy.

Consequently, to get correct estimate of the policy effect, we must ensure that the policy must be exogenous, which means that it can't be correlated with ε_{it}. To specify, ε_{it} should be not only uncorrelated with the contemporary status of implementation of the province i, but uncorrelated with the past and future status of implementation of the province i. Because we have sorted the sample provinces into two groups according to their similar economic background as well as identical and constant intensity of subsidy policy (include the subsidy proportion and scope), we believe that we have weakened the endogenous problem of our empirical analysis to some extent.

Main results Table 5 reports estimated coefficients on dummy variables in eastern five provinces one by one. Column (1) shows the only effect of the subsidies, IS is found to have positive effect on the growth of insurance premium revenue significantly, contributing to 59.13% of the average growth, which is 4.08(mean of AII). Column (2) shows the effect of the subsidies on the eastern five provinces, considering the effect of other explanatory variables, including DI, FER, PA and PAI. It shows that the effect of IS decreases to 0.79%, but still contributes to 19.36% of the average growth of the insurance revenue. In other words, the addition of other controlling variables lowers the magnitude of IS coefficient by 67.2%. To evaluate lasting effectiveness of the policy, Column (3) and Column (4) report the policy effect when considering policy years. Column (3) shows the only effect of the years, and the contribution made by the year lag of the policy are generally equal, indicating that the lasting effect of the policy seems to be strong. Column (4) shows the effect of the subsidy policy when considering other explanatory variables, including DI, FER, PA and *PAI*, and the effect of the first year is 0.84%, then decreases to 0.44% in the second year, and increases to 0.86% in the third year. Both Column (3) and Column (4) indicates that there is a seemingly lasting effect of the policy, contributing to the growth of the insurance revenue significantly.

Table 5 reveals the strong effectiveness of the policy in the five eastern provinces, and significant lasting effect of the policy. Actually, these five provinces all have strong economic basis and agricultural production, added with the proliferation of agricultural insurance in these regions, it is arguable that the policy has a positive lasting effect on the growth of the insurance purchase.

Table 6 reports the estimated coefficients of the dummy variables in mid – western five provinces one by one. Here, we must explain that when we use Disposable Income (*DI*), Fertilizer (*FER*), Planting Area (*PA*) and Proportion of Agricultural Insurance (*PAI*) to the model, the coefficients of *DI* and *FER* are far from significant, with p – value over 0.8, and make the model less reasonable. So we discard these two variables when modeling the mid – western five provinces and find that the new model is optimal, it means that this model can explain the data well. Column (1) shows the only effect of the implementation of the policy, which is 1.54%, contributing to 36.16% of the average growth in insurance revenue. Column (2) demonstrates the effect of the policy, considering other significant explanatory variables, including *PA* and *PAI*, which decreases to 0.38%, and only contributing to 8.90% of the growth. It also suggests that the addition of controls lowers the magnitude of the *IS* coefficient by 66.6% and also improves the precision of the estimated coefficient by 75.57%. Similarly, we need to evaluate the lasting effectiveness of the policy, so Column (3) and Column (4) reports the effect of the policy when considering policy years. Column (3) shows the only effect of the years, and it indicates an increasing contribution to the growth as time passed by, from 0.82% in the first to 1.67% in the second year and to 2.14% in the third year. Column (4) reports the effectiveness of the time when considering other explanatory variables, including *PA* and *PAI*. And it shows that the effect gradually decreases when considering additional variables from 0.48% in the first year to 0.24% in the second year and to −0.30% in the third year, indicating a decrease in the insurance revenue.

By comparing the different effect of the implementation of the central financial subsidy policy on agricultural insurance in five eastern provinces and five mid – western provinces, we can analyze the results roughly. Both groups witness significant increase in the insurance purchase in the first year of implementation, which proves that the policy did have some positive effect but the effect varies according to different provinces. For those who have strong economic basis (enable peasants to buy insurance) and prevalence of the agricultural insurance (peasants are more willing to buy insurance) like the eastern five provinces, the effect appears evident. However, for those whose economic basis and agriculture insurance market is relatively backward like the five mid – western provinces, the effect will be smaller, despite higher subsidy proportions. One possible explanation could be that peasants in less developed provinces have less disposable savings and lower acceptance of agricultural insurance, so the policy will hardly incentivize the purchase in these regions. On the other hand, the relatively weak agriculture productivity and anti – risk strength also provides a potentially larger market in these regions and it is easier to keep the lasting effect. But since the insurance markets are active in developed provinces, a stimulation will gain large increase in insurance purchase. Their relatively prosperous agriculture also explains the lasting effect of the central financial subsidy.

One thing that we find interesting is that when we consider controlling variables in long run effect estimation of the five mid – western provinces, the long run effect decays gradually, even to – 0.30% which bellows 0. This phenomenon, showing the less effectiveness of the subsidy, contradicts to what we have analyzed above. But on the contrary, this is reasonable, actually, most provinces in China suffer from this kind of ineffectiveness, and only a small amount of provinces can keep the long run effect. We will discuss this contradiction in the following part.

IV. Contradiction

What we found above makes us in some extent believe that the central financial subsidy policy on agricultural insurance did has positive and lasting effectiveness. However, in our further research, some phenomena interest us, which is contradictory with the above results.

Fieldwork study actually, all the contradictions originated from our fieldwork in Hunan province which is one of the first provinces receiving the central financial subsidy on agricultural insurance. And 6 months before our fieldwork, a drought over one month had just caused great losses to the local agricultural production. Surprisingly, during our visit in over 30 villages with a relatively well – developed[①] agricultural production spread around four major grain – producing counties, more than 80 percent of interviewed peasants including some large – scale contract peasant households expressed that they haven't purchased agricultural insurance, especially the crop insurance, very different from what we learnt from the news reports or government figures. This is the same as what we learnt from the interview with a high – class administrator who has ever been a branch's president in the town – level for the last 10 years in one of the local rural financial institutions that the crop insurance has a relatively low coverage and slow growth in fact while the livestock insurance has almost covered all the raisers quickly after the implementation of the central financial subsidy policy in Hunan. The situation further reflects on the self – burden of loss for the most of the local peasants in the drought, which made them complain the government's absence and call for financial help to compensate their loss.

On the other hand, when we interviewed some village cadres, they also complained that the disinclination of the local peasants and the target set by their high – level government for the purchase of the agricultural insurance made them in a dilemma. So some of them had to cooperate with those who is willing to pay the premium (always the large – scale contract peasant households) to put money together and the rural community finance help to fill the vacancy which is caused by those who didn't pay the insurance premium. But those peasants who didn't pay the premium are unconscious of the fact that their farms have already been insured. As a result, even they suffered a loss of

---

① Here we refer to those villages which have large – scale contract peasant households, or agricultural cooperatives, or national experimental fields, or characteristic agriculture.

agricultural production, they didn't have proof to claim payment from the insurance company, even didn't know their insurance at all. And we found that every local government always convenes meetings about grain production with those large - scale contract peasant households in the county and propagate the central financial subsidy policy on agricultural insurance at the beginning of every year. But when we interviewed those large - scale contract peasant households, most of them told us that they didn't purchase the agricultural insurance and basically their agricultural production loss caused by disasters was borne by themselves.

Such a complicated and disordered situation indicated that the central financial subsidy policy did have some problems which impeded the realization of its efficiency for the development of agricultural insurance. But did it just happen in Hunan province? What about other provinces which the DID method didn't select as our sample? We decided to use a relatively crude method to approximately appraise whether it is a single problem just happened in Hunan or not.

Intuitive analysis to figure out the above problem and evaluate the effect of the policy on a larger scale, we research on the annual agricultural insurance premium revenue for each province directly and compare the increase rate of the revenue before and after the subsidy intuitively. Figure 3 illustrates the annual agricultural insurance premium revenue before and after the subsidy for the rest of the provinces that are not in the DID model. In each graph, the blue solid lines with dots are annual agricultural insurance premium revenue before the implementation of the crop subsidy, and the red dashed lines with square marks demonstrate the revenue after the subsidy. We can see in the graph showing the annual agricultural insurance premium revenue of Hunan province that the revenue increased rapidly in the first policy year but decreased significantly after the first year of the implementation of the central financial subsidy policy, and that witnesses our finding in fieldwork study that few peasants relative to the news report purchased the insurance.

The slopes in the graphs all become bigger after the first year of the implementation of the subsidy policy and decrease gradually as time goes by, which indicates that the policy incentivized the purchases of the insurance at the right year of the subsidy, and kept less significant increase in purchase of the insurance. Some provinces, to some extent, did perform well after the policy implementation and kept a steady growth in the agricultural insurance premium revenue, for instance, Anhui, Hebei, Heilongjiang and Jiangsu. However, some provinces' revenue data stagnated or even declined, like Xinjiang, Hubei, Henan, Hunan, and Jilin, in particular. Conclusions can be drawn that at least in these provinces the central financial subsidy policy did stimulate the purchase in the first year but hardly had lasting effect on agricultural insurance premium revenue.

Drawbacks of DID in our research of the efficiency of the policy, we develop a DID model to evaluate it and find the lasting effect of the subsidy policy. However, to get net effect of the subsidy, we discard samples of provinces whose central financial subsidy proportion has changed in case that the change in the agricultural insurance premium revenue may be brought by the proportion increase instead of the subsidy itself. Consequently, we get a sample set that only includes 10 provinces for 6 years, making a sample set with sample size of 60. What's more, we need to divide the samples into two parts according to the difference of central financial subsidy on livestock insurance in each group. Eventually, we have two small sample sets with sample size of 30 and 30 separately. The DID model based on these two small sample sets is not powerful enough to illustrate the effect of the policy on the whole country, because data of these 5 eastern provinces and 5 mid – western provinces can only indicate situations in these areas and we can't prove sufficiently that these provinces in sample can represent the development of agricultural insurance market of the whole country with broad area and uneven development.

What is more, compared to other DID researches with large sample size, our model seems less convincing because we only have 30 samples in each model when using the provincial data. To improve this model, we can use municipal data or county data, but those data are inaccessible. To specify, model based on municipal data or county data also illustrate situations in these 10 provinces merely. So even the DID method reflects the lasting effect of the central financial subsidy on agricultural insurance premium revenue, we still have reservations about what we get from this method which is lack of enough credibility when it comes to the efficiency of the policy at the national level. We tend to believe that the implementation of the central financial subsidy policy really has problems in some of the provinces while in some other provinces the policy produced an positive and lasting effect on the growth of the agricultural insurance premium revenue and there is still room for the improvement of its efficiency according to our fieldwork study and the intuitive graphs which seems superficial but obvious. And our fieldwork experience will help us surmise what caused the contradiction and propose advice on the improvement of the central financial subsidy policy for our government.

V. Speculation and Improvement

Finally, according to what we conducted before, we speculated boldly that those provinces whose agricultural insurance didn't develop as well as we expected, without a lasting effect on the growth of the agricultural insurance premium revenue after the implementation of the central financial subsidy, may encounter these problems as followed which impeded the efficiency of the policy:

1. The local government focused on the implementation of the policy in the first year which can reflect its political achievements more as well as respond to the central government, but after that, it may not attach great importance to this policy, but to take the implementation of other latest policies seriously.

2. What's more, due to the higher – level government's objectives set, the primary organization and cadres had to try their best to finish their tasks which caused the behavior of raising premium only from some of the peasants without guidance on the purchase of the agricultural insurance and filling a vacancy from the governments at the villages and towns level. And the premium revenue must decline after the higher – level government minded this policy less.

3. Or the county or city government who is the primary organization of the subsidy policy cooperated with the local insurance company to swindled higher – level government, the central and provincial government out of the financial subsidized capital.

4. The county or city government was unable to support the sustained development of the agri-

cultural insurance due to its relatively weak fiscal solvency. And the subsidy from the government at this level couldn't be in place after the first year of the implementation which affected the efficiency of the central financial subsidy.

These are by no means exhaustive or complete but are the major problems we assume based on our research. And in order to improve the efficiency of the central financial subsidy on agricultural insurance, we propose advice as followed to settle the problems above:

1. When formulating plans about performance evaluation of agricultural insurance premium subsidy, the Ministry of Finance should not only pay attention to the current year, but also attach importance to the annual change in the later years. In other words, the efficiency evaluation should be built as a long – term mechanism.

2. Avoid setting specific objective for the lower – level government, but pay more attention to guide and encourage the large – scale contract peasant households who can obtain more subsidy on the insurance premium to purchase agricultural insurance to formulate a demonstration effect, which can bring those who has a relatively small production scale but a potential need on agricultural insurance to purchase the insurance.

3. Issue strict rules and punish those who cooperated with the local insurance company to swindle central and provincial financial subsidized capital, especially the local government officials. Subsidize the operating expenses of the local insurance company to reduce the management burden on the insurance company with agricultural insurance business.

4. Given the different fiscal solvency in municipal and county level government, the central and provincial financial had better appropriate special fund to help those local government with relatively weak finance to ensure the implementation of the subsidy policy. And only after the local financial subsidy has been in place, the provincial and central financial subsidy would be given in place one after another.

References

1. Ahsan, S. M., Ali, A. A., & Kurian, N. J. (1982). Toward a theory of agricultural insurance. *American Journal of Agricultural Economics*, 64(3), 510 – 529.

2. Card, D., & Krueger, A. B. (2000). Minimum wages and employment: a case study of the fast – food industry in New Jersey and Pennsylvania: reply. *American Economic Review*, 1397 – 1420.

3. Chen, S., & Wang, J. (2014). Rural Tax Reform: Agricultural Productivity and Local Public Finance. *Available at SSRN* 2374923.

4. Shi Hong. (2008). Review of researches on fiscal system for agricultural insurance in the USA & comments on China's fiscal system to agricultural insurance. *Insurance studies*, (4), 91 – 94.

5. Guozhu Tuo & Junsheng Zhu. (2005). Discussion on several important issues about the construction of China's agricultural insurance system. *Chinese Rural Economy*, (6), 46 – 52.

6. Huihua Nie, Mingyue Fang, Tao Li (2009). Effect on corporate behavior and performance of VAT Transformation. *Management World*, 5, 17 – 35.

7. Kai Wang & Sheng Wan. (2009). An Empirical Analysis of multiple factors affecting the development of China's agriculture Insurance. *Insurance Studies*, (4), 101 – 105.

8. Kudamatsu, M. (2012). Has Democratization reduced infant mortality in Sub – Saharan Africa? – Evidence From Micro Data. *Journal of the European Economic Association*, 10(6), 1294 – 1317.

9. Lian Zhou, Ye Chen. (2005). Effectiveness analysis on China's reformation of rural taxation system: based on difference – in – difference model. *Economic Research*, (8), 44 – 53.

10. Mishra, P. K. (1996). *Agricultural risk, insurance and income: a study of the impact and design of India's comprehensive crop insurance scheme.* Avebury.

11. Wenli Feng. (2004). China's agricultural insurance Market failure and system supply. *Journal of Financial Research*, (4), 124 – 129.

12. Wright, B. D., & Hewitt, J. A. (1994). All – risk crop insurance: lessons from theory and experience. In *Economics of agricultural crop insurance: theory and evidence* (pp. 73 – 112). Springer Netherlands.

13. Xinhua Yang & Xiangyang Wei. (2010). Fiscal incentives on agricultural insurance in China. *Insurance Studies*, (3), 89 – 93.

14. Yonghui Pan. (2008). International comparison of fiscal support on agricultural insurance and China's choice. *Agricultural Economic Issues*, (7), 97 – 103.

15. Youhai Fei. (2005). Deep roots of the development dilemma of agricultural insurance in China – the analysis based on the perspective of welfare economics. *Journal of Financial Research*, (3), 133 – 144.

16. Yuehua Zhang & Haiying Gu. (2004). Nature of the quasi – public goods, externalities and agricultural insurance – Discussion on agricultural insurance policy subsidy theory. *China soft science magazine*, (9), 10 – 15.

17. Zhongxin Wu, Ya Zhang. (2009). Agricultural Insurance subsidies review. *Economic Perspectives*, (11), 120 – 124

Appendix

Figure 1: Annual agricultural insurance premium revenue

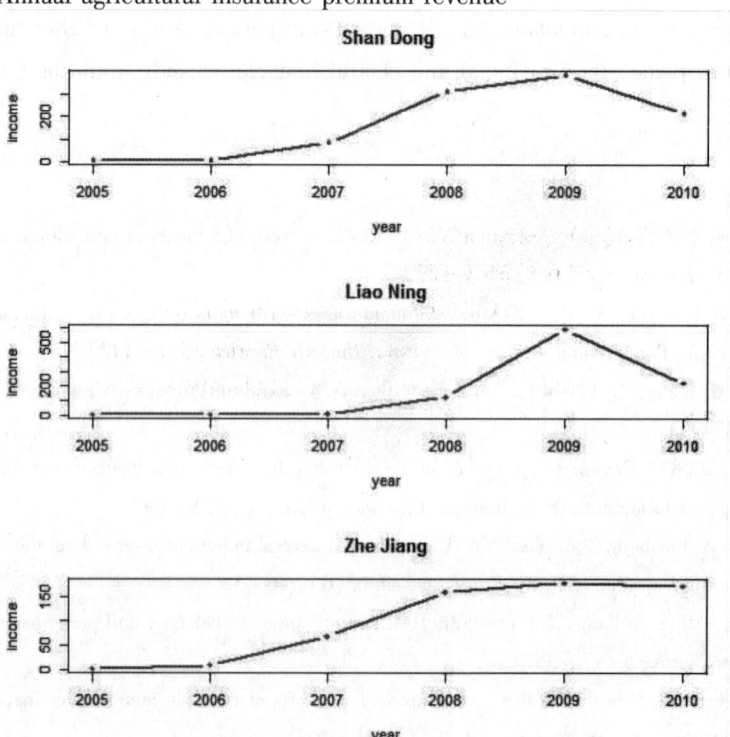

Figure 1(Continued): Annual agricultural insurance premium revenue

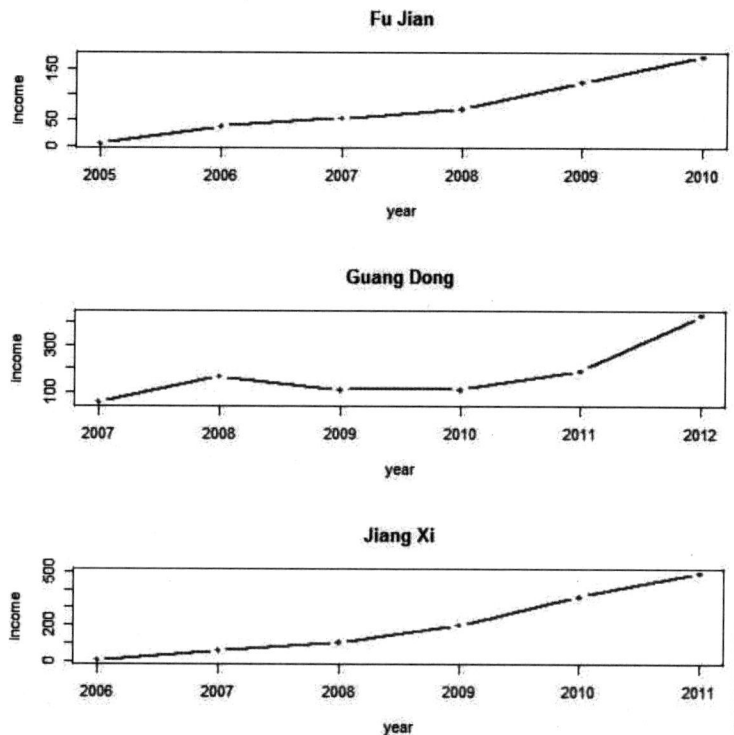

Figure 1(Continued): Annual agricultural insurance premium revenue

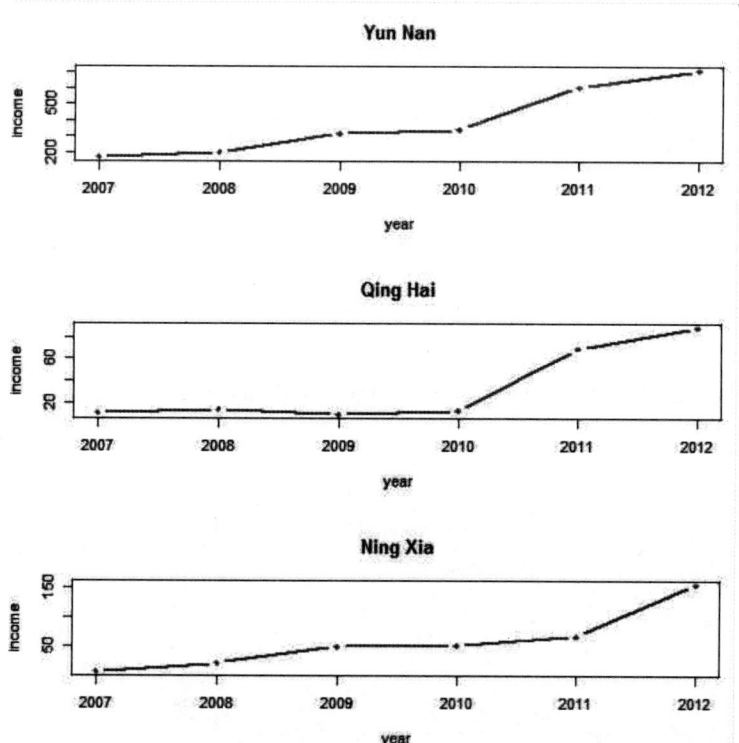

Figure 1(Continued): Annual agricultural insurance premium revenue

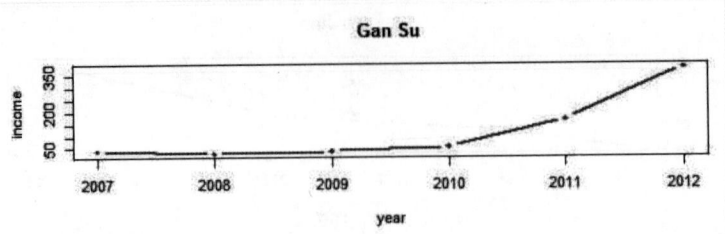

Figure 2: Natural logarithm of the annual agricultural insurance premium revenue

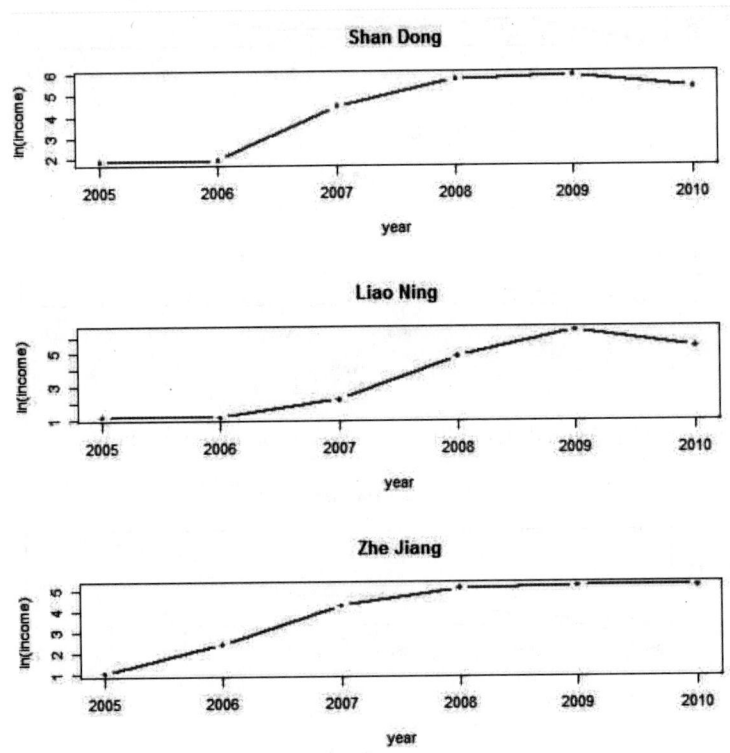

Figure 2(Continued): Natural logarithm of the annual agricultural insurance premium revenue

Central Financial Subsidy of Agricultural Insurance in China: the Efficiency and Improvement for the Government

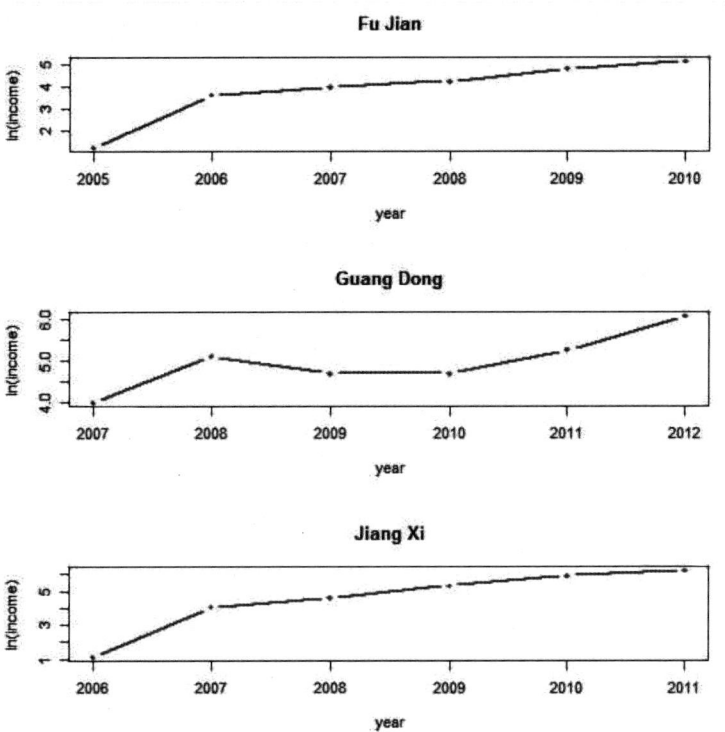

Figure 2 (Continued): Natural logarithm of the annual agricultural insurance premium revenue

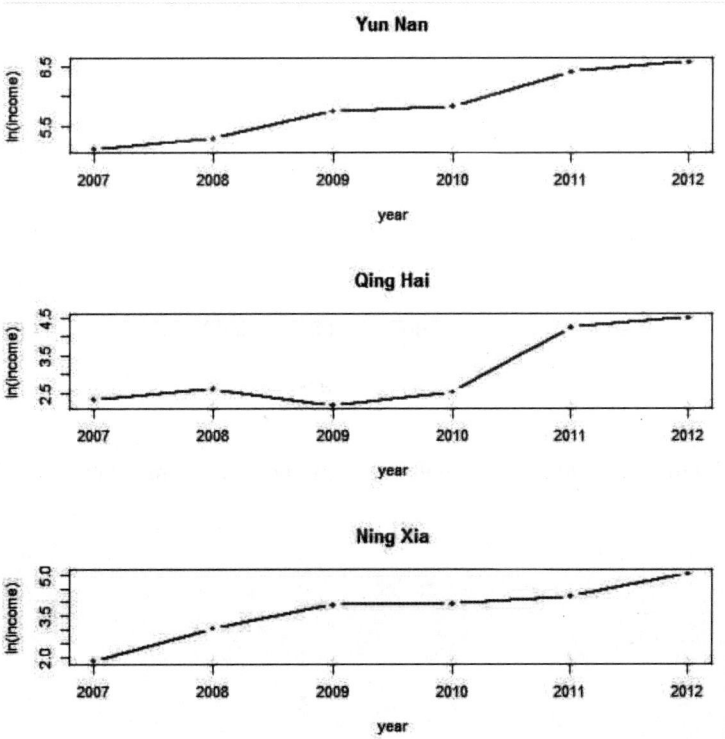

Figure 2(Continued): Natural logarithm of the annual agricultural insurance premium revenue

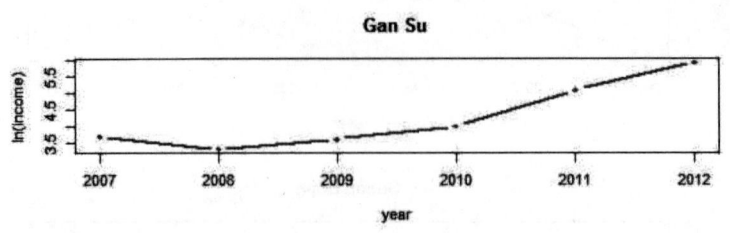

Figure 3: Annual agricultural insurance premium revenue before and after the subsidy – Anhui

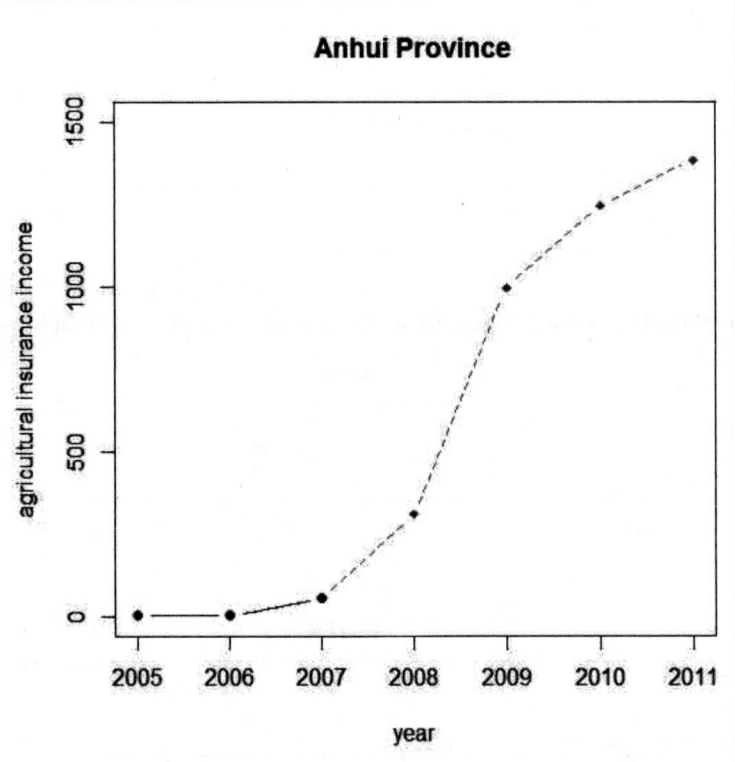

Figure 3 (Continued): Annual agricultural insurance premium revenue before and after the subsidy – Hebei

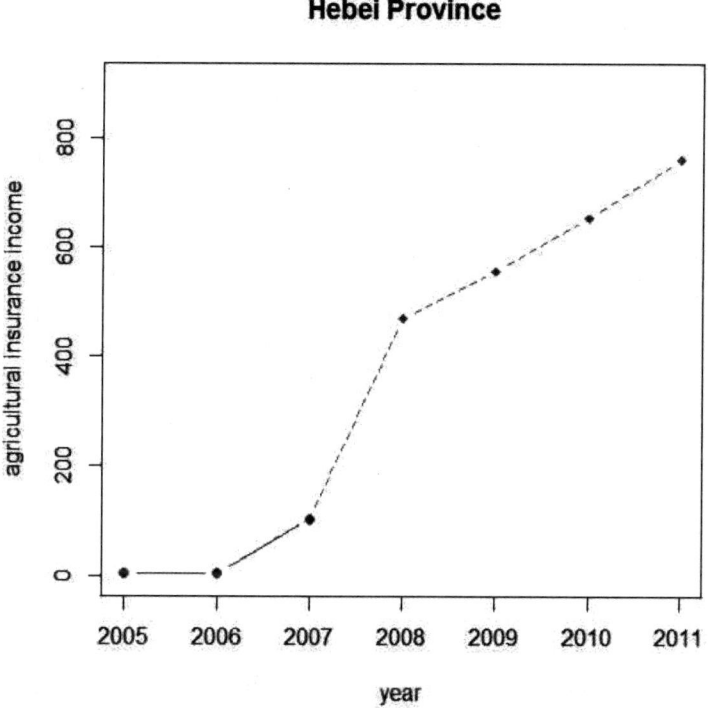

Figure 3 (Continued): Annual agricultural insurance premium revenue before and after the subsidy – Heilongjiang

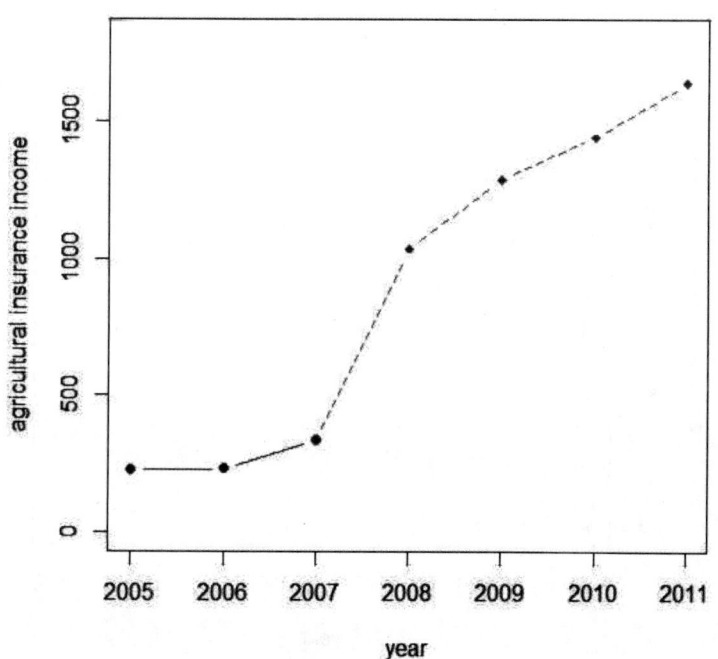

Figure 3 (Continued): Annual agricultural insurance premium revenue before and after the Subsidy – Jiangsu

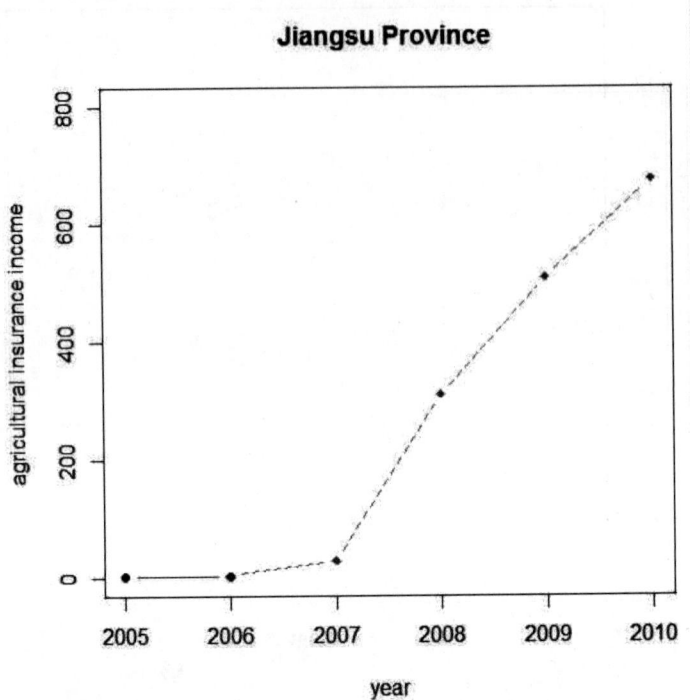

Figure 3 (Continued): Annual agricultural insurance premium revenue before and after the subsidy – Inner Mongolia

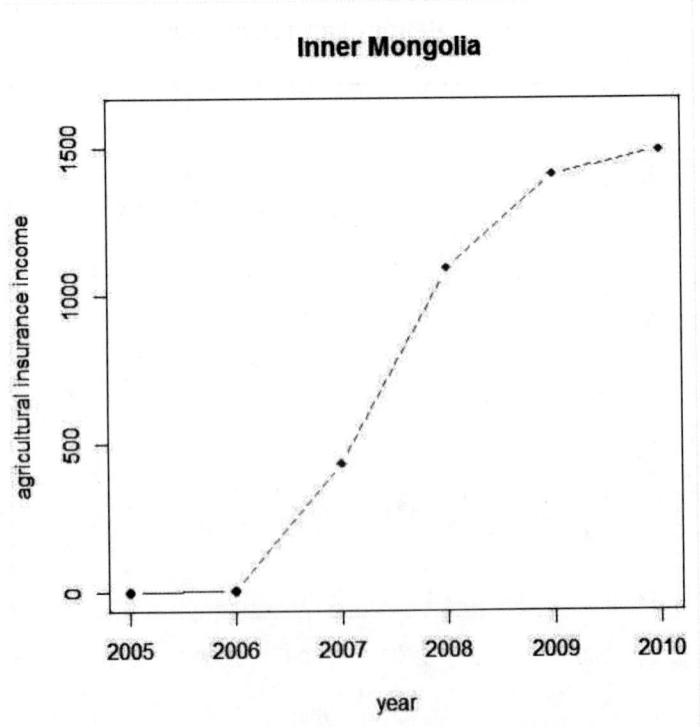

Figure 3 (Continued): Annual agricultural insurance premium revenue before and after the subsidy – Henan

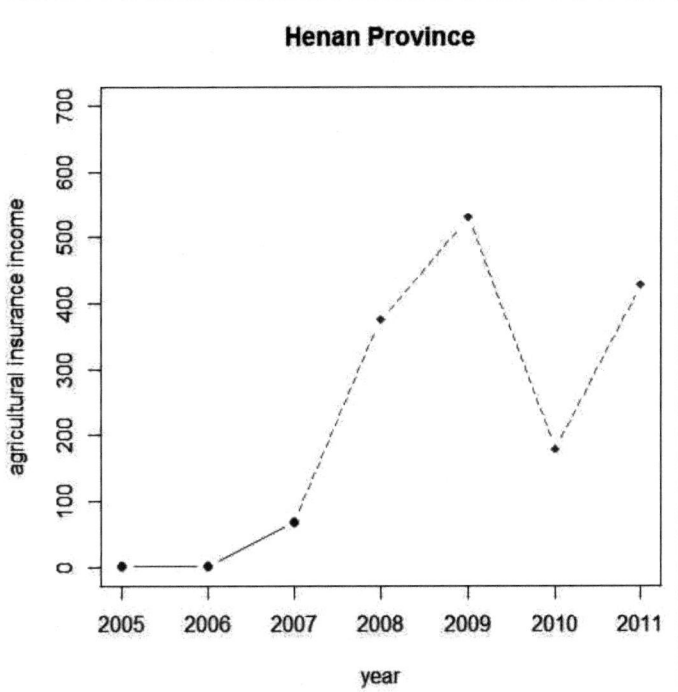

Figure 3 (Continued): Annual agricultural insurance premium revenue before and after the subsidy—Hubei

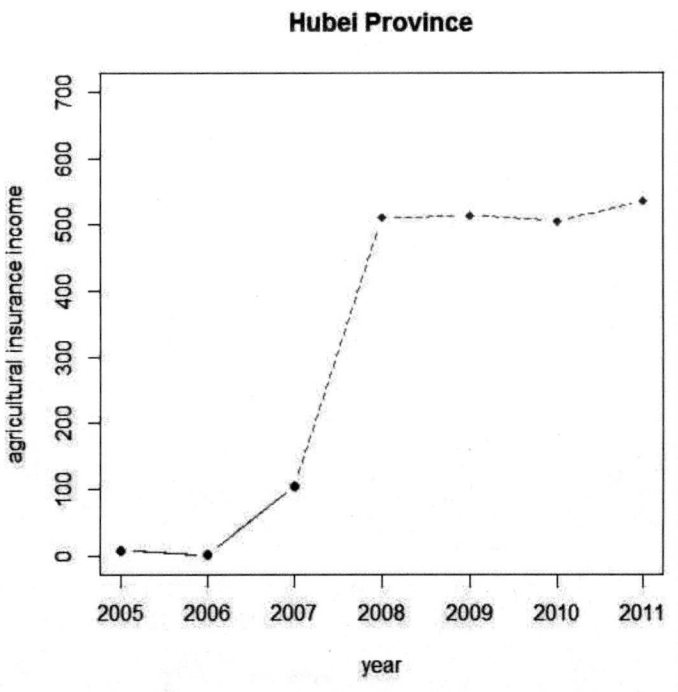

Figure 3 (Continued): Annual agricultural insurance premium revenue before and after the subsidy—Hunan

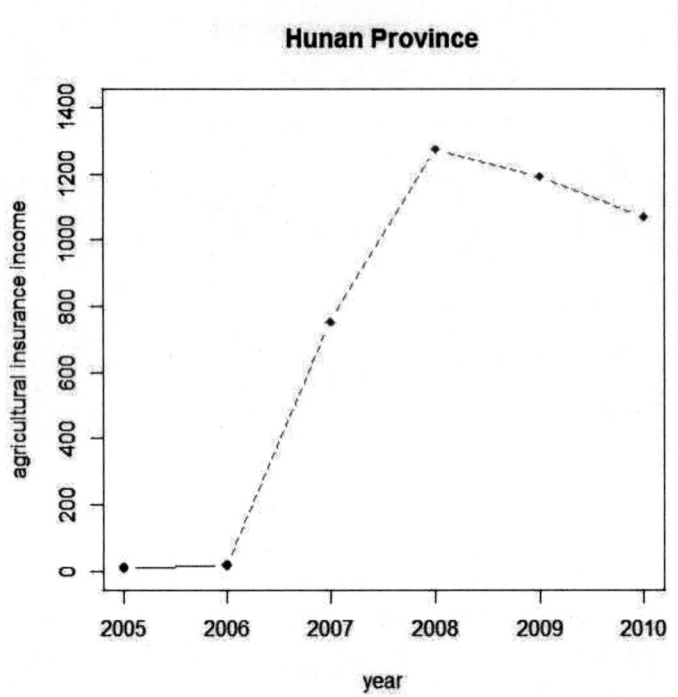

Figure 3 (Continued): Annual agricultural insurance premium revenue before and after the subsidy – Jilin

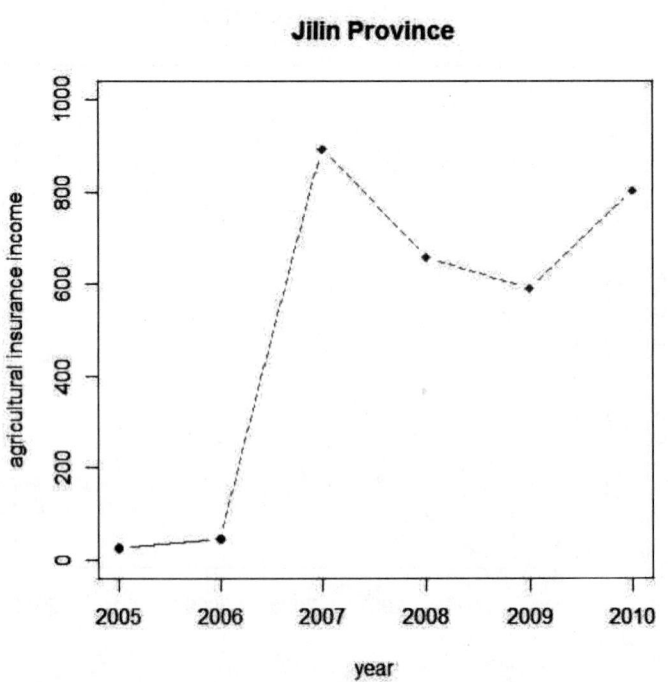

Figure 3 (Continued): Annual agricultural insurance premium revenue before and after the subsidy – Sichuan

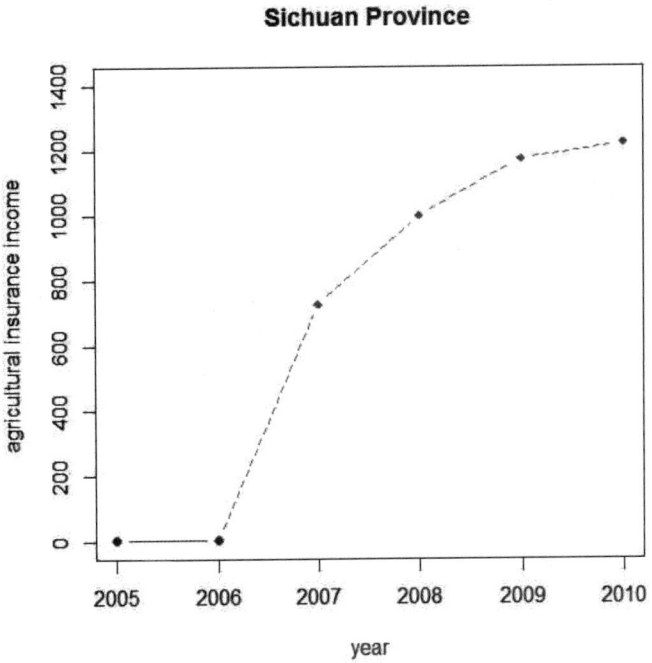

Figure 3 (Continued): Annual agricultural insurance premium revenue before and after the subsidy – Xinjiang

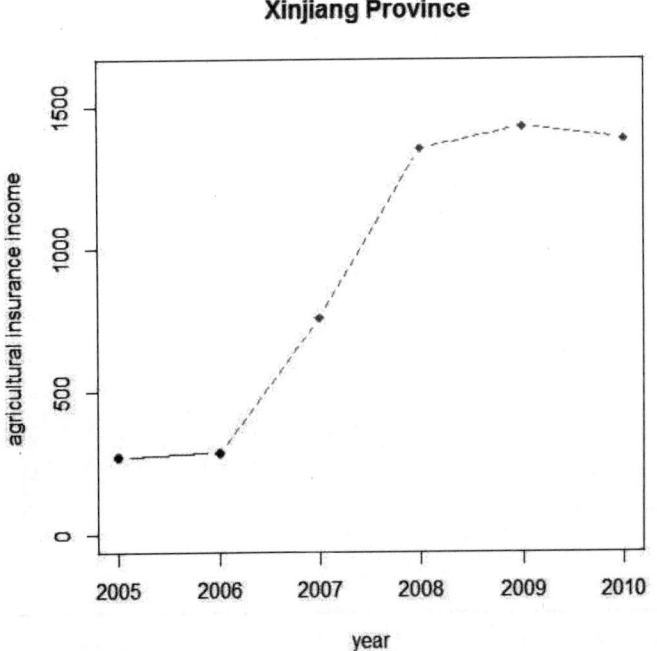

Table 1 Progress of subsidy

Year	Provinces
2007	Jiangsu, Jilin, Inner Mongolia, Hunan, Sichuan, Xinjiang
2008	Shandong, Anhui, Heilongjiang, Henan, Hebei, Shanxi, Liaoning, Hubei, Zhejiang, Fujian
2009	Jiangxi, Hainan
2010	Yunnan, Gansu, Guangdong, Qinghai, Ningxia
2011	Shanxi, Guangxi
2012	Xizang, Guizhou

Table 2 Subsidy proportions for provinces

Year Provinces	2007	2008	2009	2010	2011	2012
Jiangsu	25%	35%	35%	35%	35%	35%
Jilin	25%	35%	40%	40%	40%	40%
Inner Mongolia	25%	35%	40%	40%	40%	40%
Hunan	25%	35%	40%	40%	40%	40%
Sichuan	25%	35%	40%	40%	40%	40%
Xinjiang	25%	35%	40%	40%	40%	40%
Shandong		35%	35%	35%	35%	35%
Anhui		35%	40%	40%	40%	40%
Heilongjiang		35%	40%	40%	40%	40%
Hebei		35%	40%	40%	40%	40%
Shanxi		35%	40%	40%	40%	40%
Liaoning		35%	35%	35%	35%	35%
Hubei		35%	40%	40%	40%	40%
Zhejiang		35%	35%	35%	35%	35%
Fujian		35%	35%	35%	35%	35%
Jiangxi			40%	40%	40%	40%
Hainan			40%	40%	40%	40%
Yunnan				40%	40%	40%
Gansu				40%	40%	40%
Guangdong				40%	40%	40%
Qinghai				40%	40%	40%
Ningxia				40%	40%	40%
Shanxi					40%	40%
Guangxi					40%	40%
Xizang						40%
Guizhou						40%

Table 3:

Provinces	Year of subsidy	Years observed	Group
Shan Dong	2008	2005 – 2010	1
Liao Ning	2008	2005 – 2010	1
Zhe Jiang	2008	2005 – 2010	1
Fu Jian	2008	2005 – 2010	1
Jiang Xi	2009	2006 – 2011	2
Yun Nan	2010	2007 – 2012	2
Guang Dong	2010	2007 – 2012	1
Qing Hai	2010	2007 – 2012	2
Ning Xia	2010	2007 – 2012	2
Gan Su	2010	2007 – 2012	2

Table 4   **Summary statistics**

	(1)	(2)	(3)
Provinces	All	Group 1	Group 2
implementation of subsidy	0.5 (0.50)	0.5 (0.51)	0.5 (0.51)
first year	0.1667 (0.38)	0.1667 (0.38)	0.1667 (0.38)
second year	0.1667 (0.38)	0.1667 (0.38)	0.1667 (0.38)
third year	0.1667 (0.38)	0.1667 (0.38)	0.1667 (0.38)
average income (yuan)	5346.32 (2043.06)	6588 (1996.78)	4104 (1146.06)
Fertilizer (10000 ton)	150.40 (127.46)	211.3 (145.410)	89.48 (65.03)
planting area (1000 hectare)	4134.23 (2822.14)	4777 (3155.67)	3491 (2321.50)
proportion of agricultural insurance	0.0207 (0.02)	0.0093 (0.01)	0.0321 (0.02)
Agricultural insurance Premium revenue (AII) (million yuan)	4.18 (1.54)	4.08 (1.64)	4.27 (1.45)
Sample	60	30	30

Table 5   Estimated regression models for five eastern provinces

	(1)	(2)	(3)	(4)
Implementation of subsidy(IS)	2.4136 * * * (0.4066)	0.7911. (0.4176)		
1st year of implementation			2.0392 * * (0.5875)	0.8387. (0.4573)
2nd year of implementation			2.6423 * * * (0.5875)	0.4361 (0.5870)
3rd year of implementation			2.5593 * * * (0.5875)	0.8562 (0.5609)
Disposable Income (DI)		0.0003 * * (0.0001)		0.0003 * * (0.0001)
Fertilizer(FER)		0.0186 * * (0.0052)		0.0190 * * (0.0053)
Planting Areas (PA)		−0.0007 * * (0.0002)		−0.0008 * * * (0.0002)
Proportion of Agricultural Insurance (PAI)		68.86 * * * (13.95)		74.13 * * * (15.45)

Significant code: '* * *' 0.001, '* *' 0.01, '*' 0.05, '.' 0.1

Table 6   Estimated regression models for mid-five western provinces

	(1)	(2)	(3)	(4)
Implementation of subsidy(IS)	1.5439 * * (0.4545)	0.3825. (0.2191)		
1st year of implementation			0.8200 (0.6315)	0.4848. (0.2381)
2nd year of implementation			1.6685 * (0.6315)	0.2353 (0.2973)
3rd year of implementation			2.1432 * * (0.6315)	−0.3016 (0.3936)
Planting Areas (PA)		−0.0003 * * * (0.00004)		−0.0003 * * * (0.00004)
Proportion of Agricultural Insurance (PAI)		51.97 * * * (6.439)		63.63 * * * (8.582)

Significant code: '* * *' 0.001, '* *' 0.01, '*' 0.05, '.' 0.1

Indicators Analysis of Ping An Insurance Group
——Based on its Global Systemically Importance

Huiran Ma Yumeng Zhou

Abstract: This paper is based on the fact that Ping An Insurance Group was rated as one of the global systemically important insures (GSIIs) in 2013. The paper mainly focuses on explaining why Ping An became one of the GSIIs by analyzing selected indicators and Ping An investment portfolio. What's more, the paper also pays attention to its non-traditional business and the financial-related risk. Facing the global financial environment change, the analysis provides a new coordinate for insurance companies. The conclusion is that Ping An is delicate to comprehensive finance mode and has made great innovation in internet finance. Ping An connects with the whole finance system mainly through investment business, whose operation risk and related transactions risk shall be emphasized. It is the involvement of NTNI business and internet finance that makes Ping An a systemically important institution.

Key words: Ping An, GSIIs, Financial related risk, Non-traditional business

Part I INTRODUCTIONS – RESEARCH PURPOSE AND IMPORTANCE

The Financial Stability Board (FSB) issued the initial 9 global system importance insurers (G-SIIs) name list in August 2013, with Ping An Insurance being the only-selected insurance institution in Asia, and also the only-selected institution in the developing country and emerging insurance market. Insurance is nearly the largest long-term capital provider and the most important institutional investor in the financial market. Under the influence of subprime crisis, Asia, even the global economy suffered from a serious shock. People started to pay more attention to the stable operating ability of the financial institutions. Though Ping An Insurance does not have the optimal financial indicators and largest business volume in Asian area, it gradually became the most important one to influence the world in this area, and the reason shall be researched.

Under the background of digitalization and integration, the revolution brought by the emerging market cannot be underestimated. We must pay attention to the butterfly effect in new market revolution. The study on typical subject – Ping An Insurance – of Chinese insurance industry will have the

---

① 18th Asia-Pacific Risk and Insurance Association Annual Conference, Moscow, 2014.
② Graduate students of Central University of Finance and Economics, Beijing, China.

significance of learning and reference. For the past decades, Chinese insurance industry has been developing itself by learning from other countries´ experience. Nowadays, Chinese insurance industry has evolved to be of great uniqueness, which is worthy for foreign insurers to take into consideration. Ping An provides new coordinate and reference point for the foreign financial groups, helping them reposition themselves and respond to the change of the global financial environment.

Part II LITERATURE REVIEW

A. Indicators and Assessment Methodology of GSIIs

International Association of Insurance Supervisors (IAIS) found that insurers that operate traditional insurance can absorb financial systemic risk, while those who operate non – traditional non – financial business are more likely to be influenced by market, to spread, to zoom and even to lead to financial crisis. Based on the Global Systemically Important Insurers: Proposed Assessment Methodology, IAIS chose five catalogues including 20 indicators as assessment indicators, which reflects the importance of insurance funds and the relevance between insurer investment and financial market. The indicators are shown in table1. Size indicates the insurer´s ability to influence the market and to provide financial service. Global activity measures insurer´s participation in the global risk transfer and also measures its foreign influence. Interconnectedness mainly reflects the degree of internal financialization and internal cross impacts between different departments. Non – traditional and non – insurance activities (NTNI) pay attention to high – risk investment and speculation. Substitutability[①] uses data of credit insurance, aviation insurance and marine insurance to measure insurers´ global impact.

Table 1 　　　　　　　　**Assessment Indicators of GSIIs**

Category	Individual indicator	Indicator weighting
Size	total assets	2.5% – 5%
	total revenue	2.5% – 5%
global activity	Revenues derived outside of home country	2.5% – 5%
	Number of countries	2.5% – 5%
interconnectedness	Intra – financial assets	4.3% – 5.7%
	Intra – financial liabilities	4.3% – 5.7%
	Reinsurance	4.3% – 5.7%
	Derivatives	4.3% – 5.7%
	Large exposures	4.3% – 5.7%
	Turnover	4.3% – 5.7%
	Level 3 assets	4.3% – 5.7%

---

① Hao Yansu, Explaining and evaluation of global systemically important insurer, http://finance.sina.com.cn/money/insurance/bxrw/20130813/140916432722.shtml.

续表

Category	Individual indicator	Indicator weighting
non – traditional and non – insurance activities	Non – policy holder liabilities and non – insurance revenues	6.7% – 8.3%
	Derivatives trading	6.7% – 8.3%
	Short term funding	6.7% – 8.3%
	Financial guarantees	6.7% – 8.3%
	Variable annuities	6.7% – 8.3%
	Intra – group commitments	6.7% – 8.3%
substitutability	Premiums for specific business lines	5% – 10%

B. Research on global system important institutions

Foreign researches of GSIIs concentrates on global system important banks, mainly on the "too big too fall" issue. Segoviano& Goldhart(2009) used network analysis method to evaluate GSIIS; Adrian& Brunnermeier (2009) measured risk premium of GSIIs by cov – VaR. V. Acharya et al (2010) examined the GSIIs marginal contribution to the finical market by MES method. Chinese scholars pay attention to the monitoring level of global system important banks. Chen Jing, Chen Ruoqing(2012) analyzed monitoring indicators of The Royal Bank of Scotland and provided suggestions for Chinese government. Yue Yi(2012) analysed Bank of China in 4 aspects – bank capital, Compliance costs, risk management and Industry competition – to propose development strategy. However, researches on global system important insurers are rare. Researches based on GSIIs Indicators and financial relevance risks is basically a latest field.

C. Research on typical insurers in Chinese market

Scholars have done a lot of research about Chinese typical insurers. As for Ping An, researches including corporate governance, development strategy, marketing strategy, insurance funds investment and competitive ability, such as Li Zhuyong (2009), Wang Kai(2011), Jin Yongde (2008). These papers, however, did not analyze Ping An's non – traditional business or its integrated business risk under framework of global system important institutions.

Therefore, based on the framework of GSIIs and indicators provided by IAIS, this paper mainly analyses comprehensive performance of Ping An Insurance Group in Chinese market, then focuses on business(mainly on insurance funds investment) that have close connection with financial system risk, and also pays attention to its NTNI business.

Part III COMPREHENSIVE ANALYSIS OF PING AN INSURANCE

A. Indicator Selected

Based on Basel Committee requirements and IAIS's insurance standard, indicators were selected to reflect corporate governance, financial requirements and market behaviors. Ping An Insurance is a comprehensive financial Group, whose core business is insurance. As a GSII, the paper firstly analyses insurance business by its scale, financial asset, profitability, solvency and embedded value.

B. Data Sources

Data used in the paper are selected from annual reports of Ping An Insurance group(2006 – 2013), China Insurance Yearbook and published reports from China Insurance Regulatory Commission.

C. Analysis and Results

1. Scale and Organization

Ping An Insurance Group

Insurance	Banking	Investment	
Ping An life insurance		Ping An Trust	
Ping An property insurance		Ping An Securities	
Ping An Annuity	Ping An Bank	Ping An Asset Management	
		Ping An Overseas Holdings	
Ping An Health		Ping An Asset Management(Hong Kong)	
Ping An Hong Kong		Ping An UOB funds	
Shared Platform			
Ping An Technology	Ping An processing and Technology	Ping An Financial Technology	Ping An Channel Development

Figuer1 Ping An Insurance Group

Ping An develops from an insurance company to an integrated financial services conglomerate with three core businesses: insurance, banking, and investment, and also pays attention to make full use of internet finance to develop non – traditional business.

Ping An Insurance Group has owned assets of 3360. 3 billion Yuan, earned premium of 335 billion Yuan, and realized net profit 28. 154 billion Yuan in 2013. Ping An life insurance has 13. 6% market share, and 44. 16 million Yuan of the 219. 4 billion Yuan premium is new business, which has increased by 14. 1%; Ping An property insurance has a market share of 17. 8%, and earned premium of 115. 7 billion Yuan, being the second in Chinese property insurance industry. The amount of insurance funds investment is 1230. 4 billion Yuan. So far, Ping An has provided insurance, banking and investment services for over 80 million customers.

2. Profitability

Ping An Life Insurance has been performing well in recent years and has excellent overall profitability, ranking at the forefront of the industry.

Table 2   Indicators of Profitability – Ping An Life Insurance

year	Expense ratio	investment yield	net profit (in million Yuan)	net profit/total asset	net profit/ Owner's equity
2013	23.40%	5.00%	12219	1.04%	28.31%
2012	22.95%	2.80%	6457	0.62%	16.04%
2011	21.99%	4.10%	9974	1.17%	33.31%
2010	23.02%	5.00%	8417	1.10%	36.72%
2009	25.12%	6.70%	10374	1.72%	36.00%
2008	21.94%	-2.40%	-1464	-0.31%	-12.62%
2007	22.59%	14.20%	7831	1.86%	25.83%
2006	18.80%	7.80%	5671	1.72%	30.06%

(1) Insurance business. The expense ratio is a negative indicator to reflect business quality, including commission fee for insurance (excludes reinsurance), development expenses and insurance taxes and license fee. For Ping An Life Insurance, the expense ratio aresmooth and close to the industry average level.

(2) Investment. As it is shown in table 2, investment yield fluctuated a lot in recent years. The yield has close connection with Chinese macroeconomic. Due to financial crisis and unwise investment in Fortis, Ping An has resulted in a huge amount of loss in 2008. Chinese stock market and interest rate stayed in a down cycle in 2012, also influencing the investment yield. More detailed analysis will be in part C.

(3) Indicators related to net profit. Table 2 shows 2 indicators related to net profits, whose denominator are total asset and owner's surplus separately, reflecting profits contribution to the operation. When the growth rate of net profits exceeds that of total asset or owner's equity, the ratio would increase, otherwise it will stay stable. Since total assets and owner's equity also increased stably except for 2008 and 2012, those ratios of Ping An Life perform well in recent year.

Table 3   Indicators of Profitability – Ping An Property Insurance

YEAR	Combined cost ratio①	Combined loss ratio②	investment yield	net profit/ total asset	net profit/ total income	net profit/ Owner's equity
2013	97.3%	60.40%	5.40%	3.67%	6.02%	18.95%
2012	95.3%	59.40%	3.30%	4.76%	7.81%	23.73%
2011	93.5%	57.80%	3.90%	4.56%	7.45%	22.25%
2010	93.2%	55.40%	4.20%	4.86%	4.86%	22.25%
2009	98.6%	57.00%	5.40%	1.32%	2.23%	7.29%
2008	104.0%	68.10%	7.00%	1.31%	2.14%	7.51%
2007	101.8%	61.10%	14.70%	4.77%	8.09%	26.51%
2006	101.8%	63.90%	5.30%	2.51%	4.88%	16.43%

(1) The combined cost ratio and combined loss ratio are special ratio for non – life insurance. Ping An's combined cost ratio is decreasing in recent years, while combined loss ratio stays at a level of 60%. This trend indicates that Ping An has done a lot of work in controlling cost to increase its profitability. Although these two ratios almost equal to the average level of Chinese industry, non – life insurers in China have relatively low loss ratio compared with other countries.

(2) Investment. Ping An premium income has increased in 2013, as does investment yield. For the investment portfolio, Ping An increased weights of fixed income assets Due to the increasing rate for fixed income assets weights and the overall upturn economic cycle, its investment business performed well in 2013.

(3) Indicators related to net profits stays at the forefront of the industry except 2008 and 2009, which is largely affected by the financial crisis. Chinese economy has a lower growth rate for the reason of adjusting policy, while property insurance industry became more competitive in 2013. What's more, Ping An transferred resources to build internet channel. For those reasons, the net profits of Ping An property insurance decreased in 2013.

3. Solvency

---

① Combined cost ratio = (claims paid – reinsurers' share of insurance claims paid + reserves + reinsurance expenses extraction + non – investment – related business tax and surcharges + insurance fee and commission expenses + non – investment – related business and administrative expenses – Refund of reinsurance premium ceded + impairment losses of non – investment assets) / earned premiums.

② Combined ratio = (claims paid – Compensation payout refund + Insurance liability reserve refund) / earned premiums.

Indicators Analysis of Ping An Insurance Group

Table 4   Indicators of solvency

YEAR	Ping An Life Insurance			Ping An Property Insurance			Ceding premium/ premium income
	Asset – liability ratio	Solvency adequacy ratio	Change in reserve/equity	Asset – liability ratio	Solvency adequacy ratio	Change in reserve / equity	
2013	96.3%	171.9%	204.6%	80.65%	167.1%	38.6%	14.34%
2012	96.1%	190.6%	167.9%	79.93%	178.4%	45.2%	12.34%
2011	96.5%	156.1%	232.7%	79.52%	166.1%	73.8%	12.56%
2010	97.0%	180.2%	263.8%	78.14%	179.6%	89.3%	10.92%
2009	95.2%	226.7%	136.1%	81.82%	143.6%	78.0%	12.76%
2008	97.6%	183.7%	98.3%	82.57%	153.3%	38.1%	17.89%
2007	92.8%	287.9%	252.8%	81.99%	181.6%	52.4%	16.56%
2006	94.3%	183.1%	295.7%	84.72%	131.3%	74.1%	21.42%

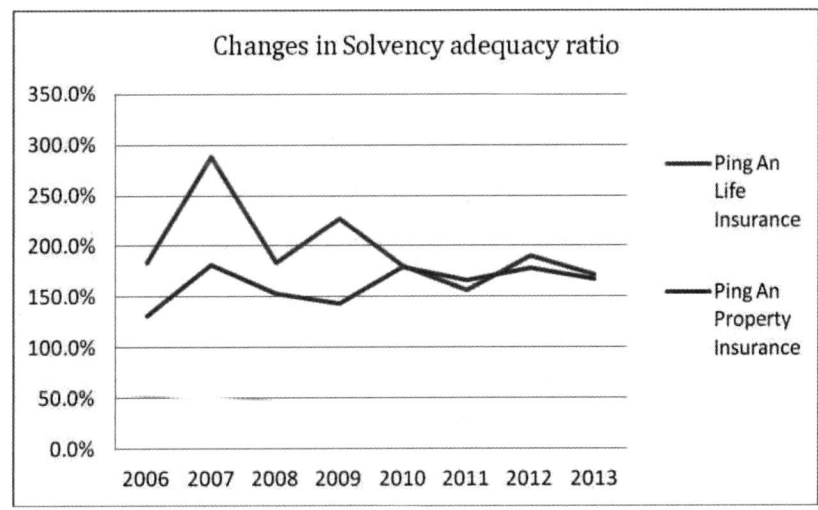

Figure 2   Changes in Ping An Insurance Solvency adequacy ratio

(1) China Insurance Regulatory Commission (CIRC) divided insurance company into 3 catalogues according to its solvency adequacy ratio. Ping An insurance has always been in solvency adequacy II level.

As shown in figure 2, Ping An solvency adequacy ratio has changed a lot in 2007, 2009 and 2012. In 2007, new released accounting standards changed the measurement of the insurance company's assets and liabilities, resulting in dramatic changes in the value of the industry's solvency. Ping An solvency ratio rose to 287.9% in 2007 since it issued 1.15 billion shares by 33.8 Yuan / share, dramatically increasing its capital. Ping An increased registered capital of 2 billion Yuan in 2009 to be consisted with the increasing premium. In 2011 and 2012, Ping An issued 4 billion subordinated debt to replenish its capital and increased registered capital of 5 billion Yuan to meet the requirement of CIRC.

The solvency ratios of both Ping An life and non - life insurance decreased compared with those of 2012, even though issuing 26 billion convertible bonds. The main reason is Ping An concentrated on expanding new channels, and the fair value of financial assets available for sale also declined in 2013. What's more, Ping An Life and Property Insurance share out dividends of 6 billion and 2 billion respectively to the Group, also making the solvency reduced.

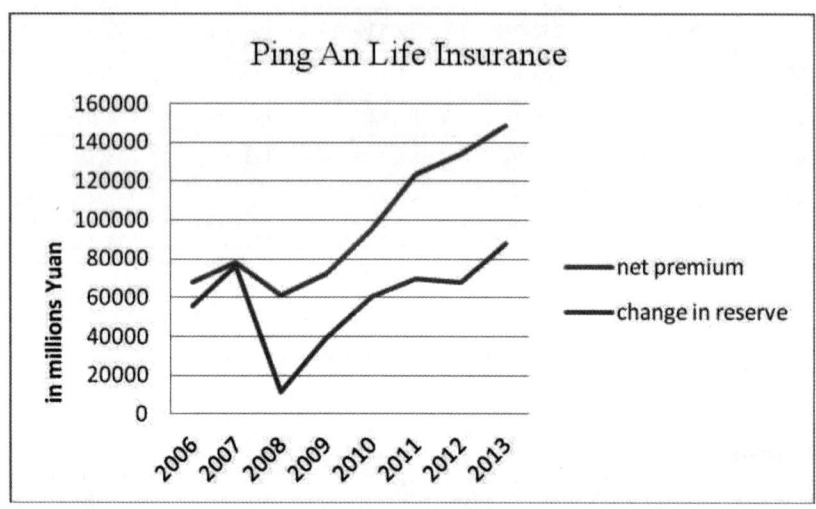

Figure 3　Change in reserve of Ping An Life Insurance

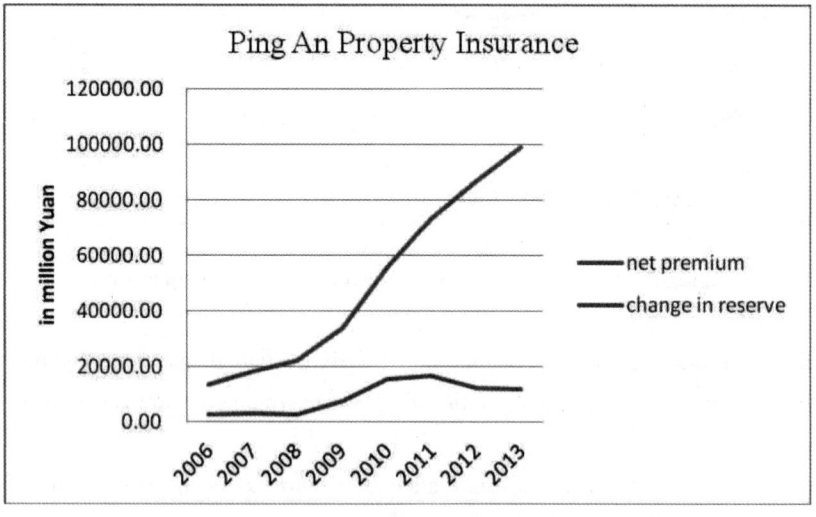

Figure 4　Change in reserve of Ping An Life Insurance

(2) Change in reserve reflects insurance responsibility for outstanding liability. It has close relationship with annul profits, especially for Life Insurance Company. The increase of change in Reserve will reduce net profits, therefore reducing net assets, then further impact solvency. So it is a

negative indicator. For the amount, change in Reserve of Ping An Life has been rising at a higher rate since 2008, while that of Ping An property became slow down after 2011. The rapid growth rate of change in Reserve in Ping An Life came from the expanded premium income. The change in reserve of Ping An Property Insurance stays stable, reflecting business's good quality.

(3) Most of insurance funds comes from debt —— premium income, so assets – liabilities ratio has been high. For the policyholders, the safety of funds is the first priority; for the operators, asset – liability ratio has high financial leverage. The fluctuation of asset – liability ratio may add internal risk. Neither Ping An Life or non – life insurance has a fluctuating ratio, reflecting a good condition in capital.

(iv) Ceding premium/premium income indicates the quality of non – life insurance, also indicates a company's connections with whole industry. For this ratio, Ping An Property Insurance has certain connection with whole market and transferred risk properly.

4. Embedded Value

Table 5   Changes In Ping An Embedded Value (million Yuan)

	2013	2012	2011	2010	2009	2008
Embedded value of life insurance at Jan. 1 2013	177460	144400	121086	100704	69643	73407
Annual Value Increase of life insurance	13025	22700	7960	6095	19359	-8172
New business value of life insurance	18540	16340	17343	16310	12654	9348
Life insurance's dividends to group	-5987	-5990	-1989	-2023	-952	-4940
Embedded value of life insurance at Dec. 31, 2013	203038	177450	144400	121086	100704	69643
Embedded value of non – life insurance at Jan. 1 2013	108414	91230	79900	54554	53216	76904
Annual Value Increase of non – life insurance	16173	14420	7406	10706	3194	-3059
Embedded value of non – life insurance at Dec. 31, 2013	124587	105650	87306	65260	56410	73845
Dividends to shareholders	-3958	-3166	-4245	-3440	-1102	-5142
Embedded value of Ping An group①	329653	285870	235627	200986	155258	122859

① Embedded value of Ping An group = Embedded value of life insurance (at beginning of the year) + Annual Value Increase of life insurance + new business value of life insurance – dividends to group + Embedded value of non – life insurance (at beginning of the year) + Annual Value Increase of non – life insurance + dividends from life insurance – dividends to shareholders.

续表

	2013	2012	2011	2010	2009	2008
Share capital	7916.7	7914.5	7906.9	7642.1	7358.2	7356.8
Embedded value per share	41.64	36.12	29.8	26.3	21.1	16.7

Embedded value is the value of a company's current outcomes without considering further new business. It can also be considered as liquidation value. Table 5 shows the change of Ping An embedded value in recent 5 years.

(1) Ping An insurance business has contributed stable dividends to the group, showing that Banking and Investment business still rely on insurance.

(2) Insurance is a significant business for Ping An group and has potential to develop. Take 2013 as an example. Firstly, premium of the new business in life insurance is 59 billion, having 30.8% profit rate. Secondly, taking the decline in the fair value of investment assets of life insurance into consideration, the proportion of life insurance embedded value in tthe Group is still above the 60%. Thirdly, there are favorable policies for insurance funds investment. So life insurance would still hold an important position in the Group in the next few years.

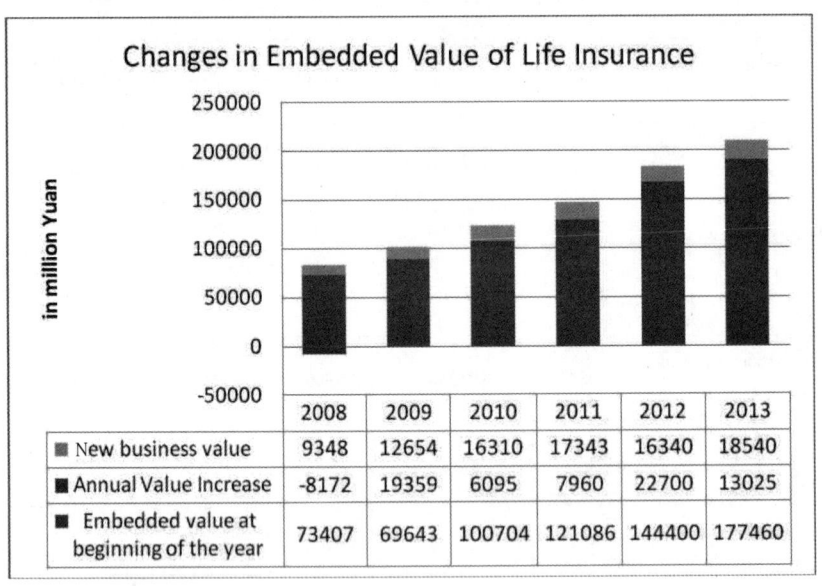

Figure 5 Changes in embedded value of life insurance

(3) The annul value increase contributes a lot to the change of embedded value in life insurance, as it is shown in figure 5. The reason is: a. adjustment of market capitalization value b. Differences in investment returns. c. Changes in assumptions and models. The adjustment of income tax raising the embedded value in 2012, and change of major diseases incidence rate led to the decline of embedded value in 2013.

Part IV ANALYSIS OF BUSINESS CONNECTED WITH FINANCIAL SYSTEM RISK

Ping An insurance group has connected with financial system risk via its investment business, as well as the internal connection among insurance, banking and investment. Furthermore, its non-traditional non-insurance (NTNI) business has expanded a lot, leading to an increasing risk reacting on the financial system.

A. Investment portfolio of Ping An Insurance Group

1. Overall Analysis

Ping An Insurance Group has investment funds of 1230.4 billion Yuan in 2013, increasing by 15.45% compared with that of 2014. Figure 6 shows the investment portfolio in 2013 and table 6 shows the detail numbers.

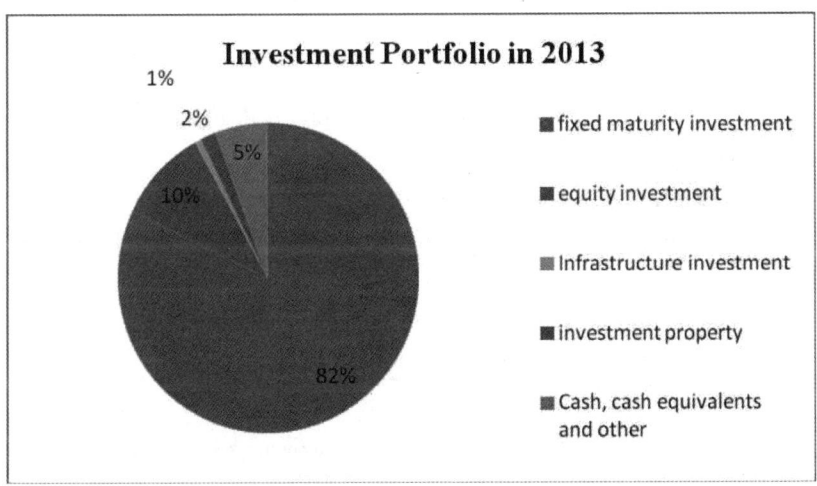

Figure 6 Investment portfolio of Ping An Insurance Group in 2013

Table 6 Investment portfolio of Ping An Insurance Group 2013 (in million Yuan)

Category	2013	2012	Change amount	Proportion of changes
Deposits	224865	241600	-16735	-6.93%
bonds	639241	560042	79199	14.14%
Debts plans	107401	37429	69972	186.95%
Other fixed maturity investment①	40186	35165	5021	14.28%
fixed maturity investment	1011693	874236	137457	15.72%
Securities Investment Fund	33247	25099	8148	32.46%

① Including Redemptory monetary capital for sale, policy loans, restricted statutory deposits and so on.

续表

Category	2013	2012	Change amount	Proportion of changes
Equity Securities	87250	76371	10879	14.24%
Equity investment	120497	101470	19027	18.75%
Infrastructure investment	8686	8802	-116	-1.32%
Investment property	20349	16385	3964	24.19%
Cash, cash equivalents and other	69142	73295	-4153	-5.67%
Total investment	1230367	1074188	156179	14.54%

(1) Most of the funds are invested in the fixed maturity investment. The 1011.6 billion Yuan fixed maturity investments reaches about 80% of the total funds.

(2) Investment funds have increased by 156.2 billion in 2013, mainly investing Yuan in bonds and debt plans. The debt plan accounts for 8.7% of the whole portfolio, increasing 5.2% (by 699.7 billion) compared with 2012.

(3) Cash and cash equivalents declined in the portfolio both in amount and proportion, reflecting the investment strategy.

(4) Property investments continue to expand. Ping An Group has made the first overseas acquisitions of real estate - buying Lloyd's building in order to obtain stable rental returns.

2. Analysis for Equity investment

Table 7　　　　Top-10 Available-for-sale Financial assets(2013)

	Initial investment amount(ml)	Changes in amounts(ml)	Net book value(ml)	Proportion to total equity
Industrial and Commercial Bank of China	20499	6787	17529	14.55%
Agricultural Bank of China	14911	662	13741	11.40%
China Construction Bank	13826	1403	11877	9.86%
Yunnan Baiyao	1407	0	6629	5.50%
Bank of Communications	4372	-174	3623	3.01%
Ageas	23874	0	3153	2.62%
Shanghai Pudong Development Bank	2491	1481	2785	2.31%
China Life Insurance	731	731	696	0.58%
China Cinda	468	468	623	0.52%
Midea Group	536	-494	595	0.49%
total	83115	10864	61251	50.83%
Sum of Financial stock	81172	11358	54027	44.84%

The top 10 available-for-sale financial assets have a total book value of 61.25 billion Yuan, accounting for 50.85% of the whole equity. From table 7 we can find two characteristics. Firstly, investment strategy prefers to financial stock. There are 5 banks, 1 asset management company and 2 insurance companies in the top 10 equities. Ping An has increased the investment in ICBC, ABC and CCB in 2013. Secondly, stock investment gradually concentrated. The top 10 stocks accounted for more than half of the entire equity investment, while in 2009 it was only 30.5%.

The fact that the allocation of Ping An investment in available-for-sale financial assets concentrates on financial stock might lead Ping An to be more sensitive to the financial system risk. Nowadays, banks play a significant role in Chinese financial market and have larger scale than the sum of security and insurance. When considering development potential, Ping An should pay more attention to the stocks of insurance and security and also add stocks on new energy and medicine fields in order to reduce cyclical risks caused by excessive concentration.

3. Analysis for Real Estate Investment

Ping An shows an increasing enthusiasm to invest in real estate since it is a proper way to meet long-term returns requirements of Asset-liability management. By the end of 2013, the total value of real estate investment was 18.264 billion Yuan, 4 times more than that by the end of 2007, which was 4.05 billion Yuan. Policy from CIRC is becoming more favorable since it increases upper limit on real estate investment and permits insurance fund to invest in overseas property. Therefore, Ping An has greater motivation and ability to invest in real estate.

B. Development of non-traditional non-insurance business

2013 is a significant year for Ping An Insurance Group since it has distributed several important non-traditional non-insurance businesses to connect with internet finance. As for NTNI business, Ping An Group might be the most forward-looking company in China. The core part of Ping An's comprehensive financial strategy is to take the advantage of internet finance to penetrate into NTNI business, realizing mutual promotion and transferring customers. "Transferring customers" means the transformation between traditional customer and non-traditional customers. In this way, Ping An expect to provide each customer with numerous services only through one account efficiently. Since the NTNI business is still in the early stage, the whole business is basically at loss. Data shows Zhongan Online, the associate, has a net profit of -25 million Yuan; Ping An Fu, the mobile payment systems, still has negative profits.

The Ping An NTNI business contains 5 parts - Lufax (Shanghai lujiazui international financial asset trading co. Ltd), Wanlitong integration system, Ping An Haoche online trade, mobile payment system and Mobile-social financial system.

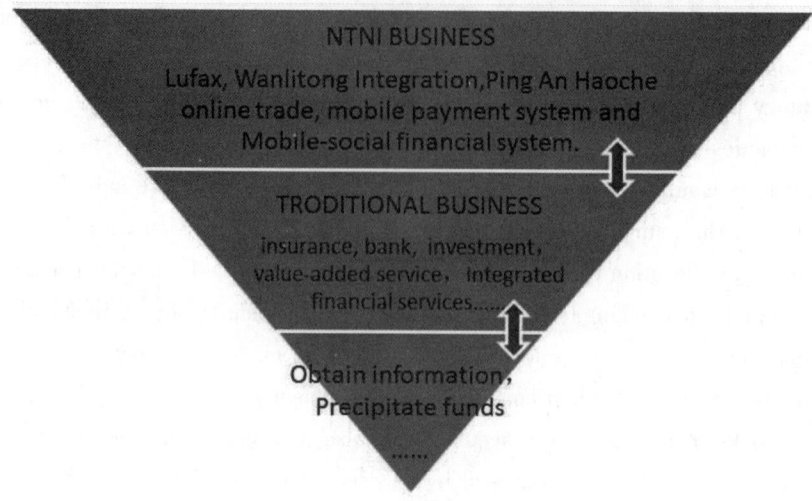

Figure 7 Ping An Integrated financial stratgy

a. Lufax starts from peer – to – peer lending platform, also target at non – traditional market such as B2B, B2C and F2F.

b. Wanlitong offers discounts and other value – added integration services to Ping An members, the integration can be used in online shopping webs and associates.

c. Ping An Haoche is an online used – car market, using O2O commerce model to trade vehicles. It has also built up 11 offline stores for car trading.

d. Mobile payment system is an essential adjunct to all consumptions.

e. Mobile – social financial system called "Tianxiatong" is advanced by Ping An Technology Co., mainly focusing on integrating the existing resources and enhancing connections between customers.

The 5 parts have close connection with customer's life. By promoting the 5 platforms, Ping An expects to attract more customers, to get more information and to build integral files so as to strengthen the customer loyalty. Furthermore, the NTNI business will interact with traditional parts. The whole business would form a funnel – shaped layout to accumulate capitals. In order to coordinate with the NTNI business, Ping An Bank set up Retail Business department of major clients to advance the customer transferring.

C. Major financial risk of Ping An business

1. Market Risk

(1) Interest rate. China had been in low interest rate for the past few decades, promoting the expanding of insurance industry by low cost. However, nowadays China is in a period of increased interest rate. The influences are mainly on liquidity of insurance business and solvency adequacy rate. For one thing, the needs for insurance products decrease when interest rate begins to rise, and surrender rates of traditional insurance policy also rise, causing liquidity pressures. On the other hand, the passive asset and liability management mode can bring an increasing cost of financing bur-

den, therefore affecting solvency.

(2) Exchange risk. With the opening up of Chinese economy, Ping An becomes more active and involved into the international financial markets. Ping An foreign asset concludes deposits, bonds, stocks and funds that are accounted in foreign currency. The debt also contains claim reserves for foreign business. The foreign insurance can be signed to pay insurance claims in the same foreign currency to avoid exchange risk. However, Ping An suffered some loss of the overseas portfolios due to RMB appreciation. One of the similar cases was that Japan Insurance industry has experienced great depression because of the rapid appreciation of the currency.

(3) Cyclical equity risk. The equities held by Ping An are faced with system risk, since Group held a great proportion of finance stock, which has same cyclical fluctuations. Although Ping An has estimated the risk by VaR, but it is hard to diversify system risk.

2. Credit Risk

(1) Credit risk related to insurance business. Ping An Group has a huge amount of receivable premium. It accounted for 8.99% of premium income by the end of 2013. The proportion is over 10% in Ping An Property insurance. The receivable premium mainly comes from credit insurance and liability insurance. In the Chinese market, insurance companies often agree insured to postpone paying the premium so as to get more project business. Once the project completed, receivable premiums are easily deteriorate to bad debt.

(2) Loan risk. Policy loans subject to credit risk. Furthermore, Ping An Bank dedicated to develop mini finance mode, those small and medium enterprises have higher possibility to cause performing loans.

(3) Risk related to investment. Ping An is cautious in investment and has a robust invest strategy. Group chooses counterparty and projects that have high credit rate, especially in real estate project. All maturity projects have realized expected returns. The property investment has cashed more than 20 billion Yuan.

(4) Cross credit risk within Group and subsidiaries. Within the group there are subsidiaries operating different business, as well as branches in different management levels. The cross – shareholdings between subsidiaries can transfer and magnify the credit risks. Ping An Group should set up firewalls among different business.

3. Operation Risk

It is the operation risk related to investment that Ping An Group should pay attention to. Operation risk can be magnified by Internet finance rapidly, as well as causing unexpected huge loss. Compared to the severity of operational risk, market risk and credit risk are too small to be mentioned. That's why ING Group and Germany's Allianz Group (ANZ) divide group management risk into two categories —— assets and liabilities risk management and operational risk management. Ping An has to be aware of the severity and establish mechanism to prevent operational risk.

4. Related Transactions Risks

As an integrate financial group, Ping An uses related transactions to bring efficiency and reduce transaction costs. As disclosed in annual report, the counter party of Ping An transactions is its subsidiaries and shareholders. Ping An injects capital to subsidiaries, gets dividends from insurance business, and purchases technology from associates. Under China separate supervision system, transactions parties shall comply with the contract principles and be supervised separately. Each subsidiary shall operate independently without being fully controlled by head office. The Group must set up risk management mechanism and disclose information correctly and timely.

5. Unknown Risk Brought By Internet Finance

Internet finance creates a new environment for financial innovation and capital allocation, but it also brings new, unknown risks. There are mutual promotion between financial disintermediation and product innovation, but regulatory also exists vacuum. Blind innovation may bring unpredictable liability such as long – tail risk. The effect can also be magnified by internet. Take Lufax as an example. Lufax is a not only a peer – to – peer financing platform, but also open to financial companies and enterprises. However, a well – organized internet financing platform needs credit system to support. China does not build up a Sound credit system at the present stage. So it is harder and risker to examine qualification. What's more, Lufax allows the original creditor to transfer debt on the secondary bond market when the creditor needs to obtain liquidity. This form of debt – based Secured lending relationship increases finances leverage. What's more, the debt relationship is inclined to form a chain. Once a party defaults, the whole system is likely to cause a chain reaction. Although Ping An Financing Guarantee Company is the guarantee for the loan of Lufax members, the default risk is still inside the Group.

Part V   MAIN CONCLUSIONS

A. The core business of Ping An is still the life insurance, for which the profitability is satisfactory while the solvency need to be monitored more closely.

1. The core business of Ping An is still the life insurance. In general, Ping An life insurance and Ping An property insurance keep a high ranking among the Chinese insurance companies, with its market increasing constantly. The life insurance is still the main business for Ping An, which plays an important role of balancing with the banking and investment sector in the group.

2. The profitability is satisfactory. Ping An made more investment in fix – income securities to stabilize the general returns when the capital markets went down, and put a stricter control on the cost to reduce the cost rate in order to triumph over other competitors. That's why Ping An still gained a satisfactory profitability even though both the premium growth rate and market share of life insurance went down.

3. The solvency needs to be monitored more closely. Although Ping An has experienced a hard time during the finance crisis as well as heavy loss on investing Fortis in the past five years , it still keeps to the solvency adequacy II standard. However, solvency condition was kept by passive capital injection. By adding registered capital and issuing Subordinated debt, Ping An successfully reduced accumulated leverage risk, also causing excessive volatility on solvency. The volatility will effect investor's stable expectation. What's more, According to solvency calculation rules, annual growth rate of a large insurance company can consume 10% to 15% solvency adequacy, the volatili-

ty of Ping An solvency has clearly exceed this range.

B. The insurance fund would put more weight on the equity investment, adjust the portfolio structure and increase the real estate investment to be more correlated to the financial market.

The China Insurance Regulatory Commission has loosened the regulation on the insurance fund utilization gradually these years. The China Insurance Regulatory Commission (CIRC) released 13 regulations on the insurance fund utilization in 2012, which broaden the investment area and proportion, including equity, real estate, financial derivatives, stock index future and overseas investments. It also lifted the upper limit of insurance investments. In general, the Chinese insurance fund investment has a feature of high stability but low efficiency. Given this, there would be 2 features of the investment trend for Ping An group.

1. Much potential for the equity investment to increase. The entire Chinese insurance industry, not only Ping An, has put more proportion of investment on fix – income securities, and the ease of regulation would definitely lead to a rise in equity investment. For example, the proportion of equity investment in all the investment of Ping An in 2013 is 9.8% by contrast to 30% as stipulated by the China Insurance Regulatory Commission, which shows a great potential. As to the portfolio structure of equity investment, Ping An would try to avoid concentrating on the financial industry stocks, especially the banking stocks.

2. Ping An is more active to the real estate investment, especially overseas investment. According to the analysis by Ping An Trust, real estate investment can meet the requirements of long – term stable income for insurance companies. According to No. 69 and No. 92 regulations, the real estate investment of Ping An has risen enormously, but it would take some time before we conclude that these investments would generate stable returns in the long run. Another thing is about Ping An purchasing Lloyd's building, which was not only based on the consideration of long – term investment return, but also symbolized the expectations from Chinese government under the China Going Out policy for all industries including insurance due to the unique position of this building in global insurance industry.

C. Ping An group is rated as an GSII mainly based on the Chinese emerging market, also due to the high correlation among each business sector within the group as well as the involvement of non – traditional non – insurance business.

1. Unique economic environment. China has been keeping a high economic growth rate since the opening and reforming policy started to be applied, generating a growing influence on the global economy. During this particular period of time, due to the limited openness and highly regulation of Chinese market resulting in less competition, Ping An, as one of the most important Chinese financial institutes, has gained a really advantageous position in the whole market.

2. Ping An group has a highly correlated business structure. Ping An group is one of the first few financial institutes which are authorized with all licenses and acting as the experimental samples for the integrated operation in the current background of separate operation. Banking and investment business expand quickly by the advantage of insurance business. Assets and liabilities in the finan-

cial system have increased, as well as financial derivative assets. The proportion of reinsurance stays steadily. There is also a sharp rise in third – level assets compared with that in 2012. Moreover, the proportion of equity investment is growing largely, mainly focusing on financial industrial stocks, like banking and securities. Meanwhile, the real estate investment is also increasing. Considering the more and more easing investment policy in China, the correlation with outer environment is predictably ascending in the future.

3. Ping An group has a deep engagement of non – traditional and non – insurance business. Liabilities for non – policyholders and revenue generated from other financial business have been growing. The private wealth management business of Ping An Trust also expanded. Ping An Security gains qualifications of OTC equity swaps, OTC options trading and stock collateral repo transactions at Shanghai and Shenzhen Stock Exchanges. Besides, Ping An Securities take financial guarantees for Lufax. And derivatives trading significantly are improved, so does short – term financing business.

Ping An will take the advantage of internet finance to promote comprehensive finance. By the 5 web platforms, Ping An can get more customers information and build integral files so as to interact with traditional parts.

D. The main aspect of risk for Ping An group related to the financial market is about its investment sector, however, the operation risk, related transactions risk and the unknown risk brought in by the internet finance ought to be at a higher exposure of attention.

1. The impact on Ping An group from the financial market is primarily about all kinds of risk associated with investment. The traditional risks such as market risk(interest rate, exchange rate, equities etc.) and credit risk(policy holder, reinsurance, loan borrower etc.) would be transferred to the financial market through insurance sector or investment sector of the group, which need to be under real time monitoring via asset debt management, pressure test, sensitivity test etc. In particular, the currency risk, which belongs to the market risk, should be paid long – term attention to. The receivable premium, if reaching a large amount, would also become a credit risk. The same attention should be paid to those mini – enterprises credit appraisal as well.

2. Compared with the traditional risks, the operation risk, the related transactions risk and the unknown risks brought in by the internet finance are more difficult to quantify and manage, which deserves more discreetness. To some extent, it is considered that the traditional risks would only be aroused by the financial market and exert an impact on the group operation in a one – way mode, however, contrastingly, the harm caused by the non – traditional risks would punch back to the financial market, leading to a more tremendous and more severe threat. For example, the Lufax, a non – traditional business, would possibly enlarge the operation risk via the internet finance, which needs to be treated discreetly.

E. Ping An has always been delicate to developing a comprehensive business mode and making a great progress in internet finance.

1. Comprehensive business mode. Ping An has developed a Big Data platform, which plays a vital role in insurance and banking service sales. The Personal Finance is focusing on improving the

clients' user experience while the Group Finance puts much effort on providing the enterprises client with an all – inclusive service package. Besides, Ping An also got a powerful technology team to back up, which created the mobile insurance Technology (MIT) to develop the business in a more low – carbon and more regulated way, and "YI pay" to support the self – claim process.

2. Internet finance and continued innovation. Ping An has developed the LUfax、Wanlitong、Ping An online car trading market、mobile payment system、mobile – social financial system and also set up an online insurance company Zhongan Online with Alibaba and Tencent. Ping An has always been making its best effort to be as innovative as possible. No matter to be the first company to bring in the life insurance agency system or to be the forerunner in the internet finance relay, Ping An has proved to its clients and to China that only innovation would be the constant engine power.

Reference

1. Renbao Chen, Kie Ann Wong, the determinants of financial heatlth of asian insurance companies, Journal of Risk and Insurance, Vol71, 469 – 499

2. VivianJeng, GeneC. Lai, MichaelJ. McNamara, "Efficiency and Demutualizaiton:Evidence from the U. S. Life Insurance Indystry in the 1980s and 1990s", the Journal of Risk and Insurance, Vol. 74, No. 3, 683 – 711, 2007

3. J. DavidCummins, Maria Rubio – Misas, " Deregulation, Consolidation, and Efficiency: Evidence from the Spanish Insurance Industry", Journal of Money, Credit, and Banking, Vol. 38, No. 2, 2006

4. William W. Cooper, Lawrence M. Seiford, Kaoru Tone Data envelopment analysis second edition, Springer Science + Business Media, LLC

5. International Association of Insurance Supervisors(IAIS), Global Systemically Important Insurers: Initial Assessment Methodology, 2013 – 6 – 18

6. International Association of Insurance Supervisors(IAIS), Global Insurance Market Report (GIMAR), 2012

7. Philip Hardwick, "Measuring Cost Inefficiency in the UK Life Insurance Industry", Applied Financial Economics, 7, 37 – 44, 1997

8. Wang Yi, Ping An profitability mode[J]. Journal of Jinan University(Social Science) No 4, 2008

9. Cao Minjie, LuoJianzhao & Zhang Baoshan, Comprehensive evaluation of Chinese insurance core competitiveness [J]. Journal of Xian Jiaotong Unniversity (social science), No. 5 2008

10. Ye Xin, Xue Weixian, the competitiveness ranking of insurance company in Shanghai [J], Commercial Research, No. 4 2007

11. Fullerton Insurance Research Center of California State University, Insurance companies in Asia Competitiveness Ranking in 2013, 21 Century Business Herald reported, No. 2, 2009

12. Li Sha, Wang Wei, Zhang Jiangang, Insurance company's capital structure analysis – take Ping An Insurance Group as an example [J], Insurance Research, No. 9 2009

13. China Insurance Yearbook Committee, China Insurance Yearbook [M], 2005 – 2013

Intuitive Chartist and Chart Intuition[①]

Yidian Liu　Shuainan Du[②]

Abstract: Price charts are pervasively used in today's security analysis. In this paper, we argue that where there is a chart, there is more or less an "intuitive chartist" – investor whose forecasts are partly based on his or her "chart intuition". Asking subjects to forecast simulated stock price series, we find some characteristics of their chart intuition: People normally extrapolate at the same direction to the latest price change, while in some special cases they do not simply extrapolate, but follow the general trend which is determined by their judgment of price series' peak and trough. Then we introduce information and find that people do largely rely on their chart intuition when forecast – even there is more reliable information. Furthermore, if all investors are intuitive chartists in some degree, efficient market hypothesis might be challenged behaviorally, since "all" market participants make "inefficient" decisions.

I. Introduction

Chartists, investors who believe 'the past behavior of a security's price is rich in information concerning its future behavior' and thus are trying to understand 'patterns' of price behavior and predict future prices 'through careful analysis of price charts' (Fama, 1965, p 34), have long been an important part of participants in security markets. There are various mature chartist theories, for example, the Dow Theory, and some of them are proved to be extremely useful at a certain period. Some immature theories also get a bunch of followers, especially theories developed by those so called 'folk masters' in Chinese stock market.[③]

As the underlying assumption of chartist theories stands in sharp contradiction to efficient market hypothesis, how many people today are still chartists? We deem that almost all investors are more or less intuitive chartists. The intuitive chartists here do not necessarily mean those 'professional' noise traders who try to find rules from past price patterns, but they refer to investors who are somehow affected by their chart intuition in different degrees. Chart intuition means investors'

[①] International Finance and Banking Society (IFABS) Conference, Lisbon, 2014.
[②] School of Insurance, Central University of Finance and Economics, Beijing, China.
Email: edan.yd.liu@gmail.com; sxdushuainan@gmail.com.
[③] It is very common to see online lessons, discussion groups, or advertisements teaching people how to read candlestick charts on Chinese websites.

expectations of future stock prices, but these expectations are only based on patterns of past price series. We can also say that the investor is extrapolating the price series, but our findings of extrapolation are slightly different from prior studies.

Our theory is: where there is a chart, there is more or less an intuitive chartist. Price charts are pervasively used in today's security analysis. Even a person does not mean to follow a chartist theory to read the chart, he still looks at the chart when he makes decisions. As long as he is looking at it, he is very likely to be affected by its price patterns. From a psychological perspective, image information like chart may have a framing effect on people and thus could distort their decisions. Tversky and Kahneman (1986) suggested that optical illusion could manipulate preferences to subject to contexts. For example, if an investor observes a stock's price goes up one day and goes down the next day, and for a long time it just goes up and down one day after another, he might think its price will keep this pattern in the future, at least in the very near future. In this case, he becomes an intuitive chartist. Real 'investors' do not even need a chart. They should only rely on fundamentals, since it is information that leads the price to where it should go. For example, it is said that Warren Buffett, the greatest investor today, never reads charts when he picks a stock. If an investor forms expectation in front of a chart, the chart may well have an impact on his judgment, and in this case the investor is (partly) performing extrapolation. We will empirically test this theory in Section 4.

An increasing amount of empirical and theoretical research in behavioral finance has turned to human expectations to account for several pervasive anomalies, such as excess volatility (LeRoy and Porter, 1981), equity premium puzzle (Mehra and Prescott, 1985), low correlation of stock returns and consumption growth (Hansen and Singleton, 1982), and predictability of stock returns (Campbell and Shiller, 1988). An important start point, also the base of these works, is the extrapolative expectations people hold (Case et al, 2012; Greenwood and Shleifer, 2013).

Extrapolation is also called positive feedback strategy (Cutler et al., 1991). Positive feedback traders buy stocks as prices rise while sell them when prices fall (DeLong et al., 1990). Lakonishok et al. (1994) used several measures of past growth (i.e., earnings, cash flow, sales, and stock return) to test extrapolation, and found that the actual future growth rate was largely consistent with the predictions of the extrapolation model. Based on some statistical and psychological evidence, Barberis, Shleifer, and Vishny (1998) presented a model in which investors underreacted and overreacted to news. When the investor observed a series of positive earnings surprises, he might expect a further increase, whereas when a negative surprise followed a positive one, the investor was more likely to believe the earnings were mean-reverting. Extrapolation bias suggested that people's expectations put too much weight on recent changes, which were naive intuitive expectations. A quasi-rational model, natural expectation, was proposed by Fuster et al. (2010). Their agents formed intuitions as if they were using a small number of lagged variables to estimate growth regressions. Recently, Barberis et al. (2013) proposed an X-CAPM model (Extrapolative Capital Asset Pricing Model), pointing out that "extrapolators'believe that the expected price change of the stock market is a weighted average of past price changes, where more recent price changes are weighted more heavily" (Barberis et al., 2013, p3).

In this paper, we experimentally test how individuals make one-step-ahead forecasts of price series, and report some new and more detailed findings of extrapolation and forecast. At the first phase, our experiment controlled the fundamental information variable and established a clean environment where only price patterns mattered. Every subject was asked to perform a forecast task of a simulated series of stock price which was generated by ARIMA model. About one-half of them faced a positive series, which contained 20 initial data and 130 separately predicted data generated by ARIMA, based on every twenty data prior to each period (from the 21th to the 150th), maximizing R square. Others did a negative series which was right the opposite of the positive series. By observing how subjects form expectations through reading chart, we could get some extrapolation characteristics of their chart intuition.

Then, at the second phase, we introduced information (earnings surprise) in our additional experiment to examine to what extent investors' forecasts are subject to past price patterns. In other words, this is to test whether chart intuition matters in real decision making. We found that, at least for some not-so-striking information and for Chinese investors[①], people do still largely rely on their chart intuition even they have more reliable fundamental information. Hence our findings of extrapolation behavior reveal some significant characteristics of how people form expectations in real security market.

Several prior experiments have also looked into people's expectations of financial time series. Some used a random walk or stylized patterns as the basic data to be forecast, and specially informed subjects about its unpredictable nature (Eggleton, 1982; Dwyer et al., 1993; Bloomfield and Hales, 2002; Rötheli, 2011). Others gave subjects real data or simulated a real market (e.g., Schmalensee, 1976; DeBondt, 1993; Maines and Hand, 1996; Hommes, 2011). However, both types of the basic data in the experiment have some problems. First, asking subjects to forecast a random walk, or an unpredictable series, may be confusing. Even if classic theories suggest that financial series in reality are random walks, noise traders often believe there is a rule and assume themselves have got it, and they expect to make money by following the rule. If subjects are clearly informed about the unpredictability of the series in an experiment, however, they will have much weaker tendency to assume a predictable rule exists here. People could suspect classic theories, but they are less likely to doubt the experimenter. Hence the task to forecast an unpredictable series seems confusing to subjects, and it is not like what real noise traders do. Besides, some experimental random walks only change one unit every time, thus we cannot see how much people extrapolate from different magnitudes of changes. Second, we argue that it is not the best idea to use real historical data to study forecast behavior in our experiment. As we mentioned in footnote 2, real stock price may be shocked by some seemingly unrelated information, and these shocks are noises in a

---

① Chinese stock market is irrationally sensitive to some news which is supposed to be essentially unrelated to stock price. Some important "information" has striking impact on stock prices. For example, in March 2013, after media covered that China's first lady, Peng Liyuan, wore clothes from domestic brands, prices of almost all apparel firms' stocks in mainland China's stock market dramatically surged in the following days (South China Morning Post, March 26, 2013). Here we do not test this kind of information, but those concerning stock's intrinsic value.

clean chart. We are not trying to say that investors are totally ignoring all information, but they do partly rely on chart intuition. To some degree, extrapolation may play a more important role in forming expectations than some fundamental information such as earnings surprises. Hence at the first phase, we use ARIMA model to simulate a price series and ask subjects to find its rule. This is a clean environment without any fundamental information for subjects to intuitively read a chart. As nobody knows the exact rule of real stock prices, if it has any, it is appropriate to use ARIMA to simulate the series. However, this is based on the assumption that chart intuition does matters, and we will then test this hypothesis at the second phase.

In a more recent study, Beshears et al. (2013) also used ARIMA process to set basic data. They used two fixed models to generate time series which were regarded as standards to judge forecasts. Our models are not fixed, but they are selected by a constant rule. And we do not use the basic data as criteria to see how well subjects perform forecasts[1], but only a foundation for subjects to form expectations and thus elicits their extrapolation characteristics. We also test the assumption of intuitive chartist which lies under many similar experimental studies. Only when investors are indeed affected by their chart intuition will findings in these experiments have practical significance.

We find that when people extrapolate, they almost entirely rely on the latest one period of change. Subjects' forecasts are mostly in the same direction to the latest change. The magnitude of extrapolation in this case is often around 45 (or 50) percent of last change.[2] We specially stress the impact of change of the latest period rather than 'recent periods' as most extrapolation studies suggested.

However, subjects do not always simply extrapolate. They try to recognize the general trend and then follow it to adjust their extrapolation. We mainly find two cases where subjects do not simply extrapolate as we suggest above. First, when the latest period's price[3] has already broken the reference point (i.e., exceeding last peak or below last trough. We will elaborate this term in Section 3.), subjects largely lower the magnitude they extrapolate or expect a reversal. If the latest data has not broken the reference point but has a tendency to do by simply extrapolating[4], people also adjust their normal extrapolative method in order to prevent the break, so the magnitude of extrapolation usually would also be lower. Second, when more than one reversal occur sequentially, like an 'up, down, up' pattern, and if the latest change is at the opposite direction to the general trend subjects judge, they usually follow the general trend to forecast rather than extrapolating by last change. We will elaborate our hypothesis of how intuitive chartists judge the peak and trough of price series and

---

[1] In fact, these data cannot serve as a standard to judge subjects'forecasts, because the optimal point forecast depends on the loss function of individuals. We thank this advice from Bruce Hansen.

[2] "Last change" is "the latest change". We use them alternatively in this paper. 45 percent is for the mean of all subjects' forecasts, indicated by the slope of linear regression. 50 percent is the median. We analyze both mean and median, and the median is shown in the bracket in the following parts.

[3] In our experiment, subjects observe data from period n − 20 to period n − 1, to forecast data in period n, where n ranges from 21 to 150. "The latest period" means period n − 1.

[4] We define "has a tendency to break the reference by simply extrapolating" as the forecasted price will break the reference if the subject extrapolates 100 percent of last change.

realize its general trend in Section 3. These characteristics may have an important impact on investors' judgments of future stock price in real financial markets.

Besides, our additional experiment introduces fundamental information and proves that investors are at least partly subject to their chart intuition when forming expectations – even there is more reliable information. If forecasts are 'efficient', whether there is chart or not should not induce different expectations for future stock prices, since the future is determined by fundamental information when the market is efficient. We find that people do hold different expectations with and without a chart.

Investors are partly affected by their chart intuition is the underlying assumption of this study (and also many other extrapolation studies), or revealing how people read charts will have much less practical significance. Moreover, if all investors are intuitive chartists in some degree, efficient market hypothesis might be challenged behaviorally, since 'all' market participants make 'inefficient' decisions. However, this conclusion is only based on the assumption that "all" investors are intuitive chartists. Yet we suppose it may well hold, because the chart intuition is a kind of subconscious which is hard to overcome by rationality.

The remainder of the paper is organized as follows. Section 2 presents the experiment, including the data generating process and the practice. Section 3 analyzes the data of subjects' forecasts and summarizes their extrapolation characteristics. Section 4 uses an additional experiment to prove our underlying assumption of intuitive chartist, and discusses about efficient market hypothesis from a behavioral perspective. Section 5 concludes.

2. Experimental design

2.1 Data generation

Twenty sequent closing prices of Mengniu Dairy (from April 4th, 2013 to May 3rd, 2013), a Hong Kong stock, were selected as the initial historical data. Because our subjects all came from mainland China and were not familiar with Hong Kong stocks, using data of this stock was less likely to interfere with people's forecasts. From the twenty-first period, every data was generated by ARIMA(p,d,q): using prior twenty data, we select appropriate values for p, d, q to maximize R square of the model. Once the data was generated, it was regarded as a historical data (basic data) and was then used to generate the next one. For instance, based on data from the 40th to the 59th period, we selected ARIMA(8,0,0) (adjusted R^2 = 0.827, BIC = -1.841) which had the biggest R square among all alternatives to generate the 60th basic data. Then ARIMA(10,0,0) (adjusted R^2 = 0.851, BIC = -1.631) was chosen to generate the 61th basic data based on the 51th to the 60th. Every data had two decimal places. Finally we got 150 periods of basic data in total.

The minimum of the 150-period price series was 21.45 Yuan at period 2. Maximum was 22.95 Yuan at period 7. Average change between every two periods was 0.12 Yuan (max was 0.5 Yuan, min was 0 Yuan). The average adjusted R square of the whole data procedure was 0.86825 ±0.05133.

We also created a negative series where every data was the opposite number of those in the positive series, just in order to give us richer data patterns. It might be a little confusing to say the negative series was a simulation of stock prices. However, we told subjects that the series was right opposite to a positive series which did follow a certain rule simulating stock prices, although they were negative numbers.

2.2 Practice

96 undergraduate students in Central University of Finance and Economics (CUFE) were recruited to make one – step – ahead forecasts of the price series described above, from the 21st period to the 150th. 50 of them were given the positive series, and 46 did the negative series. They were informed that the series were simulations of real stock prices, and all data, except the initial twenty data, followed a certain rule, but they did not know which rule it was. They were also not allowed to use pen or calculator to predict. For the initial twenty data, we told subjects that they were sequent twenty periods taken from of a real stock.

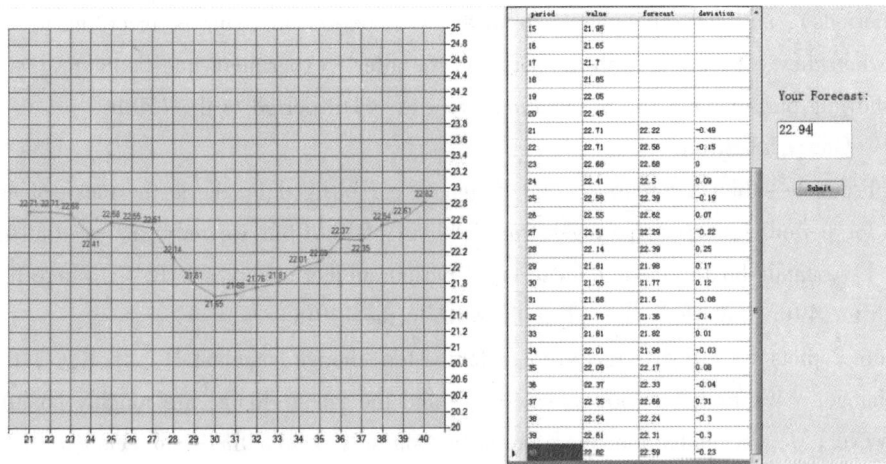

Figure1 Experimental Screen

The actual basic data was revealed after every forecast was made. As basic data was generated by ARIMA from prior twenty numbers, subjects were also asked to form expectations only based on the latest twenty periods. This was to ensure that the difficulty of the task did not change over time. All forecasts were required to keep two decimal places, since all basic data have.

Both graph and numbers were shown in a screen, as well as period, prediction, and the forecast error (forecast minus basic data). The graph only presented last twenty data in every period. Figure 1 is an example of the screen used in experiment.

The experiment is similar to the case where chartists are in. Noise traders always believe they could find out the rule of financial time series which are regarded as random walks by classic theories. In the experiment, the rule does exist, and subjects are encouraged to figure it out through studying price patterns. This design eliminates the interference of information and focuses on people's chart reading intuition. Extrapolation characteristics presenting in this clean experiment may well show in real investors' expectations in some degree. Students in CUFE are also quite similar to real traders in stock market. They have taken several investment classes, so we suppose they are potential stock traders.

If a forecast error did not exceed 0.01 (i.e., 0.01, 0, or −0.01), the subject would get 2 Yuan reward for that period. Experiment lasted an hour. The average absolute forecast error of all forecasts was 0.1156 Yuan (0.1137 Yuan for positive and 0.1176 Yuan for negative). Subjects earned 15.08 Yuan on average (positive subjects earned 15.28 Yuan and negative earned 14.87 Yuan).

3. Result

This part analyzes and summarizes subjects' extrapolation characteristics: facing a price chart, where does the investor expect the series to go next? Allowing for the process subjects need to get familiar with the price series and experiment, we cut down the initial twenty forecasts (from the 21th to 40th periods), and start our analysis from the 41th period on. This is according to subjects' reports of when they get familiar with the series in the after-experiment questionnaire. Data analyses in the following parts mainly use observations from the 41th period to the 150th.

3.1 Chart intuition

Let F denote subjects' forecasts, and R denote our basic data. $\overline{F_n}$ is the mean of all subjects' forecasts for period n, where n ranges from 21th to 150th (but we only analyze the 41th to the 150th). $F_{n,M}$ stands for the median. The latest period subject observes is R_{n-1}, where n−1 ranges from 20th to 149th (but we only analyze the 40th to the 149th).

Figure 2 plots $\overline{F_n} - R_{n-1}$, the average forecasted change, against $R_{n-1} - R_{n-2}$, the last observed change.① We find that forecasted change and the latest change are roughly positive correlated. However, we also notice that there are some "outliers": sometimes subjects expect an opposite direction of change to the last change. Besides, some spots are quite scattered. Therefore we analyze outliers separately, make some hypotheses of diverse cases where people follow different rules to form expectations, and present a parsimonious model of how people extrapolate and forecast.

Figure 2 classifies spots into five categories based on different cases they are in, which will be discussed in usual case, unusual case (containing two cases), and exceptions (containing two cases), respectively. Note that these spots are subjects' forecasts for period n, where n ranges from 41th to 150th. The cases, however, are classified only by periods before n, because data in period n has not been revealed when we judge what the case is.

However, how people recognize various cases and apply different forecasting strategies is quite a nuanced conclusion. It is actually only a conjecture but gets some experimental supports. Nevertheless, classifying spots in this pattern does explain many outliers and give us a more accurate model to predict people's forecasts.

---

① Plotting $F_{n,M} - R_{n-1}$ against $R_{n-1} - R_{n-2}$ is almost the same pattern. Here we only show the result of mean. Result of median is presented in Appendix Figure E6.

Our basic models are

$$\overline{F_n} - R_{n-1} = \beta_0 + \beta_1(R_{n-1} - R_{n-2}) + \varepsilon_n \qquad (1)$$

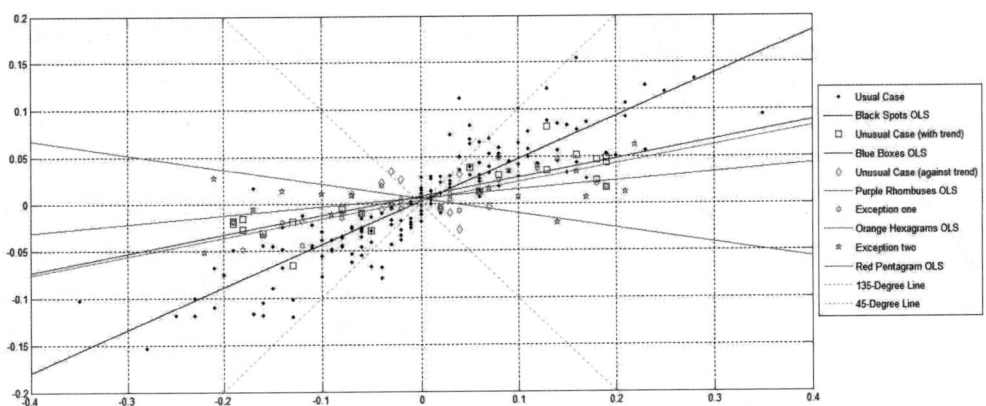

Figure 2 Mean Forecasted Change against Last Observed Change

Note: The slope of usual case (black spots) is 0.4542, with-trend unusual case (blue boxes) is 0.2014, against-trend unusual case (purple rhombuses) is -0.1556, exception one (orange hexagrams) is 0.1969, and exception two (red pentagram) is 0.09193.

Table 1   **Determinants of Forecasted Change**

$F_n - R_{n-1}$ Category	Mean (All Periods)	Median (All Periods)	Mean (Black Spots)	Median (Black Spots)	Mean (Blue Boxes)	Median (Blue Boxes)	Mean (Purple)	Median (Purple)
$F_{n-1} - R_{n-2}$	0.259574***	0.340394***	0.387654***	0.464769***	0.201354***	0.262143***	-0.155599	-0.217290*
	(16.22493)	(17.93752)	(18.73927)	(23.26716)	(7.218460)	(7.277607)	(-1.318899)	(-1.882895)
AR(1)	0.579572***	0.317980***	0.510275	0.369849***				
	(9.823661)	(4.472309)	(6.968056)	(4.754261)				
AR(2)		0.169742***						
		(2.527945)						
Constant	0.003871	0.003577	0.003052	0.001663	0.007644	0.007500	0.005344	0.006786
	(0.912410)	(0.982722)	(0.756391)	(0.527379)	(1.836162)	(1.395164)	(1.158605)	(1.503972)
$[p-val, \beta_1]$	0.0000	0.0000	0.0000	0.0000	0.0000	0.0000	0.2118	0.0842
N	220	220	150	150	22	22	14	14
R^2	0.744779	0.759524	0.835836	0.854696	0.722631	0.725891	0.126605	0.228062
F-statistic	315.1624	225.3007	371.6765	429.3934	52.10617	52.96357	1.739495	3.545295
MAE	0.023914	0.022963	0.021216	0.019054	0.013052	0.018685	0.013453	0.011258
DW	2.094094	1.982268	1.936301	1.979271	2.096779	1.501140	1.057320	2.306165

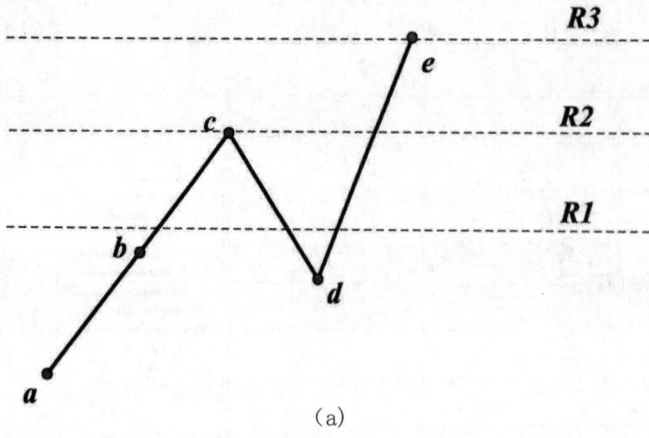

(a)

Notes: Suppose when he only observes point a and b, the upper reference is R1. Then when point c is revealed, it breaks R1 and creates a new reference R2. Likewise, point e breaks R2 and renews the reference to R3. Point d cannot break the upper reference R2. Even it is lower than R1, but R1 is not the latest reference and has been replaced by R2.

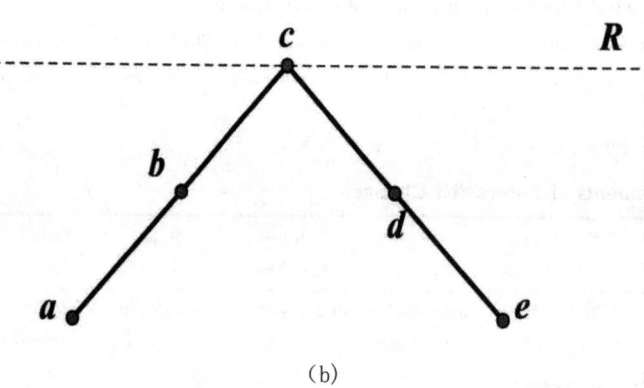

(b)

Notes: Point c is the peak, upper reference, he judges. Before point e is revealed, point c has already been judged to be the upper reference, but where point e goes might question prior judgement. This is discussed in (c).

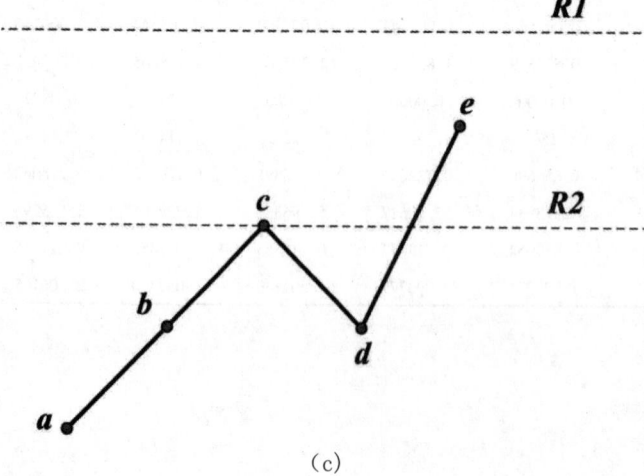

(c)

Notes: Before point e is revealed, point c is judged to be the upper reference. If point e breaks R2, it is similar to (a), but it might not break R1 which is the upper reference before he judges R2. In this case, point c is no longer the peak, but point e is also not the new reference, unless it breaks R1. In this figure the reference goes back to R1 after point e breaking R2. If point e does not break R2, it is point e at (e).

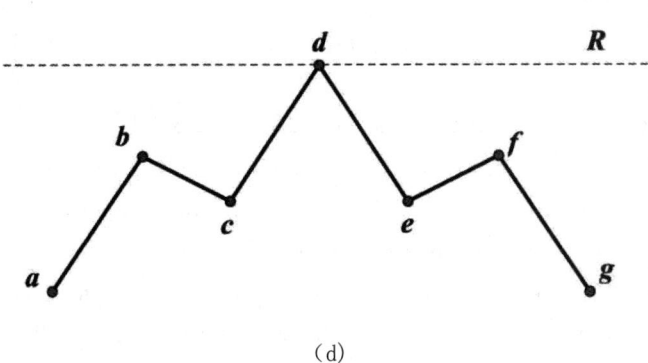

Notes: Point d is a plausible upper reference intuitively, because it is higher than nearby periods. Yet we do not have enough this kind of data patterns to draw a more general conclusion.

(d)

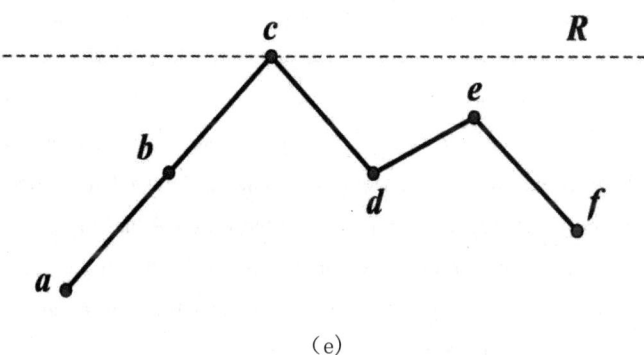

Notes: Before point e and f are revealed, point c is judged to be upper reference. The reversal of point e questions this judgement. Yet we do not know whether he thinks the series will go up or down at point e with our limited data patterns. As point f goes down, point c is further confirmed to be the upper reference.

(e)

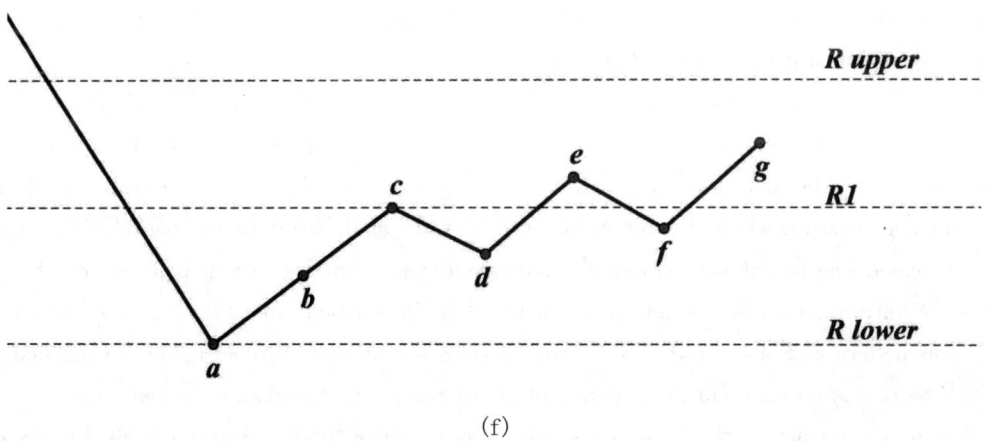

(f)

Notes: If he only observes point a, b, and c, suppose the references at this time are R upper and R lower respectively. When point d is revealed, R1 replaces R upper. If point e follows to break R1, the reference goes back to R upper. R upper also servers as the upper reference when point e, f, and g occurs, because there is no other upper references could be recognized in these unusual cases.

Figure 3　Some Examples

for mean forecast, and

$$F_{n,M} - R_{n-1} = \beta_0 + \beta_1(R_{n-1} - R_{n-2})\varepsilon_n \tag{2}$$

for median forecast.

Table 1 presents the regression results. We also regress the forecasted change, $F - R_{n-1}$, against other variables, including $R_{n-1}, R_{n-2}, \cdots, R_{n-19}, R_{n-20}, R_{n-2} - R_{n-3}, R_{n-3} - R_{n-4}, \cdots, R_{n-18} - R_{n-19}, R_{n-19} - R_{n-20}$, and some of them combined together. Those factors, however, do not explain subjects' forecasts as well as last change. Some do play a slightly better role in an unusual case which only contains a few spots, but last change could explain expectations in all cases almost perfectly. Hence we will only show our models by using $R_{n-1} - R_{n-2}$ as independent variable in following parts. Appendix Table E3 and Appendix Table E4 provide other regressions with other variables.

3.1.1 Peak, trough, and general trend

We should first define the term reference. Observing a series of historical data, a subject (suppose it is a "he" hereafter) has already formed expectations about where the next peak and trough should probably be. They are supposed to be around the reference: the level of last one. Last peak is the upper reference, and last trough is lower reference.

If a data rises to a level higher than last peak, it has broken the upper reference, and it also creates a new one at the same time. This is identical for the declining data and lower reference. Note that a declining data cannot be higher than last upper reference. If it were above last upper reference, as there must be previous data below the upper reference (or it will not be an upper reference) and the series is continuous, there would be a period has already broken the reference and creates a higher new one. Figure 3(a) helps to explain breaking the reference.

The primary thing for him to form expectations is to recognize the general trend to decide to guess up or down. When he has recognized the latest reference to be a peak or trough, the trend is thought to go against it to another reference.①

The core question is, how can he judge the peak and trough? Our hypothesis is that in four sequent periods, if only the penultimate period reverses (i.e., "up, up, down, down" or "down, down, up, up"), he then thinks the period before the reversal, the antepenultimate period, is the new reference. See Figures 3(b) for instance.② In fact, at the penultimate period before the last period revealed, he has already judged the antepenultimate period as a new peak or trough. Yet if the last period reverses again, prior judgment might be questioned. See Figure 3(c) and Figure 3(e). This pattern and other cases where more periods sequentially reverse belong to unusual cases that will be discussed later. In the experiment, most peaks and troughs are in usual cases.

Two things are noteworthy here. First, establishing a new reference does not need to break the old one (last reference), although breaking last reference also leads to setting a new one (e.g., R2

---

① First, the latest reference does not necessarily be the latest period. It is the closet reference to that period. It could either be an upper reference or an under one. Second, he can also judge the trend without realizing the reference in usual case which will be discussed later. However, the two methods are identical in essence except for different descriptions.

② There are actually five periods in Figure 3(b). Point a only serves as a foundation. We are concerning about whether point b, c, d, or e reverses.

in Figure 3(c), R1 in Figure 3(f)). Even he refers to references, once a new peak or trough has been determined, he has a new reference and the old one is replaced. No matter what the data before the reversal occurs is, either it is far from the reference or has already broken it, it is thought to be a new reference, and the reversal following it determines a new trend. Second, there are always two, and only two, references, upper and under. Once a new reference is recognized, the old one will be replaced.

Normally, our data (and so are most data in reality) are not around the reference level. If the data has broken the reference or has a tendency to break it by simply extrapolating at the magnitude of 100 percent of last change, they are referred to as two expectations. First, we discuss normal cases (i. e., cases that are not exceptions), including usual cases and unusual cases, and then we come to the two exceptions.

3.1.2 Usual case

When at most one reversal occurs in the recent three periods (i. e., 'up, down, down', 'up, up, down', 'up, up, up', 'down, up, up', 'down, down, up', or 'down, down, down') and no matter what other periods like, we refer it to the usual case. In this situation, he thinks the trend is identical to the latest period. He does NOT need to recognize the peak and trough now, so we only need recent three periods to judge the case. Most cases in experiment, and maybe also in real world, are usual. Forecasted changes in these periods are black spots in Figure 2. [1]

In usual cases, he linearly extrapolates. According to the slope of linear regression, the magnitude of extrapolation is around 45 (or 50) percent of last change. When last change is 0.1 Yuan, the predicted change may be about 0.045 Yuan (or 0.05 Yuan). If it falls by 0.2 Yuan, the forecast could go 0.09 Yuan (or 0.1 Yuan) down further.

The mean absolute error (MAE) of predictions given by our models is about 0.021 Yuan (or 0.019 Yuan), which is quite slight compared to MAE of subjects' forecasts (see Table 3) or the average change of the series (0.12 Yuan). R square of our model is 0.84 (or 0.85), indicating a good regression.

3.1.3 Unusual case

Now we turn to the unusual case. It refers to the situation when two reversals occur in the latest three periods (i. e., 'up, down, up' or 'down, up, down'). After the first reversal, he could believe the trend reverses (if it is in usual case). When another reversal comes straight after the first one, however, he revises his judgment of the trend and stops simply extrapolating.

Unfortunately we do not have enough this sort of basic data patterns to draw a more convincing conclusion of the way he judges the reference in this case. However, the rule of thumb is: when he observes a period is higher or lower than nearby periods (usually two periods on both sides), that period is the new reference. If there is no this kind of pattern recently, he will just follow the trend before the unusual pattern occurs. In other words, the trend is supposed to be that before any rever-

---

[1] Forecasts "in" period $n-1$ are "for" period n. The latest period the subject sees is period $n-1$, and he should forecast the data for period n.

sal occurs, unless a plausible peak or trough has been built during the sequent reversing process. Refer to (d), (e), (f) in Figure 3 for instances. Note that unlike usual case, he has to judge the reference in unusual case.

In unusual case, he normally extrapolates about 20 (or 26) percent of last change. This conclusion indicates that the latest change is at the same direction as the general trend, since he often follows the general trend to form expectations. Blue boxes in Figure 2 represent forecasts in these with - trend periods.

However, there do have some changes that are opposite to the trend. Forecasts in these periods are purple rhombuses in Figure 2. Among them, in 10 out of 14 (or 7 out of 14)[①] times he forecasts an opposite direction to last change in order to follow the general trend.

We also regress the with - trend spots and against - trend spots respectively. The difference between them is obvious. It is hard to draw a more general conclusion of how he forecasts when the change is against the trend with the limited data, but we assume he mostly follows the trend rather than last change. Still, we can see his hesitation to extrapolate in unusual case from the low magnitude of extrapolation. He might also try to weigh the latest change against prior general trend when conflict arises.

3.1.4 Exceptions

When the extrapolating strategies mentioned above result in a forecast might break the reference (the reference will be broken if he extrapolates at the magnitude of 100 percent), it is the first exception. Orange hexagrams in Figure 2 are these periods. Now, he will decrease the magnitude of extrapolation, in order to keep his forecast be around the reference. The magnitude is often lower than 25 percent of last change.

The second exception is that the data has already broken last reference[②], shown by red pentagrams in Figure 2. These periods are all new references. The magnitude of extrapolation is lower than other cases, around 16 percent of last change.

When the series has already reached the peak, where does he expect it to go next, going further or back? Forecasts in 13 out of 18 (or 12 out of 18) times are positive extrapolations. However, there are still 5 (or 2) times in exception two he expects the series to return. Even in the first exception which the latest data is close to the reference, we observe forecasts in three periods are opposite to last change. These results suggest he sometimes judge a new reference without a reversal. Yet we do not have enough basic data in these patterns to find out when he judge reference in this way.

We also do not have another special data pattern: data continuously break references. That is, for example, data in one period rises above the upper reference and creates a new one, but the next data keeps rising and creates another new reference. Our hypothesis is that the reference will go back to the most recently higher old reference in this case. Figure 3(c) and 3(f) provides two examples. The hypothesis is not examined. In fact this kind of price pattern is quite common in real-

---

① For median forecasts, in 4 out of 14 times he forecasts no change.
② If the data is identical to last reference, we count it in exception one.

ity, like stock prices which keep creating new peaks or new troughs. It deserves further studies.

These findings are rather nuanced. It might still be hard to draw a more general conclusion even given more sufficient data patterns. Nevertheless, at least we know that the two exceptions are different from normal cases based on our limited data.

3.2 Forecasts and ARIMA

Do people correctly perceive the series generated by ARIMA model? It is not our main objective to study this, actually. ARIMA is neither the optimal model to make forecasts nor pervasively used by normal investors in reality. It only serves a series of basic data which has a certain mathematic rule. The rule simulates the illusion that noise traders in reality hold: they have learned or have a possibility to learn a rule to predict the financial market which could lead them to win extra profit. How people behave when they are trying to follow the rule is of our major concern, not how well they perform in experiment.

However, there are still some merits to look at the forecasting accuracy. First, it could help us understand how human expectations deviate from the statistic model. It is actually another method to examine how people forecast, by comparing their expectations with statistic models which are already known to us and summarizing what the deviations like. Second, as subjects are trying to follow the rule in experiment, it is worth to test the accuracy of the result, since it could be compared to the real situation if some indexes do follow a certain rule in reality. If subjects cannot behave well under the simple experimental environment, it explains why so many people lose money in real stock market which is much more complex (even if it really has some rules and is predictable).

Table 2 **Real Change and Forecast Error**

Real change	Forecast error	Positive		Negative		All
	>0	760	28.68%	552	28.68%	24.89%
>0	0	100	3.77%	75	3.77%	3.32%
	<0	1790	67.55%	1995	67.55%	71.79%
	>0	2203	77.30%	1719	77.30%	74.17%
<0	0	95	3.33%	96	3.33%	3.61%
	<0	552	19.37%	623	19.37%	22.22%

Note: Real change is $R_n - R_{n-1}$. Forecast error is $F_n - R_n$. If real change is 0, which is not a common case, we count last change.

Table 2 analyzes individual data ($N = 10560 = 96 \times 110$)[①], and shows that subjects often underestimate a positive real change whilst overestimate a negative one. This finding may explain why so many speculators cannot succeed in reality: they do not expect the price to go up enough in bull markets, and are not pessimistic enough to recognize the decline in bear markets.

Table 3   **Mean Absolute Error of Forecast in Every Stage**

Stage (periods)	Mean (all)	Median (all)	Mean (positive)	Median (positive)	Mean (negative)	Median (negative)
1 (21–30)	0.20	0.17	0.20	0.17	0.20	0.17
2 (31–40)	0.16	0.13	0.15	0.13	0.16	0.13
3 (41–50)	0.14	0.13	0.15	0.14	0.13	0.12
4 (51–60)	0.11	0.10	0.11	0.10	0.12	0.11
5 (61–70)	0.11	0.10	0.11	0.09	0.11	0.10
6 (71–80)	0.10	0.09	0.10	0.09	0.11	0.09
7 (81–90)	0.10	0.09	0.10	0.09	0.11	0.10
8 (91–100)	0.09	0.09	0.09	0.08	0.10	0.09
9 (101–110)	0.10	0.09	0.10	0.09	0.10	0.09
10 (111–120)	0.10	0.09	0.09	0.08	0.10	0.09
11 (121–130)	0.10	0.10	0.10	0.09	0.11	0.10
12 (131–140)	0.10	0.10	0.10	0.09	0.10	0.10
13 (141–150)	0.09	0.08	0.09	0.08	0.09	0.08

Note: Every ten periods are regarded as a stage to calculate the MAE of means and medians forecast in these periods, so there are thirteen stages in total.

Table 3 shows that subjects' absolute forecast error is significantly declining during the first five stages, especially the initial four. From the sixth stage on, MAE is very stable, being around (often smaller than) 0.1 Yuan. Subjects' forecasting accuracy is improving at first. Then it stays relatively stable. Intuitive learning has some effect in short term, but it cannot keep helping subjects see the rule more clearly. It has a limit. Yet we do not know whether the accuracy could be further improved if they got more periods to forecast. Studies do point out that learning process could help investors become more rational (e.g., Gervais and Odean, 2001; List, 2003; Feng and Seasholes, 2005; Peng and Xiong, 2006). We argue that market experience may not help real traders form more accurate expectations in a long term, but it still could lead them to behave more rationally than

---

[①] We have also tried to study individuals' data in previous parts instead of mean and median. However, our findings do not apply very well to all individuals. We cannot even figure out a general rule individuals follow to forecast. Even for one subject, he might expect two totally opposite results at two different times when he observes roughly identical data patterns. A possible explanation is that subjects sometimes are trying to test some new strategies, so they do not always follow the behavior pattern we find in mean and median forecasts. Yet if we look at them as a whole, this kind of disturbance could be largely eliminated, and it reflects what a person normally will expect.

freshmen.

4. Underlying Assumption and Efficient Market Hypothesis

Our findings about extrapolation characteristics are based on an underlying assumption: almost all investors are more or less affected by their chart intuition and do extrapolation in some degree, even there is reliable fundamental information. If this assumption does not hold, these findings will be much less meaningful. If it does holds, we have revealed some important characteristics of pervasively existing intuitive chartists, and efficient market hypothesis might be partly challenged.

In this part, we empirically test this hypothesis. For a rational investor to make "efficient" decisions, his forecasts should not be different in spite of the fact that whether there is a chart or not, since classic theories claims that it should be the fundamental information that determines future stock prices rather than past price patterns. Therefore we plan to see if forecasts with and without a chart are different.

4.1 Experimental design

To prove our hypothesis, we conducted an additional experiment. Fundamental information was introduced in experiment this time, in order to see how subjects weighted information against chart intuition. It contained two treatments: chart – information treatment and information treatment. These results were compared with results we got in prior forecast experiment which was referred to as chart treatment.

We cut off four pieces of data from the positive basic data we used in prior experiment. Each piece contained twenty sequent periods, and subjects were required to forecast the next data (the 21th period's) in each piece. We also informed subjects that the series were simulated stock prices. Hence they were just doing part of prior subjects' forecast task (4 out of 130 periods). The four pieces were all cut from usual case, for we have got sufficient data and more stable result in this case. We did not reveal the 21th period's basic data right after subjects reported their forecasts, but revealed them after subjects finished all four forecasts in this experiment.

Subjects in chart – information treatment were presented with information besides the chart and twenty listed numbers. The information was revealed at the last period in the piece and before the 21th period, so it should have an impact on the period to be forecasted. We offered both "enhanced information" and "weaken information". Enhanced information means forecast based on the information should be at the same direction to forecast based on chart intuition, and weaken information might lead to opposite forecast to chart intuition. For example, if the subject was predicted to forecast a rise according to our findings of extrapolation, we gave him a bad news as weaken information and good news as enhanced information; if our findings suggested it would be a decline, then the bad news was enhanced information and good news was weaken information. Thus we could see whether the subject followed his chart intuition or information.

For the information treatment, we did not show the chart of past twenty periods to subjects, but only gave them information and those twenty numbers. They were also forbidden to draw a chart by themselves. The same price pieces and information as that in chart – information treatment were given to them. This group of subjects was not supposed to be affected by chart intuition, since they did not look at a chart when forecast. Results in the four pieces in chart treatment were also used to compare with results in these two treatments.

The information we offered was earnings surprise. The good news said that prior expected earnings per share of the stock was 1 Yuan, but now (after the 20th data was revealed but before the 21th was revealed) the company announced that the actual earnings per share was 1.2 Yuan. The earnings surprise was 20%, which was good news. In bad news, the actual earnings per share was 0.8 Yuan which meant a −20% earnings surprise.

133 subjects in this experiment were also undergraduate students in CUFE. They have taken many finance classes, so we suppose they were quite familiar with the information we provided. After the experiment, subjects received rewards according to the same rule in chart treatment.

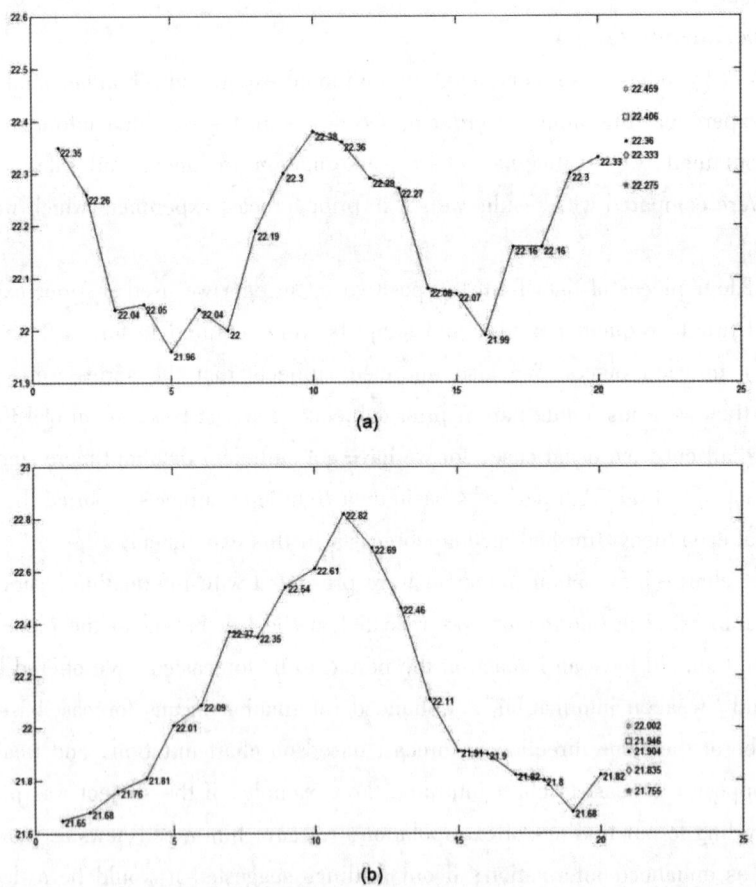

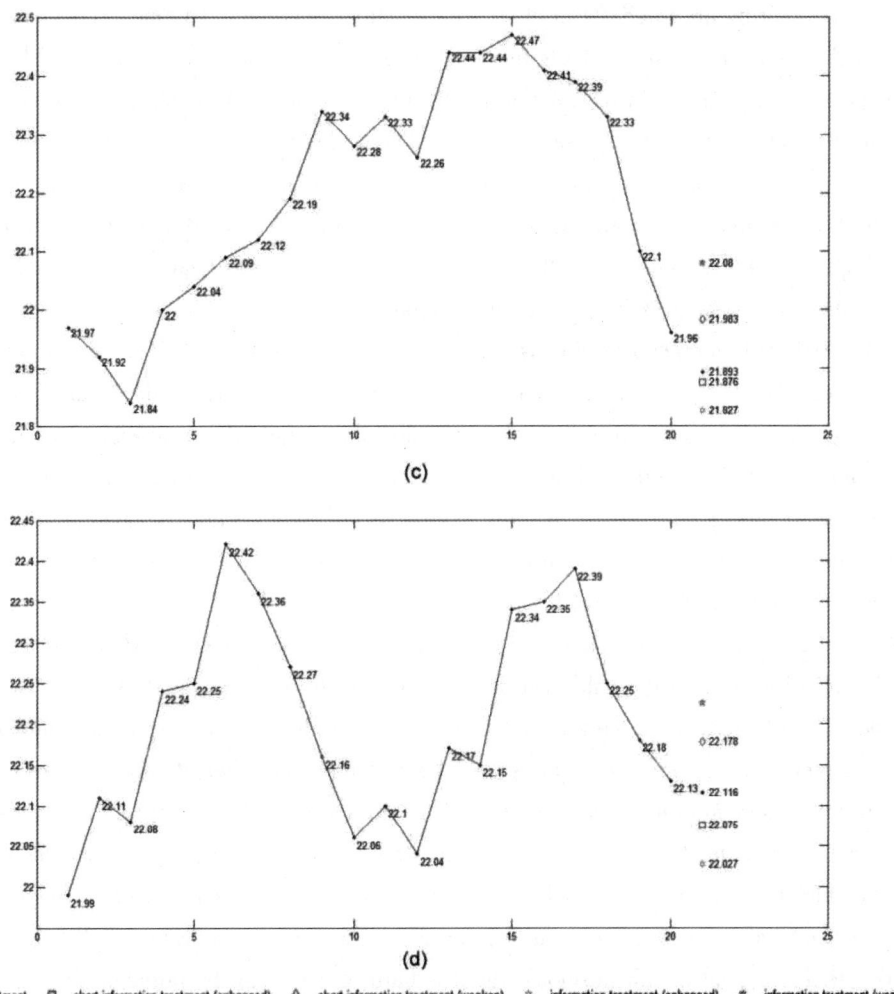

· chart treatment   □ chart-information treatment (enhanced)   ◊ chart-information treatment (weaken)   ¤ information treatment (enhanced)   ※ information treatment (weaken)

Figure 4　mean forecasts in three treatments

4.2　Result

Figure 4 shows the four pieces and subjects' mean forecasts in three treatments.① The forecasted prices in (a) and (b) are supposed to rise according to chart intuition, and in (c) and (d) are supposed to go down. Results in chart treatment are in accordance with our findings of chart intuition, and they are served as reference standards here.

Information does affect forecasts. When there is no chart, which is the case in information treatment, subjects are very sensitive to information: their forecasts are extremely high when the news is good and rather low when it is bad, compared with forecasts in chart treatment or chart – information treatment.

---

①　Figure 4 is not exactly the image we use in the additional experiment. We use screenshots in prior experiment in the additional one in order to compare their results. And the Median forecasts are shown in Appendix Figure J2.

What noteworthy are forecasts in chart - information treatment. The mean forecasts are affected by information compared with forecasts in chart treatment. Yet they are also affected by chart intuition compared with forecasts in information treatment: they are not as extreme as those forecasts only based on information, but more close to forecasts simply based on chart intuition.

Therefore, chart intuition actually serves as a base to form expectations. This also tests the statement Tversky and Kahneman (1974) proposed that intuition could serve as a starting point that biases people's beliefs. We do find that forecasts are starting from chart intuition and are adjusted by some other factors such as information on this base.

4.3 Efficient market hypothesis

Efficient market hypothesis has been fiercely argued for the past decades. Fama (1970) simply states it as: security prices fully reflect all available information. As reasonable information is hard to be decided, empirical studies always look into more visible indexes such as prices and returns. Classical researchers go directly to market to test its efficiency, and behavioral economists have turned to human psychology to explain a bunch of anomalies. Here we are trying to investigate human behavior to determine whether the market is efficient.

We find that chart could distort investors' judgment in some degree. This is an effect affecting people's subconscious, so it would also have an impact on even the smartest investor. If this holds for all people, all investors making decisions in front of a chart cannot be purely rational. Allowing for the prevalence of various price charts, we boldly conjecture that all investors are more or less subject to their chart intuition, and thus their behaviors are not 'efficient'. In this case, it is not only information that leads the price to where it should go, but also people's common chart intuition. Therefore the market may well be inefficient. However, this conclusion is only based on the assumption that 'all' investors are intuitive chartists. Yet we suppose it may well hold, because the chart intuition is a kind of subconscious which is hard to overcome by rationality.

5. Conclusion

Asking subjects to forecast a simulated stock price series without other information creates a clean experimental environment where only chart intuition matters. We find some important characteristics of extrapolation strategies used by investors. More importantly, we test our underlying assumption of intuitive chartist and prove that people are more or less affected by their chart intuition when forecast - even they have more reliable information.

Most of our data and many data patterns in reality are in usual cases, thus we see an obvious simple extrapolating behavior. When it comes to unusual cases or the two exceptions we define, people's forecast strategies become more complicated. Simple extrapolation cannot explain expectations in these cases well. We bring up the concept of reference to help understand people's judgment of general trend. Although the findings that how people recognize diverse cases and apply different forecast strategies are kind of nuanced, classifying experimental data in this pattern does explain most observations.

While our regression does a good job in predicting people's forecasts, we cannot provide more convincing conclusions with the limited data patterns. We do not have enough special data patterns to know subjects' forecasting behavior in unusual cases and exceptions, but the available data support our primary hypothesis. In fact, this study is not aim at providing an accurate model of people's forecasts, but to suggest an idea of classifying different cases and reveal some primary characters of extrapolation behavior.

Our underlying assumption about intuitive chartist is important in forecasting research, but it has not been tested before. As many prior studies also use price chart and ask subjects to forecast, it is worth testing if investors do rely on their chart intuition. We do not deny the significance of information in investment decision making, but we do find that people are at least partly affected by the chart as long as they are looking at it. Based on this finding, efficient market hypothesis might be challenged behaviorally, since 'all' market participants make not so 'efficient' decisions. However, this is based on the hypothesis that 'all' investors are intuitive chartists. Yet we suppose it may well hold, because the chart intuition is a kind of subconscious which is hard to overcome by rationality.

Actually, our initial purpose is not to study how people read a chart, so the data patterns in our experiment are too limited to draw a more general conclusion or build a more convincing model of investors' chart intuition. Further studies could generate more various data patterns, use longer period, or ask subjects to forecast for a further future, to get more specific and reliable findings of people's chart intuition.

References

1. Barberis, Nicholas, Andrei Shleifer, and Robert Vishny. "A model of investor sentiment. " *Journal of financial economics* 49, no. 3 (1998): 307 – 343.

2. Barberis, Nicholas, Robin Greenwood, Lawrence Jin, and Andrei Shleifer. *X – capm: An extrapolative capital asset pricing model*. No. w19189. National Bureau of Economic Research, 2013.

3. Beshears, John, James J. Choi, Andreas Fuster, David Laibson, and Brigitte C. Madrian. "What Goes Up Must Come Down? Experimental Evidence on Intuitive Forecasting. " *American Economic Review* 103, no. 3 (2013): 570 – 74.

4. Bloomfield, Robert, and Jeffrey Hales. "Predicting the next step of a random walk: experimental evidence of regime – shifting beliefs. " *Journal of Financial Economics* 65, no. 3 (2002): 397 – 414.

5. Campbell, John Y. , and Robert J. Shiller. "The dividend – price ratio and expectations of future dividends and discount factors. " *Review of financial studies* 1, no. 3 (1988): 195 – 228.

6. Case, Karl E. , Robert J. Shiller, and Anne Thompson. *What have they been thinking? Home buyer behavior in hot and cold markets*. No. w18400. National Bureau of Economic Research, 2012.

7. Cutler, David M. , James M. Poterba, and Lawrence H. Summers. "Speculative dynamics. " *The Review of Economic Studies* 58, no. 3 (1991): 529 – 546.

8. De Bondt, Werner PM. "Betting on trends: Intuitive forecasts of financial risk and return. " *International Journal of forecasting* 9, no. 3 (1993): 355 – 371.

9. DeLong, J. Bradford, Andrei Shleifer, Lawrence H. Summers, and Robert J. Waldmann. "Positive feedback investment strategies and destabilizing rational speculation. " *the Journal of Finance* 45, no. 2 (1990): 379 – 395.

10. Dwyer Jr, Gerald P. "Tests of rational expectations in a stark setting." *Economic Journal* 103, no. 418 (1993): 586–601.

11. Eggleton, Ian RC. "Intuitive time–series extrapolation." *Journal of Accounting Research* 20, no. 1 (1982): 68–102.

12. Fama, Eugene F. "The behavior of stock–market prices." *Journal of business* (1965): 34–105.

13. Fama, Eugene F. "Efficient capital markets: A review of theory and empirical work *."? *The journal of Finance*? 25, no. 2 (1970): 383–417.

14. Feng, Lei, and Mark S. Seasholes. "Do investor sophistication and trading experience eliminate behavioral biases in financial markets?." *Review of Finance* 9, no. 3 (2005): 305–351.

15. Fuster, Andreas, David Laibson, and Brock Mendel. "Natural expectations and macroeconomic fluctuations." *The Journal of Economic Perspectives* 24, no. 4 (2010): 67–84.

16. Gervais, Simon, and Terrance Odean. "Learning to be overconfident." *Review of Financial studies* 14, no. 1 (2001): 1–27.

17. Greenwood, Robin, and Andrei Shleifer. *Expectations of returns and expected returns.* No. w18686. National Bureau of Economic Research, 2013.

18. Hansen, Lars Peter, and Kenneth J. Singleton. "Generalized instrumental variables estimation of nonlinear rational expectations models." *Econometrica: Journal of the Econometric Society* (1982): 1269–1286.

19. Hommes, Cars. "The heterogeneous expectations hypothesis: Some evidence from the lab." *Journal of Economic Dynamics and Control* 35, no. 1 (2011): 1–24.

20. Lakonishok, Josef, Andrei Shleifer, and Robert W. Vishny. "Contrarian investment, extrapolation, and risk." *The journal of finance* 49, no. 5 (1994): 1541–1578.

21. LeRoy, Stephen F., and Richard D. Porter. "The present–value relation: Tests based on implied variance bounds." *Econometrica: Journal of the Econometric Society* (1981): 555–574.

22. List, John A. "Does market experience eliminate market anomalies?." *The Quarterly Journal of Economics* 118, no. 1 (2003): 41–71.

23. Maines, Laureen A., and John RM Hand. "Individuals' perceptions and misperceptions of time series properties of quarterly earnings." *Accounting Review* (1996): 317–336.

24. Mehra, Rajnish, and Edward C. Prescott. "The equity premium: A puzzle." *Journal of monetary Economics* 15, no. 2 (1985): 145–161.

25. Peng, Lin, and Wei Xiong. "Investor attention, overconfidence and category learning." *Journal of Financial Economics* 80, no. 3 (2006): 563–602.

26. Rötheli, Tobias F. "Pattern–Based Expectations: International Experimental Evidence and Applications in Financial Economics." *Review of Economics and Statistics* 93, no. 4 (2011): 1319–1330.

27. Schmalensee, Richard. "An experimental study of expectation formation." *Econometrica* 44, no. 1 (1976): 17–41.

28. Tversky, Amos, and Daniel Kahneman. "Judgment under uncertainty: Heuristics and biases." *science* 185, no. 4157 (1974): 1124–1131.

29. Tversky, Amos, and Daniel Kahneman. "Rational choice and the framing of decisions." *Journal of business* (1986): S251–S278.

Research on Underwriting Cycle of Chinese Commercial Property Insurance and the Affected Factors[1]

Jing Kang[2]

Abstract: This paper examined the loss ratio of the Chinese commercial property insurance with CF filter method. The results showed that there were cycles during the progress of the Chinese commercial property insurance and the length of every cycle was between 4 and 8 years. Besides, this paper also used co – integration analysis method to reveal the affected factors. It showed that the correlation between the loss ratio and the previous year's was insignificant; neither was the last two years'. But the loss ratio was positively correlated with GDP index and interest rates. Even though the insignificance between the loss ratio and CPI, there was a high negative correlation of the loss ratio with one of the components of CPI – the added value of the real estate industry index. Results indicated external economic environment did have a deep influence on the commercial property insurance cycle, while the internal factors from the insurance operations merely had a weak impact.

Keywords: Underwriting cycle, CF filter, Co – integration Analysis

I. Introduction

Ever since China resumed the domestic property insurance business, this industry has got the development at full speed during 30 years. According to the Central People's Government of People's Republic of China website statistics, the national premium increased by more than 3000 times from 460 million in 1980 to 1.55 trillion in 2012. That indicates Chinese insurance market has become the fastest – growing one of the world. But how to keep the upward trend of the insurance industry? The insurance industry and academics begin to pay attention to underwriting cycle, which can reveal the law of the development of the insurance industry. In 2009, Ernst & Young put forward that the Chinese insurance industry was facing three major business risks, which were the non – life insurance underwriting cycle management, the channel management, climate change and catastrophic events[3], and highlight the significance to study on underwriting cycle.

---

[1] 18th Asia – Pacific Risk and Insurance Association Annual Conference, Moscow, 2014.

[2] Kang Jing, graduate student, Insurance School, Central University of Finance and Economics, China, Email address: kjsy1990@gmail.com.

I gratefully acknowledge the support and help of Professor Guan Yisheng during the creation of this paper.

[3] Ernst & Young "2009 Annual Report of the insurance industry's annual business risk".

Underwriting cycle is a phenomenon that the insurance market suffers the impact from external shocks or internal factors, which lead the underwriting profit or loss ratio to show cyclical fluctuations. The study of underwriting cycle does have practical significance for insurance operators, insurance regulators and insurance investors. More specifically, for insurance operators, they can make countermeasures effectively by discretion in terms of the state of the market. For insurance regulators, they can effectively avoid negative effects of regulatory policies delays, and take preventive measures before the arrival of the soft market to avoid severe fluctuations of underwriting profit. For insurance investors, the underwriting cycle can assist them to choose the best timing of market entry and exit. Besides, since the endogenous relationship between the development of the insurance industry and economic development, the study of underwriting cycle is beneficial for both of the insurance industry and macroeconomic.

Mainly considered two factors, this paper selected commercial property insurance to do research. One is that compared with other property insurance, the regulatory policy and legal environment have not changed remarkably since China resumed the domestic property insurance business. It means the study of the commercial property insurance is more convincing. The other is that the commercial property insurance accounts for a big part of property insurance, which has a strong influence on the whole property insurance industry. Therefore, this paper aims to research on the underwriting cycle of Chinese commercial property insurance, which may help to research on the whole property insurance's underwriting cycle.

2. Literature Review

At present, the academic circle lacks of the literature of the commercial property insurance cycle in China, but some papers examining the non-life insurance cycle through the spectral analysis and the second-order autoregressive model can be the references.

2.1 The examining of the existence of underwriting cycle

As seen from existing literature, scholars generally agree with Cummins and Outrevill (1987) who modified second-order autoregressive model for the examining of existence of the underwriting cycle. They examined thirteen insurance markets of developed countries. The results illustrated that the eight countries' property insurance markets existing underwriting cycle, six countries' motor vehicle insurance underwriting profits existing cyclical effects. They also pointed out that the underwriting cycle phenomenon would transfer to the international insurance markets through international reinsurance mechanism. Once the paper was published, it caused a strong reaction. Many scholars started to use this model for their own countries' underwriting cycle studies.

Chen, Wong and Lee (1999) conducted research on emerging markets in Asia, and pointed out that there were underwriting cycles in non-life insurance market in Singapore, Malaysia and Japan. The length was 8 years, 12 years and 14 years, respectively. Meanwhile, the fire insurance in South Korea and the motor vehicle insurance in China Taiwan also showed characteristics of cyclical.

As for our country's study of underwriting cycle, Wu Peru (1998) was the first to use the second-order autogressive model to examine the underwriting cycle of property insurance in Taiwan.

The result showed the length of the cycle was 6.06 years.

In recent years, the scholars in the mainland were also fully aware of the importance of the underwriting cycle, so many of them used the second – order autoregressive model to examine the underwriting cycle in our country. However, the research results were not perfect, some scholars' researches showed that there were cycles in our country's insurance market, some showed that our country's insurance market had not yet demonstrated underwriting cycles.

Based on twenty two years of data of our country's non – life insurance market, Wang Bo and Shi Anna (2006) did empirical research. Their results indicated that the whole non – life insurance market did not show cyclical characteristics, but the motor vehicle insurance market did and the length of it was between 6 and 8 years. Then Hu Sanming and Wu Hong (2007) also came to the conclusion that non – life insurance market did not show cyclical characteristics, which affirmed the results of Wang Bo and Shi Anna (2007).

However, based on the combined loss ratio during the period of 1980 ~ 2006, Ji Yuna and Zheng Haitao (2009) used the second – order autoregressive model and spectral analysis to examine the non – life insurance cycle. The results showed that there were cycles in the non – life insurance in China actually. Additionally, the length of the motor vehicle insurance in China was 5.76 years.

Under such circumstances which scholars used the second – order autoregressive model but came to contrary conclusions, Li Xinyu, Li Jie, and Lan Wei (2009) proposed that the general second – order autoregressive model did not apply to the Chinese non – life insurance market. Instead, they used CF filter to do examine, which showed the length of the property cycle was between 4 and 5 years. And the length of the hard market and soft market was not strict symmetry.

2.2 The causes of underwriting cycle and affected factors

Scholars hold different opinions on causes of underwriting cycle. Generally, we can make conclusions into two aspects.

One kind of statement is that insurance industry internal development and the irrational pricing of the insurers, such as underwriting capacity constraints hypothesis and price competition hypothesis. Venetian (1985) proposed naive pricing theory. He thought the pricing model of using the past loss to predict future loss would bring a substantial deviation from the competitive market price, which fundamentally caused the underwriting cycle. Berger (1988) argued that it was the excessive competition that led to solvency deficiencies and supply reductions. Anne Grown (1994) study showed the insurance capital adequacy ratio and capital flow situation would affect the underwriting cycle.

Another argument is that the underwriting cycle is caused by external shocks such as markets. This statement mainly consists of institutional intervention hypothesis, interest rate hypothesis and macroeconomic cycle hypothesis. Cummins and Osterville (1987), Lamm Tennat and Weiss (1997) are the main representatives of institutional intervention hypothesis. They proposed the setting of insurance rate and the policy delay by regulatory authorities were the causes of underwriting cycle. Because those made the insurance companies cannot adjust insurance rate in terms of market price. Doherty and Kang (1988), Doherty and Graven (1992), Haley (1993) obtained a negative correlation between the underwriting profit and interest rates. Based on Co – integration Analysis, Grace and Hotchkiss (1995) obtained that the insurance industry had a long – term relationship with the changes of national economy, which was consistent with Chen, Wong and Lee (1999). They held the opinion that economic growth was the main cause of the underwriting cycle.

At present, the causes of Chinese underwriting cycle are also varied. Based on the multivariate regression model analysis results, Zhang Lin and Zhu Liyuan (2009) held that the underwriting cycle of motor vehicle insurance market was mainly affected by the insurance industry's internal factors. By contrast, impact of external shocks such as macroeconomic development was smaller. However, Wang Lizhen etc. (2010) attempted to use the HHI index and the significant adjustment of policies and regulations to explain the generation of underwriting cycle. They concluded that the macroeconomic cycle was the leading cause of the underwriting cycle of non – life insurance in China. Besides, Xiong Haifan, Zhuo Zhi and Wang Weiming (2011) used co – integration model to study the long – term relationship between the insurance operation indicators and macroeconomic variables. The results demonstrated that Chinese insurance market presented a 'growth' cycle characteristics. In addition, there was a negative correlation between the changes of insurance operation indicators and interest rates, and the linkage between the development of the non – life insurance and macroeconomic was not too close.

3. Examine on Chinese Commercial Property Insurance Underwriting Cycle

3.1 Methodology description

As we can see from the existing literature, the majority of scholars tend to adopt Cummins and Outreville (1987) second – order autoregressive model to do research. However, I think that, compared to Western countries of which insurance markets are more mature developed, Chinese insurance market is subject to regulatory policies, macroeconomic environment development and market investors frequently entry since China resumed the domestic property insurance business. Besides, on the assumption of the model itself, the length of Chinese underwriting cycle should be fixed, which is contrary to the truth. Do not mention the time series is not long enough for the empirical analysis. Based on these considerations, I think the second – order autoregressive model is not suitable for the study of Chinese underwriting cycle. This conclusion, can be verified from the exist literatures which used the second – order autoregressive model but came to that Chinese insurance market did not show cyclical characteristics. Therefore, this paper adopts filtering method to research on the Chinese commercial property insurance.

Filtering method, favored by academics in the study of macroeconomic, can filter the original sequence into long – term trend and short – term trend, and then leaves the cyclical trend. With the emergence and development of filtering method, three influential filters are designed to detrend the data successively, which are HP filter, BK filter and CF filter. CF filter was developed by Christiano and Fitzgerald (2003). Compared with the other two methods, CF filter is more suitable for research on underwriting cycle of Chinese commercial property insurance, since CF filter has some inherent advantages.

Firstly, compared with BK filter, CF filter has no requirement for the test of the sequence stationary and symmetry. On the contrary, CF filter improves the accuracy of estimated results by non-stationary and asymmetry. Secondly, compared with HP filter, CF filter is more flexible. CF filter can use different filtering formula for different time series. And for the same time series, CF filter can also use different truncated and weights for different point estimating. Based on these advantages, this paper chooses CF filter to research on the cycle.

The principles of CF filter method for the extraction cycle:

For a given time series x_t, there must exists an orthogonal decomposition which can decomposes x_t into $x_t = y_t + Z_t$. is the kind of part of which frequency belongs to $\{(a,b) \cup (-b,-a)\} \in (-\pi, \pi)$. Z_t is the kind of part of which frequency does not belong to y_t and $0 < a \leq b \leq \pi$. y_t is the eventually filtered waveform we want, and is denoted as $y_t = B(L)x_t$. $B(L) = \sum_{j=-\infty}^{\infty} B_j L^j$, L is the lag operator. $B_j = \dfrac{\sin(jb) - \sin(ja)}{\pi j}$, $j \geq 1$, $a = \dfrac{2\pi}{p_{max}}$, $b = \dfrac{2\pi}{p_{min}}$. p_{max} is set as the maximum length of the eventually waveform, p_{min} is set as the minimum length of the eventually waveform. $\hat{y}_t = \sum_{j=-f}^{p} \hat{B}_j^{p,f} x_{t-j}$ denotes the fitted value of y_t, $f = T - t$, $p = t - 1$. $\hat{B}_j^{p,f}$ can be calculated through $\min_{\hat{B}_j^{p,f}, j=-f,\cdots p} E[(y_t - \hat{y}_t)^2 | x]$.

3.2 Data

In terms of the definition of the underwriting cycle, the underwriting profit margin is the best indicator of the study of the underwriting cycle. But there are some literatures abroad using the combined ratio and underwriting loss ratio, since there is a highly linear relationship among these three indicators. Considering the availability of Chinese commercial property insurance data, this paper chose underwriting loss ratio indicator to do research. Researching on "China Insurance Yearbook" and "China Statistical Yearbook", this paper acquired the data of Chinese commercial property insurance premium income and claims expenditure from 1985 to 2012. Then LR (represents loss ratio) is acquired by simply calculating, and Fig. 1 demonstrates the fluctuation of LR. Besides, this paper selected some indicators from China Economic Information Network database to do research on the affected factors on the underwriting cycle.

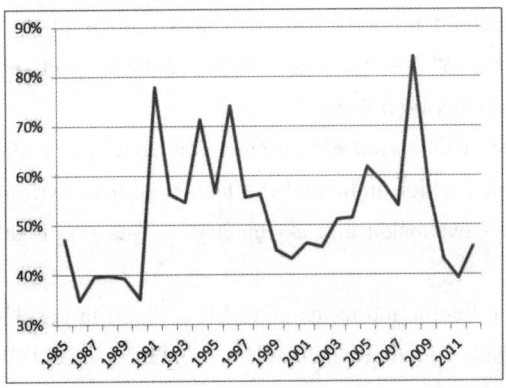

Figure 1 Chinese commercial property insurance LR (1985 – 2012)

Based on the LR in the 28 years spanning from 1985 through 2012, this paper used Eviews 7.2 software to do CF filter. According to the exist literatures home and abroad, our band was set between 4 to 8 years, and the Fig. 2 shows the CF filter result.

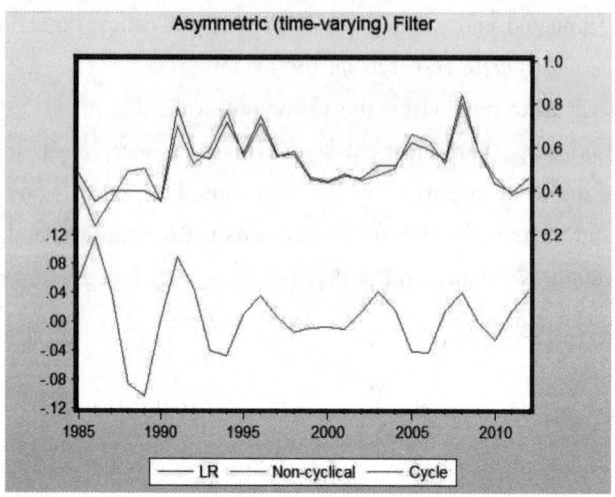

Figure 2   The CF filter result of LR

In terms of the CF filter result; this paper analyzed underwriting cycle, as seen in table 1.

Table 1   The analysis in terms of the result of LR CF filter

Peak	1986		1991		1996		2003		2008	
Trough		1989		1994		1998		2006		2010
Hard market	0		2		2		5		2	
Soft market		3		3		2		3		2

Analysis Fig. 2 and Table. 1, conclusions can be drawn as followed:

First of all, the commercial property insurance loss ratio went through four and a half cycles (1986 – 1991, 1991 – 1996, 1996 – 2003, and 2003 – 2008 respectively) from 1985 to 2012, and the length of every cycle was between 4 and 8 years.

Second, the amplitude of the peak was stronger the trough, and the length of the hard market and soft market was different, which indicated the feature of underwriting cycle of Chinese commercial property insurance was "expansion and asymmetry". This was highly consist with the study of Sun Qixiang (2010)[①].

Third, according to the fluctuation frequency, LR suffered larger fluctuations between 1986 and 1993. However, the fluctuation gradually tended to be stable since 1994. The causes of this phe-

---

① Sun Qixiang, Underwriting Cycle and Economic Cycle: International Comparison and Analysis, CCISSR, 2010: 5

nomenon should be considered in two aspects. One is that Chinese enterprises reform in the 1980s, conducted enterprises in an unstable macroeconomic environment since 1985. Thus during the period of 1986 – 1993, Chinese commercial property insurance presented strong fluctuation frequency. Second, the stable trend could be interpreted that Chinese commercial insurance market had been more mature developed since 1993.

4. The analysis of affected factors

This paper also analyzed the affected factors on the commercial property insurance cycle by using GDP index (*GDPindex*), Total Investment in Fixed Assets index (*GDZCindex*), benchmark one – year deposit rate (*R*), CPI and The added value of the real estate industry index (*REindex*) to do the co – integration analysis. All the data were gathered from the China Economic Information Network database. But the data of *GDZindex* was only acquired from 1990 to 2012. And as for R, in some years R was adjusted several times, this paper took the average of the several figures. was screened out among a sort of price indexes through correlation analysis with the Chinese commercial property insurance loss ratio respectively. They are financial added value index, industrial added value index, increasing value of transportation industry, wholesale and retail value index and catering industry increase index. Here this paper will not give the specific analysis of the screening process because it is not the precise point of the affected factors analysis. So we will analyze explicit relationships among variables and the cyclical fluctuation of the loss ratio.

Before co – integration analysis, the order of integration of each sequence should be determined. Therefore, the widely used and accepted Augmented Dickey – Fuller unit root tests were used to test each of time series first, the results are showed in Table. 2.

Table 2 **Augmented Dickey – Fuller Unit Root Tests**

Variables	ADF test value	Critical value	Prob.	Stationary or not
LR	-3.552766	-2.976263**	0.0141	Yes
GDPindex	-3.650949	-2.981038**	0.0115	Yes
R	-3.374732	-3.233456*	0.0768	Yes
CPI	-4.150625	-3.595026**	0.0157	Yes
REindex	-4.380378	-4.339330***	0.0091	Yes
GDZCindex	-2.272302	-2.642242*	0.1889	No
△GDZCindex	-5.351882	-2.679735***	0.0000	Yes

Note: Significant at: *10, **5 and ***1 per cent levels. △ represents the first differences.

As see from the Table 2, we concluded that the time series of *LR*, *GDPindex*, *R*, *CPI*, *REindex* were stationary, while the time series of *GDZCindex* was nonstationary. But the first differences of *GDZCindex* was stationary, which meant the series of *GDZCindex* contained one unit root. Therefore, we made a co – integration analysis among the time series of *LR*, *GDPindex*, *R*, *CPI*, *REindex*, as seen in Table. 3. As for the time series of *GDZCindex*, we analyze them solely.

Table 3   The result of co-integration analysis

Hypothesis	Eigenvalue	Critical value	Prob.
Hypothesized No. of CE(s)	71.23751	60.06141	0.0043
Hypothesized No. of CE(s)	34.91937	30.43961	0.0129

We can conclude from the Table. 3 that the time series of *LR*, *GDPindex*, *R*, *CPI*, *REindex* did have co-integration relationship. Therefore, we can use OLS method to do further research. The regression model was set as followed:

$$LR = C + \alpha_1 LR(-1) + \alpha_2 LR(-2) + \alpha_3 GDPindex + \alpha_4 GDPindex(-1)$$
$$+ \alpha_5 GDPindex(-2) + \alpha_6 R + \alpha_7 CPI + \alpha_8 REindex + \varepsilon$$
$$LR = C + \beta_1 \Delta GDZXindex + \beta_2 \Delta GDZCindex(-1) + \beta_3 \Delta GDZCindex(-2) + \varepsilon$$

Table 4   The result of regression 1

Variables	Coef.	
C	-3.115190	(-1.642817)
LR(-1)	-0.025286	(-0.100518)
LR(-2)	-0.246967	(-0.998214)
GDPindex	0.033971**	(2.152695)
GDPindex(-1)	0.021299	(0.947560)
GDPindex(-2)	0.003767	(0.319960)
R	0.034297*	(1.872296)
CPI	-0.017986	(-1.548308)
REindex	-0.008730*	(-2.031976)

Notes: The figures in the ( ) represent t-value. Significant at: *10, **5 and ***1 per cent levels.

Table 5   The result of regression 2

Variables	Coef.	
C	0.543759***	(20.25722)
ΔGDZCindex	-0.005148	(-1.053917)
ΔGDZCindex(-1)	0.001089	(0.229106)
ΔGDZCindex(-2)	-0.002142	(-0.444095)

Notes: The figures in the ( ) represent t-value. Significant at: *10, **5 and ***1 per cent levels.

According to the regression results, conclusions can be drawn as followed:

First, the coefficients of the loss ratio lagged one period and the lagged two periods were insignificant, which indicated the operating condition was not the right reason for underwriting cycle of Chinese commercial property insurance. Therefore, the underwriting cycle was not generated by irrational pricing behavior.

Second, loss ratio had a positive relationship with GDP index, but coefficients of GDP index lagged one period and the lagged period of two were insignificant, which indicated the underwriting cycle was affected by macroeconomic and was consensus with macroeconomic cycle. This was strong evidence of macroeconomic cycle hypothesis.

Third, the loss ratio and R had a positive correlation. As we know, the majority of commercial property insurance was one year period and higher interest rates will reduce the capacity to gain profits. Therefore, interest rate hypothesis can be an explanation for the generation of the Chinese commercial property insurance, which is consistent with many studies abroad.

Fourth, the correlation between the loss ratio and the consumer price index (CPI) was insignificant, but the loss ratio and The add value of real estate index (REindex) had a high negative correlation. But why was there a high negative correlation of the loss ratio with one of the components of CPI? Further research is needed in order to explain the high correlation.

Fifth, the coefficients of the total fixed assets investment index (GDZCindex), the lagged one period and the lagged two period were insignificant, which indicated the impact of social investment in fixed assets was not the reason for Chinese commercial property insurance underwriting cycle.

5. Conclusions

This paper examined the loss ratio of the Chinese commercial property insurance with the CF filter method. The results showed that there were cycles during the progress of the Chinese commercial property insurance and the length of every cycle was between 4 and 8 years. Besides, the feature of the cycle was "expansion and asymmetry", and the fluctuation gradually tended to be stable.

Besides, this paper also used co - integration analysis method to study on the affected factors. First, the coefficients of the loss ratio lagged one period and the lagged two periods were insignificant. Therefore, I infer insurers irrational pricing hypothesis did not apply to Chinese commercial property insurance. On the contrary, the development of Chinese commercial property insurance underwriting pricing is mature. Second, the coefficients of the total fixed assets investment index (GDZCindex), lagged one period and the lagged two period were insignificant, which indicated the impact of social investment in fixed assets was not the reason for Chinese commercial property insurance. Finally, loss ratio and GDP index fluctuated over the same period. And loss ratio with the one - year deposit interest rate had positive correlations. Therefore, insurance operators should take full advantages of these correlations. According to macroeconomic fluctuation, they can adjust business strategies to avoid the underwriting profits fluctuating greatly. In addition, the loss ratio and The add value of real estate index (REindex) had a high negative correlation.

I hypothesize that the real estate commercial property insurance accounted for a large proportion of the whole commercial property insurance. And compared with other kinds of commercial property insurance, real estate commercial property insurance was a high quality business. So loss ratio was relative lower. Whether the hypothesis is reasonable, I need to do further research to get precise conclusions.

Based on the above analysis, the conclusion is drawn as the external economic environment was the main affected factors on the commercial property insurance cycle, which is inconsistent with many domestic scholars. I think this is mainly because the regulatory policy and legal environment have not changed remarkably since China resumed the domestic property insurance business compared with other property insurance. The development of Chinese commercial property insurance market is mature, so the external economic environment becomes the main causes.

However, it should be pointed out that due to the lack of suitable quantitative model for the study, the length of the underwriting cycle this paper obtained was just an interval. So how to use quantitative analysis to get a precise length of the cycle is my future in-depth research of this paper.

References

1. Anne Gron, 1994, "Capacity Constraints and Cycles in Property - Casualty Insurance Markets," *The Rand Journal of Economics*, 25(1):111-127.

2. Berger, L. A, 1988, "A model for the underwriting cycle in property - liability insurance industry," *Journal of Risk and Insurance*, vol.55:pp.298-306.

3. Chen, Renbao, Kie Ann Wong and Hong Chew Lee, 1999, "Underwriting Cycles in Asia," *Journal of Risk and Insurance*, vol.66:29-47.

4. Cummins, J. D, and F. Outreville, 1987, "An International Analysis of Underwriting Cycles in Property - Liability Insurance," *Journal of Risk and Insurance*, vol. 54: pp. 246-262.

5. Doherty, Neil A. and Han Bin Kang, 1988, "Interest Rates and Insurance Price Cycles," *Journal of Banking and Finance*, vol.12, pp.199-214.

6. Doherty, Neil A. and James Garven, 1992, "Insurance Cycles: Interest Rates and the Capacity Constraint Model," *Journal of Business*, vol.68, pp.383-404.

7. Grace Martin F. and Julie L Hotchkiss, 1995, "External Impacts on Property - Liability Insurance Cycle," *Journal of Risk and Insurance*, vol.62, pp.738-754.

8. Haley, Joseph D, 1993, "A Cointegration Analysis of the Relationship Between Underwriting Margins and Interest Rates: 1930-1989," *Journal of Risk and Insurance*, vol.60, No.3, pp.480-493.

9. Lamm Tennant J. and Weiss, M. A., 1997, "International Insurance Cycles: Rational Expectations/ Institutional Intervention," *Journal of Risk and Insurance*, vol.64, No.3, pp.415-439.

10. Ursina B. Meier and J. Francois Outreville, 2010, "Business cycles in insurance and reinsurance: international diversification effects," *Applied Financial Economics*, 20,659-668.

11. Venezian, Emilio, 1985, "Ratemaking Methods and Profit Cycles in Property and Liability Insuranc," *Journal of Risk and Insurance*, 52:477-500.

12. Han Xiaofeng, Chen Cheng, 2010, "The empirical analysis of Chinses insurance circle and the contributions of insurance industry - based on HP filter and VAR model," *Western Business Review*, 2:99-111.

13. Hu Sanming, Wu hong, 2007, "The study on Chinese Non-life Underwriting Cycle," *Insurance studies*, 9:19-21.

14. Ji Yuna, Zheng Haitao, 2009, "Study on the Existence of Underwriting Cycles in Chinese Non – life Market," *Journal of Beijing University of Aeronautics and Astronautics(Social Sciences Edition)*, 04: 1 – 3.

15. Li lisong, 2011, "The empirical analysis of Chinses property insurance circle – based on the modle of Cuminms – Outrellvie," *Insurance studies*, 2:40 – 47.

16. Li Xinyu, Li Jie, Lan Wei, 2009, "Study on Underwriting Cycles in Chinese Non – life Market: Base on Filter Model," *CCISSR*, 11.

17. Rong Xing, Chen Yue, Yang Hui – chao, 2012, "Research on the Impacts of Economic Cycle on Non – life Underwriting Cycle in China," *Insurance studies*, 4:14 – 24.

18. Sun Qixiang, 2010, "Underwriting Cycle and Economic Cycle: International Comparison and Analysis," *CCISSR*, 5.

19. Wang Bo, Shi Anna, 2006, "The study on the non – life insurance underwriting cycle and the existence in China ," *Shanghai Finacial*, 7:37 – 40.

20. Wang Lizhen, Li Xiufang, Guo Siwen, 2010, "The exploration of Chinese non – life insurance underwriting profit fluctuations," *Insurance studies*, 9:21 – 27.

21. Wang Ya – ting, 2012, "Cyclical Fluctuations and Anti – cyclical Regulation in Insurance Industry: A Literature Review" *Insurance studies*, 9:120 – 127.

22. Wu Hong, 2011, "Insurance Fluctuating and Economy Fluctuating: Pro – cyclically or Counter – cyclically?" *Economic Review*, 5:69 – 78.

23. Wu Peiru, 1986, "The study on Chinese property insurance circle," *The Insurance Master Thesis of Feng Chia University*.

24. Xiong Haifan, Zhuo Zhi, Wang Weiming, 2011, "Study on the Existence of Underwriting Cycles in Chinese Market by Cointegration Model," *Insurance Studies*, 06:36 – 42.

25. Zhang Lin, Zhu Yuanli. 2009," The Regression Model Analysis of the U/W cycle in Automobile Insurance," *The theory and practice of finance and economics*, 2:32 – 36.

Insurance Group Risks Transmission Mechanism and Risk Management Between the Head Firm and Its Subsidiaries
——Based on the Characteristics of Liquidity Supply and Demand and Transmission Analysis[①]

Meiyi He[②]

Abstract: With the popular trend of mixed operation of economics and finance all over the world, without doubt, China's major financial groups operating mode have developed rapidly, including insurance industry. With the process of the promotion of the insurance financial groups diversified business mode, the insurance groups risks change speedy and complexly. Currently, the construction of a relatively complete and comprehensive risk management system is an important issue for insurance groups to solve.

This paper focusd on the liquidity among the insurance group, especially, between the head firm and subsidiaries, of course, including liquidity between the subsidiaries. We try to discuss the insurance group internal liquidity from a view of supply and demand of liquidity, risks with the cash flow and the risks management. In this paper, we study the above problems with the three – periods model which referring to the two – periods model, the Arrow – Debreu model of general equilibrium, an entrepreneurial model of moral hazard and LAPM: A Liquidity – Based Asset Pricing Model, and by the analysis of the cash flow and risks between the group company and the subsidiaries and among the subsidiaries. The point of this paper is that what risks exist in insurance group, how these risks conduction between the subsidiaries, what changes of risks and how to manage the liquidity, with the synergy of the insurance group.

Finally, because of the synergy of the insurance group, the risks have been changed a lot compared to the independent corporation. It also finds that the risks conduction path is similar to the series, parallel, and combination of series and parallel electric circuit. We conclude that the optimal first – best and second – best program in the process of the liquidity demand and supply in insurance group with the model. So after the study, in this way, do we better regulate risk facing by the insurance group and manage the liquidity between the head firm and the subsidiaries and between the subsidiaries.

---

① 18th Asia – Pacific Risk and Insurance Association Annual Conference, Moscow, 2014.
② Graduate student, School of Insurance, Central University of Finance and Economics, Beijing 100081, China. Email: meiyi1031@126.com

Insurance Group Risks Transmission Mechanism and Risk Management Between the Head Firm and Its Subsidiaries

I. Introduction

A. Insurance (Financial) Integration and liquidity

This paper is based on large group framework such as Insurance (Financial) Group. The so-called Insurance (Financial) Group (hereinafter referred Insurance Group) is an economic union, which provides comprehensive financial services. With the advantages of multiple cross-operations, kinds of channels interworking and others, this form of organization could make full use of group synergy, achieving efficiently economies of scale and economies of scope. As its name, the main business of Insurance Group is insurance but the range of its domain is across insurance, bank, securities, trust, etc. For this reason, Insurance Group combines insurance market, capital market and money market together. The structure of insurance group is so extremely complex and group company, group holding company, or head office is the core of the group, which has the right to decide, ownership and control its subsidiary corporations. These control relationships can be implemented by the means that capital transform as their bonds. Obviously, each corporations of the group must assume their responsibilities, since group company and its subsidiaries are separate legal entities, namely group holding and legal sub-industry. Note that, it is general that there must be a commercial bank in Insurance Group in the international community.

In China, several large insurance companies such as China Life and PICC could not be called Insurance Group strictly in the lack of commercial bank. Ping An Insurance (Group) Co., China, LTD may be presumably the most representative and only insurance group in China. Ping An is growing quite rapidly in the business model of this integration. The organizational structure of Ping An has been very large and complex, we choose some of its subsidiaries to draw Figure II according to its 2012 company report. At the end of 2012, Ping An Insurance (Group) Company has already owned more than 90 subsidiary companies with over 50% shareholding percentage and 28 consolidated special purpose subsidiaries. Moreover, a number of powerful subsidiary corporations set up subsidiaries by themselves. With the expanding and improving of its organizational structure, involved business fields are no longer confined to insurance, banking and securities, but also are gradually extended to the trust, IT industry and many other areas. Certainly, insurance must be the main business of the insurance (financial) group. As shown in the follow Figure I referring to the net profit proportion of Ping An (Group) Company in year 2011, insurance area has accounted for 61%, occupying dominant position.

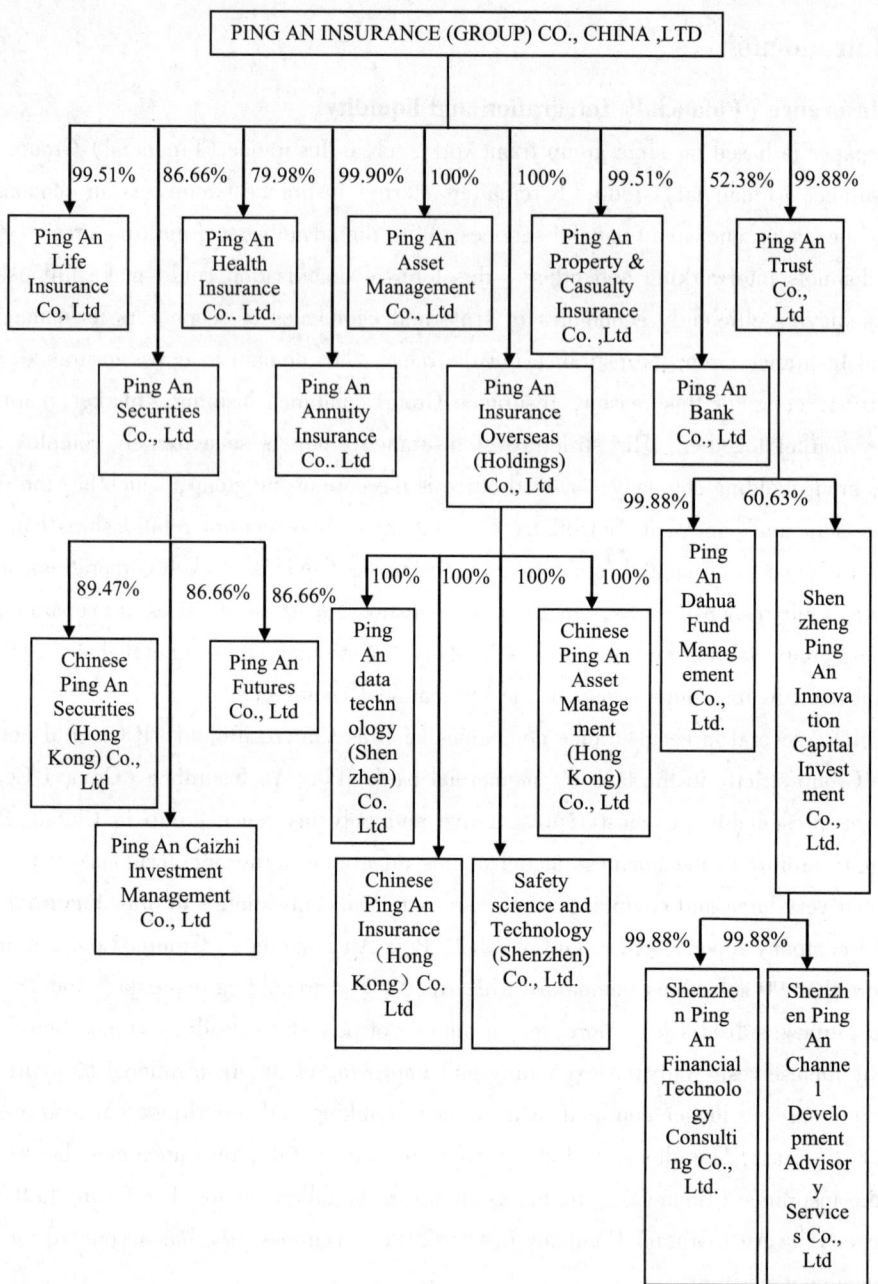

Figure I

In fact, there are a lot of insurance (financial) group such as AIG and Buffett Group in the world's top 500 enterprises.

Insurance Group Risks Transmission Mechanism and Risk Management Between the Head Firm and Its Subsidiaries

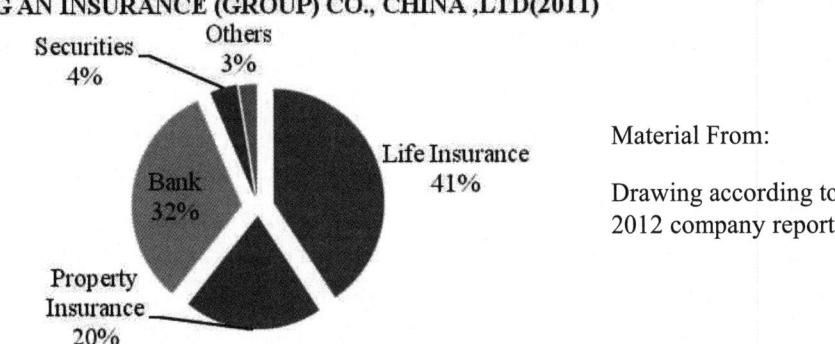

Material From:

Drawing according to 2012 company report

Figure Ⅱ

Based on 2013 AIG company report, nowadays, 647 subsidiaries are belonging to American International Group. Concluding from the table Ⅰ, which intercepted part of the whole table including several representative subsidiaries, the subsidiary corporations are across the world.

Table 1 Subsidiaries

	Subsidiary name	Country	Ownership			Source
			Direct (%)	Total (%)	Status	Date of inform
1.	AIA AURORA LLC	US	100.00	100.00	UO +	12/12
2.	AIG FEDERAL SAVINGS BANK	US	100.00	100.00	UO +	12/12
3.	AIG GLOBAL SERVICES, INC.	US	100.00	100.00	UO +	12/12
4.	AIG LIFE INSURANCE COMPANY (SWITZERLAND) LTD	CH	100.00	100.00	UO +	01/14
5.	AIG MARKETS INC	US	100.00	100.00	UO +	12/12
6.	AIG TRADING GROUP INC.	US	100.00	100.00	UO +	12/12
7.	AIUH LLC	US	100.00	100.00	UO +	09/13
8.	AM HOLDINGS LLC	US	100.00	100.00	UO +	12/12
9.	AMERICAN SECURITY LIFE INSURANCE	LI	100.00	100.00	UO +	12/12
10.	CHARTIS AZERBAIJAN INSURANCE COMPANY OJSC	AZ	100.00	100.00	UO +	12/12
11.	MG REINSURANCE CO	US	100.00	100.00	UO +	12/12
12.	CASTLE 2003 IC LLC	US	>50.00	>50.00	UO	03/14
13.	CASTLE 2003-2 TRUST	US	>50.00	>50.00	UO	03/14
14.	UNITED GUARANTY CORPORATION	US	>50.00	>50.00	UO	03/14

From: 2013 AIG Company Report

Recently, with the popular trend of financial integration, it is not difficult to foresee that such a group structure similar to Ping An (Group) Company will be common and widespread in China and Chinese insurance groups also will become international.

The word of liquidity has been widely used in the field of finance, but there is no exact meaning of it. The definition of liquidity is very ambiguous. The word has many meanings and owns different meaning under different conditions. 'no one, unambiguous, theoretically correct or all accepted definition' (Baker, 1996). In capital market, liquidity often used for describing the ability of assets could be converted into cash at reasonable price, which is matching relationship between investment time and price. But liquidity refers to the capabilities of repaying the debt on time. Lore and Borodosky said in The Professional's Handbook of Financial Risk Management (2000), liquidity is cash flow which satisfies the payment requirements. The cash flow includes assets earning and the cash borrowed from the market. Simply, liquidity is similar to 'cash'. In this paper, mostly, liquidity refers the cash flow or cash demand. The paper discusses this situation that one of the subsidiaries demand liquidity, which supplied by the head firm or other subsidiaries to cover liquidity shock and additional expenses. So how the risks with these processes conduct and how to manage liquidity.

B. Risk Transmission

In insurance group, there are three dominating cases of risks conduction. Firstly, daily related transaction in insurance group. Insurance subsidiary uses the premium to invest in the securities and bank subsidiaries or the bank subsidiary agents for the insurance subsidiary. So the risk transmits from one subsidiary to another one by internal transactions to affect the whole insurance group. Secondly, external consumers and investors view the insurance group as a whole, so when one of insurance group suffer risks, even if the others operates normally, the consumers and investors also think that the other subsidiaries have problems. If this cause the squeeze of the bank subsidiary and huge cancellation of insurance, the insurance group is on the verge of destruction. Finally, because of cyclical fluctuations in the economy or the mismatching of the subsidiaries maturity structure of assets and liabilities with expected financial needs or their own credibility downgrade or no normal finance support, one subsidiary may need liquidity from the group company and other subsidiaries. By this way, the property and timing of the funds change and form the risks transmission. This paper will analyze the third case. The debts and equity investment between different subsidiaries of insurance group are usually related with the transaction cash. When one of its subsidiaries faces liquidity shock risk, the other subsidiaries will also suffer the risks through cash flow line and internal transaction which may incur the insurance group crisis. Even though the risks conduction carriers are multitudinous, the main risks transmission of insurance group includes the cash flowing in the insurance group, internal and external information and the operating commodities. The information contains information management technology, culture of insurance group, insurance group management style and so on. It is the same judgment of the information about external environment and internal condition that the insurance group makes wrong decisions and plans. The follow part of this paper will study concretely the risks transmission and management between the head firm and the subsidiaries and among the subsidiaries on the basis of the liquidity and the model.

Insurance Group Risks Transmission Mechanism and Risk Management Between the Head Firm and Its Subsidiaries

In fact, by the introduction of the insurance group organizational structure and the path of cash flow in insurance group, as is shown in the Figure V, we conclude that the risks conduction path is similar to the series and parallel circuits in electricity. The risks transmission has four obvious characteristics.

Characteristic 1. The path dependence. The conduction of any risks must be on some carries, which seems as the cash flow we discussed follow.

Characteristic 2. Bidirectional conductivity. As the bidirectional cash flow between the head firm and subsidiaries or between the subsidiaries, the risks transmission is not mono-directional, but bidirectional with the associated liquidity and related business transaction.

Characteristic 3. The priming effect in conduction. When the risk of one subsidiary transmits to another one, the risk may lead to another new risks in the other subsidiaries. For examples, the liquidity risks of the bank subsidiary may cause insufficient solvency of the insurance subsidiary.

Characteristic 4. Amass effect in conduction. Noted firstly, 'amass' is not equivalent to 'accumulate'. It indicates that if the risks of one Subsidiary X transmit to the Subsidiary Y, the risks of the Subsidiary Y is not simply the added sum of the risks of the Subsidiary X, even maybe the risks value of the Subsidiary Y is smaller than the Subsidiary X. It means that the risks value may be modified by the conduction process with the function of the risks conduction or good risks management. Moreover, we could control the risks in the process of its conduction to insure the insurance group normal and efficient operating.

C. Research Purpose, its importance and research methodology

This paper addresses very significant issue: from a liquidity perspective, exploring how the insurance group manage their liquidity and risks between group corporation and its subsidiaries, and among subsidiaries in insurance group. Or does the group corporation or the head office acts as a crucial role or not in providing cash to cover the liquidity shortage and supervising their subsidiaries belong to the insurance group through adjustments in some areas. At the beginning, we hope to know the whole insurance organization structure and the process of the insurance group various business operation. Then through the analysis of cash flow in the group firm and subsidiaries of the insurance group, we conclude that the risks, the variation of the risks during the conduction and the risks mechanism. So we could obtain the optimal program of the demand and supply of liquidity in insurance group with the model. In this way, could we regulate the risks of insurance group and manage its liquidity better no matter for the group or for regulators.

Insurance group is not just a collection of a number of risks, it is a risk processor. Because the insurance company itself is operating risks of the enterprise, and therefore insurance group has a stronger risk conversions and risk configuration, compared to other types of financial groups. However, if the capacity of the entire group's risk allocation is weak, it is very easy to lead to transmission of financial risks within the group during the capital allocation. Therefore, insurance risk transfer and configuration group's ability is the basement of controlling risk and healthy functioning, moreover, is the biggest risk, which it facing. Insurance group head corporation must meet a lot of liquidity demand of their subsidiaries, at the same time, subsidiaries also provides the necessary liquidity with the surplus funds, and cash flow will have a circulation between the various subsidiaries and affiliates. Due to the delay in the payment of insurance, less attention paid to the insurance company liquidity. However, for the insurance group , whether the head office ,insurance company , banking subsidiaries, or securities subsidiaries liquidity shortage will cause a domino effect among the insurance group. Such as payment crisis, bank run , and credit crisis and so on will yield a series of major influence ,even a threat to the global financial system. However, global and Chinese studies and researches about this always focus on financial groups but not on insurance group, as a result, more and depth study on financial groups, less and simple on insurance group. It is not difficult to find the importance of liquidity for the financial system from a number of economic crisis, especially in the economic downturn, liquidity shortage could cause some countries finance horrible. So many economic crisis gave us a sharp warning of the importance of sound liquidity risk management and regulatory. In China, financial industry has undergone a severe liquidity shortage, brought to the adverse effects on the financial industry during June ,2013. On October 12,2011, China Banking Regulatory Commission announced the "Commercial banks' liquidity risk management approach." (plot). And China Insurance Regulatory Commission announced insurance groups management approach, which also referred to the liquidity regulation. Owing to the complex, broad and changeable of the insurance group, liquidity management and regulation are more important.

The first step of our analysis is that knowing the internal organization structure of insurance group, introduced in the above content so that understanding how the insurance group operates daily. It services for the flowing detailed study. And it explains the meaning of the liquidity in our paper in case of misunderstand for the next sections. At the last, we must hold the basic technology about the risks conduction and process of the transmission. The second step of our analysis is about the cash flow between the head firm and the subsidiaries and between various subsidiaries in insurance group. With this section discuss, we can know the process of the cash inflow and outflow and risks in insurance. The most important, it helps us to see the changes of the risks in the synergy of the whole insurance group and different risks ,different risks conduction in various subsidiaries and the insurance group. The third step of the paper is to build three – period model to study the liquidity demand and supply in insurance group. With the model and the series and parallel circuits, we study the risks transmission and liquidity management in detail. In the final part, it will state the conclusion , the limits and possible development of our study.

II. The Analysis of Insurance (Financial) Group Liquidity

A. The Cash Flow among Insurance, Commercial Bank and Security Subsidiary Companies.

This section studies insurance (financial) group liquidity. Because the current business of insurance group focused on three major aspect, insurance, banking and securities, the head firm (group corporation), insurance subsidiaries, bank subsidiaries and securities subsidiaries play a leading role in insurance group. So in order to better research, this section will analyze the cash flow of insurance group among the four main companies. In fact, insurance subsidiary premium income will accumulate much liquidity of temporarily idle, due to the characteristics and nature of insurance and the big power of the insurance company in insurance group. Therefore, the insurance subsidiary corporation acts as a liquidity provider. And since securities subsidiaries conduct the investment to expand its capital, a lot of liquidity should be supported and usually they play a role of liquidity demand. The cash flowing between the supply - side and demand - side needs commercial bank, which acts as credit intermediaries linking up the three markets. For this reason, it just said that commercial bank is necessary for insurance group. The figure III clearly demonstrates this principle.

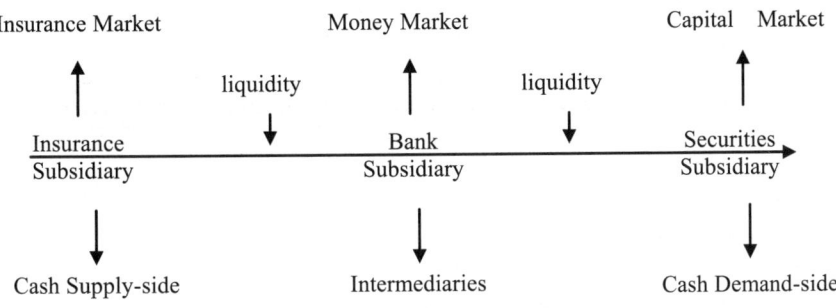

Figure III

It is particularly noteworthy that the cash flow among the insurance group owns unique characteristics and is different from that between other general companies. Cash flow is often done and achieved by the head firm in such intra - group, especially when one subsidiary generated liquidity needs, the supply of liquidity is implemented through the group corporation co - ordination arrangements. Next content will analyze the cash flow in subsidiaries in detail in order to serve for the following model and study. Two main aspects lead to liquidity demand for subsidiaries, on the one hand, serving for business development, on the other hand, making up for the shortage of capital funds. As mentioned above, the operating businesses of the securities subsidiary are mostly high - risk and high - yield investment, so it needs a large number of cash. Then this section will analyze the cash flow in the three subsidiaries through the securities company as a carrier and within the Figure IV. Insurance subsidiary could use the capital cash and various of insurance reserves to invest related financial products due to the uncertainty and time lag in the compensation and payment. Most cash flows to commercial bank subsidiary by deposit to be preserved and earned, and others may buy some safe, stable, and high - liquidity stocks and bonds. The idle assets and funds put into the bank and securities subsidiary by this means. Then most of the funds of commercial bank subsidiary can meet liquidity needs of the securities subsidiary by Interbank market, short - term financing bills, stock collateral loans and various business special loans. Moreover, when the insurance company encounter the problem of huge compensation payments and inadequate solvency, the bank subsidiary will offer loans to insurance subsidiary to prevent liquidity shortage and add the capital funds. Of course, these problems could occur rarely in practice. Figure IV shows intuitively the parallel and bidirectional cash flows between the subsidiaries in insurance group. It is interesting to note that the ways are similar to the series circuit. The group corporation plays as a power supply in the circuit to control the flow and direction of funds in such a *series circuit*.

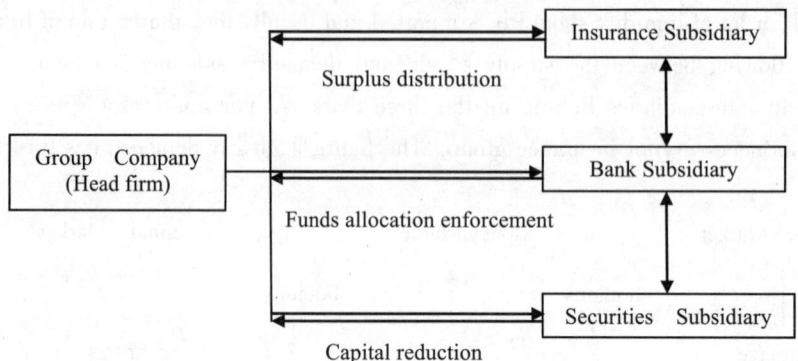

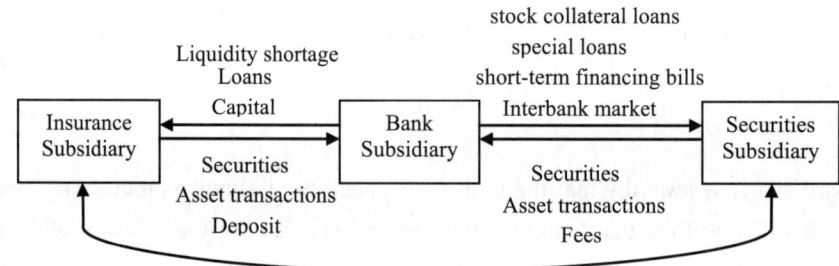

Figure IV

The surplus cash in subsidiaries will flow to the group unified accounts through kinds of ways. As is shown in Figure IV, there are three main ways including participating in the distribution of surplus funds belong to various subsidiaries as the controlling – shareholders, Reducing the capital of the subsidiaries over the minimum capital requirements of the relevant regulatory authorities, and head firm orders their subsidiaries to provide liquidity compulsorily within its power. In these ways, the group could accumulate a lot of money for investment and handling emergency situations. When the subsidiaries meet the shortage of liquidity, demand cash to develop business, or add the regulatory capital, the head firm would support them with cash considering its overall benefits. Once, the group firm does not have enough funds, it would require the other subsidiaries to offer related financial assistance to the subsidiary firm with temporarily problems. Such process is what the above context discuss that cash flow between subsidiaries. Figure IV presents to us not only the cash flow in the insurance group, but also actually the risks transmission path by the cash carrier. We will state specific process of risks conduction and liquidity management in next sections.

III. Liquidity Demand and Exogenous Supply in Insurance Group

It is known that insurance group finance function is performed by the group company through

Part I and Part II. The head firm reallocate the cash to the subsidiaries so that they could meet their demand for liquidity. Then the access to get enough cash is not only entirely through external financing, but also others for insurance group, especially for Chinese insurance group. For example, Ping An Insurance (Group) Co., China, LTD, which was listed as a whole, is obliged to provide liquidity when its subsidiaries need it. Because each subsidiary is unable to obtain funds from outside investors.

A. Model

This section will analyze liquidity problem and group liquidity risk transmission and liquidity management between group firm and securities subsidiary and between bank subsidiary and securities subsidiary by the model. ①

The model period has to extend to three from two-period investment model because of studying corporate liquidity demand and including an third stage at which needing extra funds to continue the project when it may be interrupted by an adverse liquidity shock. Timing of the model will be presented in Figure V and $t = 0, 1, 2$. There are two types of agents, Securities subsidiary and Group corporation (Head firm), and one good with no return interest if no use and used for both companies referring as cash. We assume that there is no liquidity shortage, but we will drop it because we shall study the endogenous liquidity supply in the next section.

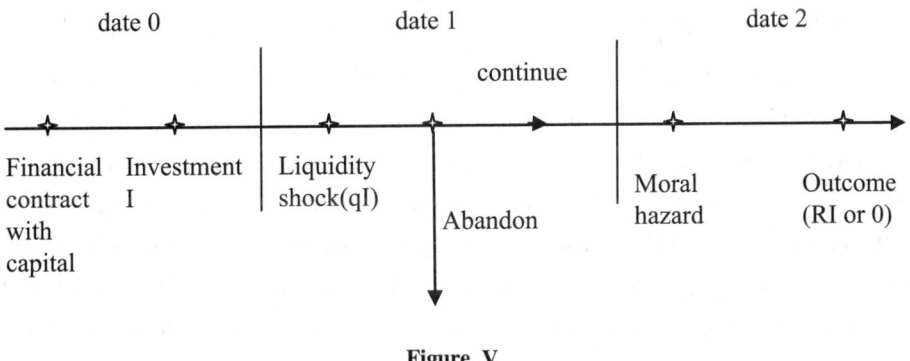

Figure V

Firstly, we assume that the securities subsidiary shall invest some project with the capital cash of A, but it demands another cash of I from the group company. That is, the head firm must invest I to the project too. The securities corporation is able to use constant earnings – to – scale techniques for the head firm the amount RI of investment I proceeds and the securities subsidiary will not get any no endowment of cash from outsiders if succeeds but nothing if it fails. The group corporation invests for the project at date 0. But at date 1 the securities subsidiary would need anther uncertainty amount $qI > 0$ to make up for operating expenditures and another cash need. The distribution function of liquidity shock ρ is described as $F(q)$, and its density function is $f(q)$. If qI is offered by

---

① The model is modified and improved on the basis of the models from Bengt Holmstron and Jean Tirole, *Private and Public Supply of liquidity*, Journal of Political Economy, Vol.106, No. 1 (Feb. 1998), pp, 1 – 40.

the head firm, the project would continue and get a final payoff Y at date 2, otherwise, the project would terminate and yield nothing (no partial liquidation). I is subjected to moral hazard in that the group company can either behave or shirk with the project succeeds probability p. The probability P_H represents the success (high) with the another investment qI and P_L without qI where $p_H - p_L \equiv \Delta p > 0$. If the head firm shirks, the securities subsidiary will obtain benefit $\alpha BI > 0$ and the group corporation will accept $(1-\alpha)BI > 0$, where a final benefit, proportional to the level of their investment funds I. It is noted that there is no endowment of cash at date 1 and date 2 except the investment from the head firm. Tentatively, we presume that the initial securities subsidiary and the head firm investment, the project result and the liquidity shock are all demonstrable. A financial contact C at date 0 included the amount the securities subsidiary will contribute, the project scale, the possibility that the project is given up at date 1 and the distribution of the proceeds from the investment. The generic contact C must tell the securities subsidiary won't get nonnegative expected return. And the securities subsidiary and group company have the limited liability : they cannot pay out more cash than they have. Because $P_H R > q$, the net present value of the overall investment from both the securities subsidiary and the group firm will be maximized by keeping on the project if and only if $q \leq q_1 \equiv p_H R$ (q_1 is referred as *first - best cutoff*). At the same time, we introduce an assumption that the net present value of the project is positive when group firm chooses to behave but to quit if it shirks:

$$\int \max\{p_H R - q, 0\} f(q) dq - 1 > 0 > \int \max\{p_L R + B - q, 0\} f(q) dq - 1 \quad (1)$$

So we just consider the situation that the head firm behaves and choose to implement the action p_H. According to the above content, we set $C = \{A, I, \varphi(q), R_s(q)\}$, where A is the level of the initial investment from the securities subsidiary, $\varphi(q)$ stands for the continuation policy which $\varphi(q) = 1$ means continue because the head firm offer another liquidity and $\varphi(q) = 0$ means abandon, and $R_s(q)$ is the amount the securities subsidiary is defrayed when the project succeeds (given to a liquidity shock q), where $R_s(q) = \alpha R$, so obviously, the head firm is left with $R_g(q)$, where $R_g(q) = (1-\alpha)R$. And if the item is failed or is abandoned, securities subsidiary and group firm proceeds are zero.

Next we will choose optimal financial contact $C = \{A, I, \varphi(q), R_s(q)\}$ to solve the *second - best program*:

$$\max I \int p_H R_s(q) \varphi(q) dF(q) - A \quad (2-1)$$

Subject to the head firm's break - even constraint (2 -2)

$$I(1 - \int \{p_H R_g(q) - q\} \varphi(q) dF(q)) \leq A \quad (2-2)$$

And for every q

$$R_s(q)(p_H - p_L) \geq \alpha B \quad (2-3)$$

We assume that the optimal continuation if and only if $q \leq \dot{q}$. Then substituting (2-2) into (2-1), we can deduce the securities subsidiary's net return as

$$U_s(\dot{q}) = n(\dot{q})I \quad (3)$$

Where the *marginal net social return* on the head firm investment:

$$n(\hat{q}) = \int_0^{\hat{q}} \Delta q dF(q) - 1 \qquad (4)$$

$\Delta q = q_1 - q$, It is easily found that the function of marginal net social return is quasi–concave and when $\hat{q} = q_1 \equiv p_H R$, it maximizes $n(\hat{q})$.

We can conclude that $n(q_1) > 0$ from the assumption (1). And then $n(\hat{q})$ is also strictly positive because $q_1 = \hat{q}$ is feasible in program (2) (for small enough I). We could infer from (3) that the securities subsidiary would like to select $R_s(q)$ to maximize I because of $n(\hat{q}) > 0$, that setting $R_s(q) = R_b \equiv \alpha B / / \Delta p$. At the same time, it can pay the head firm, which (per unit invested) is $q_0 \equiv p_H [R - \alpha B / \Delta p)]$, referring as the *pledgeable unit return* from investment at date 1. Then return to the break–even constraint, it is found that the cutoff $\hat{q} = q_0$ maximize the left–hand side of (2 –2). Because sometimes the subsidiaries of overall listed insurance group can not self–finance, we introduce (5) to ensure that the policy does not provide the head firm an expected marginal return that is larger than the marginal cost of their date 0 investment, which is that

$$\int_0^{q_0} (q_0 - q) f(q) dq < 1 \qquad (5)$$

When $q_0 = q$, $B = 0$. Hypothesis (5) is not consistent with assumption (1). In fact, the positive difference $q_1 - q_0 > 0$ is necessary to rule out self–financing for the securities subsidiary. So the maximum amount of the investment can be achieved at date 0 at $\hat{q}$. It is

$$I = e(\hat{q}) A \qquad (6)$$

Where the *equity multiplier* is

$$e(\hat{q}) \equiv \frac{1}{1 + \int_0^{\hat{q}} qf(q) dq - F(\hat{q}) q_0} \qquad (7)$$

The denominator of $e(\hat{q})$ specifies the cash amount which the securities subsidiary must offer to offset the shortfall suggested by (5) in per unit investment. $e(\hat{q})$ achieves its maximum at $\hat{q} = q_0$ from the property of $e(q_0) > 1$ and quasi–concave. $e(\hat{q})$ may be less than one when setting $\hat{q}$ very high and it is optimal if the project needs large liquidity demand. In that case, the total investment from the group company (which including the initial investment and the expected liquidity shortage) will not be larger than the securities subsidiary capital A. So we must assume that the total investment must be less than the capital A.

Then we will get the securities subsidiary net payoff

$$U_s(\hat{q}) = n(\hat{q}) e(\hat{q}) A \qquad (8)$$

Next we will find out the second–best threshold to maximize (8). Known from the above context, $e(\hat{q})$ and $n(\hat{q})$ are both quasi–concave and at $q_1 : n(q)$, reaches the maximum and at $q_0 : e(q)$, achieves the maximum. So the second–best threshold q^* must be landed in the interval $[q_0 : q_1]$. If $q < q_0$, both the securities subsidiary and the head firm prefers to continue ex post. And if $q > q_1$, the net present value of continuing is negative and there exists Pareto–optimal to abandon the inefficient item. The securities subsidiary faces a trade–off in $[q_0 : q_1]$. It can raise $\hat{q}$ to withstand higher liquidity shocks at date 1 thence increasing the marginal return $n(\hat{q})$ at date 0, or lower $\hat{q}$ to raise the investment level $e(\hat{q})$. However, because the break-even constraint, the securities firm cannot do both at the same time. Due to $n(q)$ is strictly increasing at q_0 and $e(q)$ is strictly decreasing at q_1, the trade-off should be achieved by choosing q^* within $[q_0:q_1]$. The threshold q^* could be interpreted as the outcome of (second-best) risk sharing. To characterize q^*, we can write out the firm's net payoff $U_s(\hat{q})$ using (4) and (7).

$$U_s(\hat{q}) = n(\hat{q})e(\hat{q})A \quad and \quad F(\hat{q}) = \int_0^{\hat{q}} f(q)dq$$

Then (8) divide through by $F(\hat{q})$, shows:

$$U_s(\hat{q}) = \left(\frac{q_1 - q_0}{\frac{1 + \int_0^{\hat{q}} qf(q)dq}{F(\hat{q})} - q_0} - 1 \right) A \tag{10}$$

As is shown that

$$q^* \min imizes \frac{1 + \int_0^{\hat{q}} qf(q)dq}{F(\hat{q})} \tag{11}$$

Also because,

$$\frac{1 + \int_0^{\hat{q}} qf(q)dq}{F(\hat{q})} = \frac{1 - \int_0^{\hat{q}} F(q)dq}{F(\hat{q})} + q$$

(11) gets minimum just simply means threshold q^*,

$$\int_0^{q^*} F(q)dq = 1 \tag{12}$$

We may be surprised to note that the threshold q^* doesn't decided by q_0 or q_1 as long as it falls in $[q_0, q_1]$. Thus the additional cash to cover the liquidity shortage and expenditures is available if q_0 increase would all be used to expand the project scale rather than to add liquidity.

Therefore, we can conclude that, the securities subsidiary net proceeds,

$$U_s(q^*) = \frac{q_1 - q^*}{q^* - q_0} A \tag{13}$$

the head firm investment,

$$I^* = \frac{1}{F(q^*)(q^* - q_0)} A \tag{14}$$

Interesting consequence, We can derive from (13) that,

$$U_s(q^*) = \left(\frac{q_1 - q_0}{q^* - q_0} - 1 \right) A \tag{15}$$

For example, the liquidity shock becomes more dangerous in the sense of a mean-preserving spread in the distribution F. Equation (12) reveals that the cutoff q^* declines but $U_s(q^*)$ is higher seeing from (15). The reason for this counterintuitive consequence is that the option to terminate the project makes a riskier distribution more valuable.

Insurance Group Risks Transmission Mechanism and Risk Management Between the Head Firm and Its Subsidiaries

B. Risk conduction and liquidity management between the head firm and subsidiaries.

The insurance group funds are usually contributed by the various subsidiaries. For our study, we

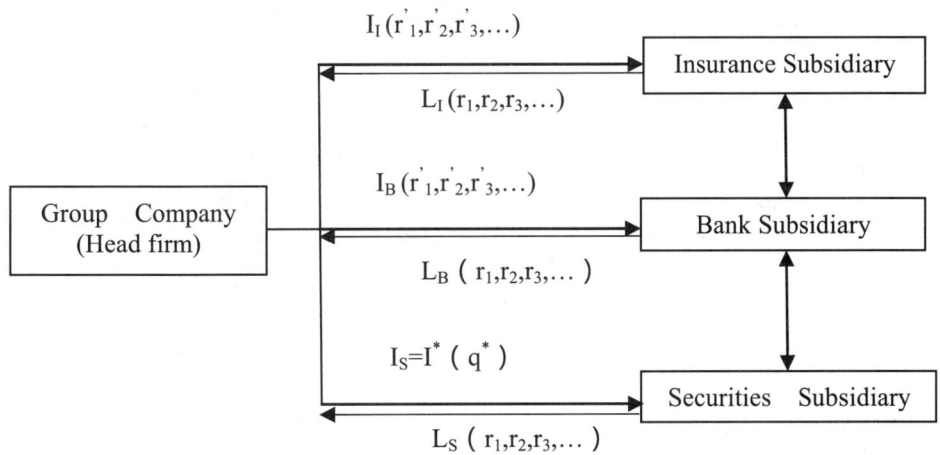

Figure VI

assume that the cash of insurance group is coming from the insurance, bank and securities subsidiary, as illustrated in Figure IV_1, that is $L = \{L_s, L_B, L_I\}$. ① But in the process of the funds flowing from the subsidiaries to the head firm, it also exists the risk which caused by the capital repeat computing leading the waste of the funds resource. On the other hand, the capital repeat computing maybe cover the risks of the capital cash insufficiency. At the same time, we must match the capital in insurance group to the risks faced by the group in case of assets value shrinking to bring about the shutdown of the subsidiaries and even the whole insurance group. But because of the complex stock rights structure and many related and corporate business, it is difficult for the insurance group to compute the real capital so that bringing out huge risks for the group operation. Drawn from the Figure II which reveals the net profit proportion of Ping An (Group) Company in year 2011, the main cash of insurance group is consist of the funds from the insurance subsidiary. So the characteristics of insurance group funds are similar to that of insurance subsidiary. Table 1 gives us the risks which insurance, bank, and securities subsidiary face. From the Figure VI, we can see the cash outflow of the insurance subsidiary includes insurance business funds and investment business funds.

---

① $I = \{I_I, I_B, I_S\}$ and $L = \{L_I, L_B, L_S\}$ is the risks conduction function between the group company and the various subsidiaries.

Table I

		Risks				
$L_I(r1,r2,r3,\ldots)$	Credit risk	Market risk	Liquidity risk	Operational risk	Legal risk	Reoutational risk
$LB(r1,r2,r4,\cdots)$	Underwriting risk	Reserve risk	Interest risk	Operational risk	Legal risk	Credit risk
$L_S(r1,r2,r5,\cdots)$	Market risk	Operational risk	Credit risk	Liquidity risk	Legal risk	Systemic risk

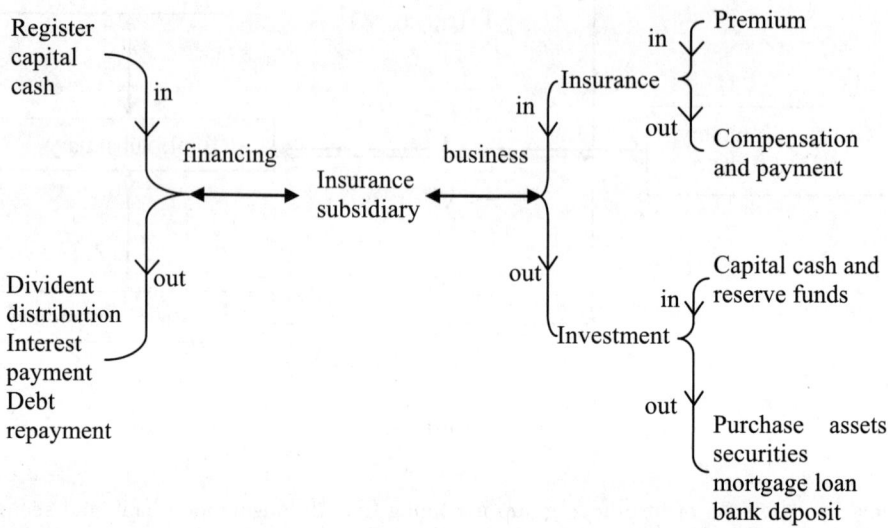

Figure Ⅵ

The point of risks management of the insurance company is matching insurance cash to investment cash. However, it is the synergy that changes the property and function of funds $I = \{I_s, I_B, I_I\}$, of insurance group, leading to mismatching between investment and debts for the insurance subsidiary. And as discussed in the above model, the securities subsidiary need the head firm to provide liquidity when it demands cash and meets liquidity shock q. But the liquidity supply engenders main risks. The first one, equivalently, the head firm uses the cash from the insurance subsidiary premium to invest into the securities subsidiary avoiding regulation in the process of supplying liquidity to the securities subsidiary by the group company. But this means converts the properties and characteristics of the funds and brings about the lack of capital of the insurance subsidiary and the insurance group. And it easily leads to solvency deficiencies if the large claims happen to insurance company. The another one, the securities subsidiary prefers to invest in projects with high – risks and high – returns if it can obtain low – costs funds. Therefore, how to manage the risks occurring and risks conduction with the above model. We should understand that what the amount of investment I is to supply liquidity to the securities subsidiary guaranteeing the maximum of the net profits value of the securities. When the securities subsidiary need the liquidity from the group corporation, the head firm should consider the possible liquidity shock q in the future and the scale of the project which the securities subsidiary will invest in. Known from the model, the optimal amount of the investment is $I_s = I^* = \dfrac{1}{F(q^*)(q^* - q_0)} A$, and the best scale of the project at the beginning with the liquidity shock q^* (11) which can be covered by the liquidity amount $q^* I$.

IV. The Endogenous Supply of Liquidity From Subsidiaries in Insurance Group

The head firm may be unable to invest to the securities subsidiary with cash for the lack of the cash of the group company or any other plans. So the group company may require other subsidiaries to support it to suffer the liquidity shock or the securities subsidiary would like to ask other subsidiaries belong to insurance group for help by itself. In practice, when the securities subsidiary faces liquidity demand, it is usually provided by bank subsidiary. And its form is usually mortgage securities loan guaranteed by the head firm. Therefore we embed the section III model in a general equilibrium framework to study in detail the endogenous supply of liquidity among the subsidiaries. So firstly we assume that there is no cash from the group corporation. As is discussed in the section II (also demonstrated in the Figure V), with no cash, we are going to study the subsidiaries can be financed by market instruments such as additional claims at date 1 or stakes in other subsidiaries. In this section, we assume that the q is self-reliant, that is, there is no aggregate uncertainty. $F(q)$ is served as the probability that the securities subsidiary faces the liquidity shock below q and the realized fraction of subsidiaries with liquidity shock below q. So the securities subsidiary liquidity need

$$N(q) \equiv I \int_0^{q^*} qf(q) dq \quad (16)$$

In Section II, we will discuss the liquidity among the subsidiaries with markets instruments in that insurance group is equivalent to a financial market, especially for the listed insurance group as a whole.

At the beginning, let us see how much the securities subsidiary can obtain by selling their new securities at date 1 to meet their liquidity shortage. It is $p_H(R - \alpha B/\Box p)I = q_0 I$ that the securities market value enables the company to continue and also reflects a minimum stake $R_b I$ as an inside claim. We set up S as the value of the market portfolio at date, which is identified. The securities corporation could continue with $q \leqslant q^*$. $F(q^*)$ represents the securities subsidiary continue probability. Then the total value of external claims is

$$V = F(q^*) q_0 I \quad (17)$$

Due to credit line, the value S should be

$$S = V - N = [F(q^*) q_0 - \int_0^{q^*} qf(q) dq] I = I - A > 0 \quad (18)$$

At date 1, the securities subsidiary can stand liquidity shock when

$$qI \leqslant q_0 I + S \quad (19)$$

If $qI = q^* I$, we must have

$$q^* + \int_0^{q^*} qf(q) dq < [1 + F(q^*)] q_0 \quad (20)$$

Insurance group forms an economy – wide conglomerate pooling several subsidiaries together. If insurance group follows the second – best program, each independent subsidiary continue if and if only $q \leqslant q^*$. The securities subsidiary has to raise N (reveal in [16]) to offer the liquidity demand. Since $F(q^*)q_0I - N = S$, which $S > 0$, the securities subsidiary can obtain the needed cash to set the second – best policy to effect. In the insurance group, which is equivalent to a small capital market, one of the realized ways to cover the liquidity demand of the securities subsidiary is that it can apply mortgage stock loan to the bank subsidiary within the guarantee by the head firm. In other words, the securities subsidiary mortgages their stock with the market value of S to the bank subsidiary, and acquires low – interest loans L from the bank subsidiary. We assume that γ is the mortgaged loan pledge rate. Financial regulator usually requests the γ must be below 60 percent.

$$L = \gamma S = \gamma(V - D) = \gamma[F(q^*)q_0 - \int_0^{q^*} qf(q)dq]I \qquad (21)$$

C. Risk conduction and liquidity management between various subsidiaries.

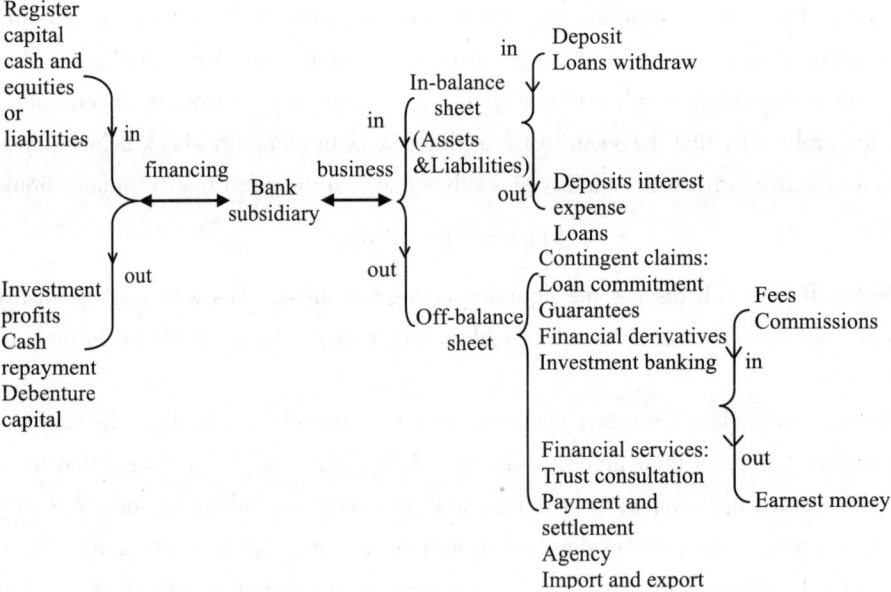

Figure Ⅶ

The bank subsidiary plays a key role in the liquidity supply when other subsidiaries occur liquidity shortage and shock as a intermediation in the insurance group. As can be seen from the follow Figure Ⅶ, the cash inflow of the bank subsidiary contains register capital cash and equities or liabilities, deposit and loans withdraw, and different kinds of business fees and commissions. On the other hand, we also know the outflow including loans and investment as listed in the Figure Ⅶ. However, the function and characteristics of cash inflow to the bank subsidiary have been changed in the insurance group, an economy conglomerate. Bank company should remain high liquidity to pay for deposits anytime, so it must invest in short – term and stable and high – liquidity projects. In the insurance group, the insurance subsidiary offer funds for the bank subsidiary. So with the stable and a great number of premium and reserve, the bank subsidiary is able to invest high‑returns and high‑risks projects for the expectation of high profits without restraints. Therefore, the amount L'_1 (shown in the Figure IV_2) flowing to the bank subsidiary from the insurance subsidiary includes more and higher risks than the cash flow in common bank company. At the same time, the quondam properties and characteristics of L_1' are also converted. On the other hand, it is unfrequent that the bank securities subsidiary supply liquidity to the insurance securities. If this happens, it implies bad news. The liquidity is structural. The liquidity shortage of the insurance subsidiary reflects the ability of solvency deficiency and the problems of assets structure. The bank subsidiary supply I'_1 (demonstrated in the Figure IV_2) to the liquidity and capital cash shortage of the insurance subsidiary through the head firm not only cover the risks of solvency deficiency, but also changes the terms of the bank subsidiary loans from short‑term to long‑term.

Then we can understand that how the cash inflow and outflow in the securities company illustrated in the Figure VIII. From the Figure VIII, the cash flow of the securities subsidiary is consisted of the financing cash and cash of the four prime business. As we all known, the cash inflow in the securities subsidiary not only increase the capital, but also provides liquidity for its business development, which is the different from the insurance subsidiary and the bank subsidiary. The risks of the securities subsidiary business, especially the self‑business and the securities underwriting, are more than other finance sectors and the cash of that is not stable. The amount of the securities subsidiary funds may be up and down with the high‑risk and high‑returns business and unstable cash and the affects of the economy cyclical fluctuation. $I'_S(r'_1, r'_2, r'_3, \cdots)$ in the Figure IV_2 stands for the investment function of the risks from the bank subsidiary to the securities subsidiary. When the securities subsidiary gains the liquidity supplied by the bank subsidiary, the process means the funds of the bank subsidiary withstand higher risks and less returns. Although the short‑term and high liquidity properties of bank funds, the characteristics and risks of the liquidity by the function of $I'_S(r'_1, r'_2, r'_3, \cdots)$ from the bank subsidiary to the securities subsidiary in insurance group have been changed to long‑term and high‑risk, once invested in the capital market. But the returns of the low‑interest loan is mismatching with the high risks. Moreover, with low‑cost funds and less limits for the business of securities subsidiary, it will invest in the higher risks projects to obtain more returns. But the risks transmit to the depositors by the function $I'_S(r'_1, r'_2, r'_3, \cdots)$. In insurance group, the commercial bank subsidiary corresponds to the currency market and the securities subsidiary operates in the capital market. According to the theory of conflicts of interest, there are four asymmetries in the incorporation of the money market and capital market including timing asymmetry, earning asymmetry, risk asymmetry and information asymmetry. This is also the reason why the funds the bank invest into the securities subsidiary could not be exceeded its own capital. But the risk conduction function $L'_S(r_1, r_2, r_3, \cdots)$ in the Figure IV_2 illustrates that the risks of the securities subsidiary will affect the funds security and business of the bank securities subsidiary. One of the financing ways between the bank and securities subsidiaries is mortgaged stock loans discussed in the above model in Section IV. With the model, we assume that the market price of the mortgaged stock loan rate is S, the amount of the mortgaged stock is N and P represents the average closing price of the stock in the seven market days before. That is,

$$S_M = N^* P \tag{22}$$

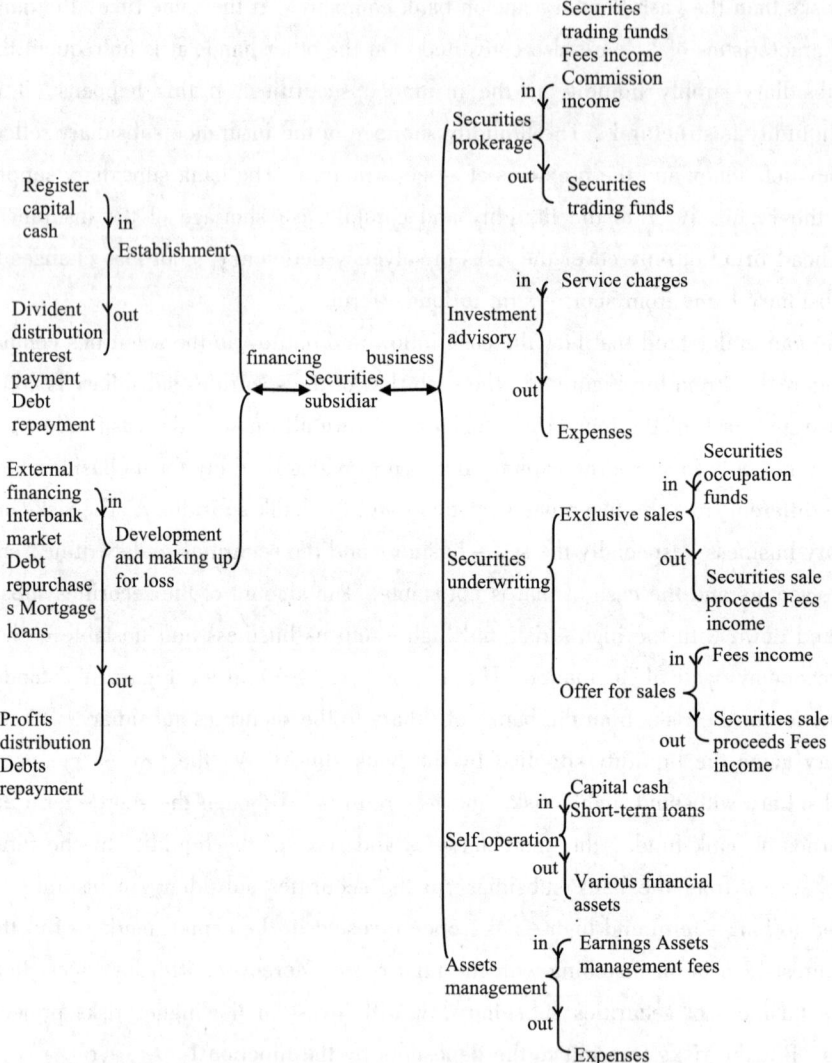

Figure VIII

Because there may be some bad information in the marker for consumers and investors about the liquidity shortage and operations of the securities subsidiary, even the insurance group, if the group-company require the others to supply liquidity to the securities subsidiary. So sometimes the stock of the securities subsidiary would not be viewed well. So,

$$S_M \leq S \tag{23}$$

It is possible that the securities subsidiary cannot withstand the liquidity shock q^*, even if the bank subsidiary offer it stock mortgaged loans. The situation discussed in Section Ⅳ generates some risks. That is, it conveys the lack of the head firm capital to the market and weakens the whole insurance group capital sufficient. This means raises the insurance subsidiary financial leverage, the ability to pay for the debts makes the subsidiaries withstand large pressure and there is no protection from the debts financing. From the view of the bank subsidiary, this funds are used to cover the liquidity shock and expenses, which in fact, to make up for the investment deficit, are not to satisfy regular business development. The another solution is that the insurance subsidiary and bank subsidiary buy the low-liquidity assets (low-quality assets) from the securities subsidiary at high price by the requirement of the head firm. In fact, it is the typical transmission of the benefits that precisely assets replacement, which the high-liquidity and high-quality assets are replaced of the low-liquidity and low-quality assets. It couldn't be done in normal market transaction but could realized if and only if in the insurance group. The process damage the structure of the bank subsidiary and the insurance subsidiary assets. The amount is so huge that destroy the matching between the assets and debts to face more stress to payoff of other assets projects. ①

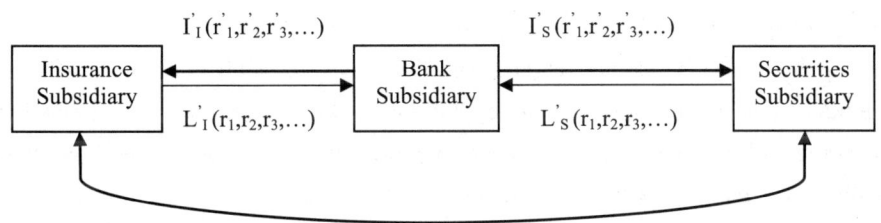

Figure Ⅳ$_2$

Ⅵ. Summary and Conclusion

The characteristics, properties, risks, risks conduction, liquidity management operation of an insurance conglomerate are different from the single firm. On the basis of the liquidity supply and demand and the cash flow in the insurance group, we study the risks, the risks transmission and liquidity management in the group. We have concluded those results as follow in our analysis.

A insurance group must include commercial bank subsidiary and insurance must be the main business. In insurance group, commercial bank serves as an intermediation, which links the insurance market, capital market and currency market to take advantage of synergy. Most funds of insurance group come from the insurance subsidiary, so the characteristics and properties of the group company are similar to that of the insurance subsidiary. And the properties and characteristics of the cash flow are decided by the properties and function of the financial institutions. There are big difference in the term structure, risks characteristics and fluctuation of the cash. This is the basic and premise for the synergy of the insurance group. But at the same time, they are the main risks resource. And we analyze the risks conduction similarly to the series and parallel electric circuits.

---

① I' = {I'$_S$, I'$_B$} and L' = {L'$_S$, L'$_B$} is the risks conduction function between the subsidiaries.

With the model, we obtain the optimism first-best program and second-best program. The maximum amount of the liquidity supplied from the head firm to the subsidiaries. But in practice, because of complex circumstance, the amount of the investment should be below the optimal value. The liquidity supplied by the group company is made up of two parts, one for the initial scale o f the project and the other part for covering the liquidity shock q* and expenses. This the good basement for our liquidity management in insurance group. Then we discuss the detail risks and risks transmission with the model and conduction path. We should know that the risks conduction is a double-bladed sword. The good risks management can decrease the risks in the process of the transmission but the bad quality of the path can increase the risks. So risks management on the conduction and liquidity management is very important for the insurance group. The existence of risks in insurance group is objective and inevitable with the corporate and related business within insurance group, the series and parallel circuits of cash flow, internal source and shared information. Moreover, the liquidity demand of the subsidiaries and the liquidity supplied by the group company and other subsidiaries is a essential process for the insurance group. Because this is not only the embody of the synergy of the whole insurance group, but also the root and path of the risks conduction. Even worse, this liquidity shortage and shock may easily lead to the crisis of insurance group.

However, this paper is not perfect and something may be studied further and more deeply. Firstly, the funds from the insurance subsidiary and the bank subsidiary solve the problem of liquidity of the securities subsidiary must be transitory, otherwise they would affect the liquidity of the both other subsidiaries. Timing is a key consideration for the risks and risks transmission of the insurance group, but in this paper, it has not been studied in detail. It is exactly needing to be studied in the future. Secondly, as shown in the Figure IX, it is said that the financial conglomerate is so common today rather than views the whole economy organization as a whole one.

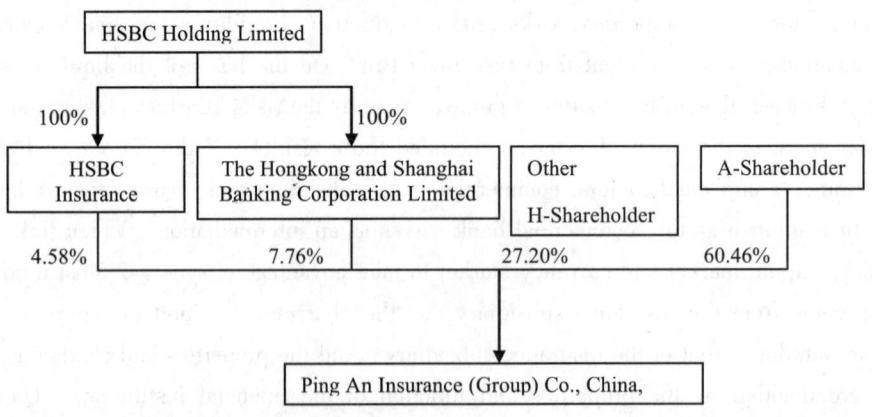

Figure IX

As we setting the above example of Ping An Insurance(Group)Co.,China, LTD, we draw that other companies and other groups may have some percentage of the stock of financial group such as the insurance group. So this paper just study the liquidity and risks conduction in insurance group as a whole. But external sectors may affect the insurance ,too. We also debt the risks transmission between the insurance group and the other financial sectors due to the structure of the stock rights. Therefore it is also significant for us to discuss the problem of the risks conduction and liquidity management with the stock shares outside the insurance group.

References

1. Bengt Hlmstrom , Moral Hazard and Observability, The Bell Journal of Economics, Vol. 10, No. 1 (Spring, 1979), pp. 74 – 91

2. Bengt Holmstrm and Jean Tirole, LAPM: A Liquidity – Based Asset Pricing Model, *The Journal of Finance*, Vol. 56, No. 5 (Oct. , 2001), pp. 1837 – 1867

3. Bengt Holmstrm and Jean Tirole, Private and Public Supply of Liquidity, *Journal of Political Economy*, Vol. 106, No. 1 (February 1998), pp. 1 – 40

4. Bengt Holmstrm and Jean Tirole, Liquidity and Risk Management ,*Journal of Money, Credit and Banking*, Vol. 32, No. 3, Part 1 (Aug. , 2000), pp. 295 – 319

5. Banerjee, Abhijit V. , and Maskin, Eric S. "A Walrasian Theory of Money and Barter."*Q. J. E.* 111 (November 1996): 955 – 1005.

6. Berglof, Erik, and von Thadden, Ernst – Ludwig. "Short – Term versus Long – Term Interests: Capital Structure with Multiple Investors." *Q. J. E.* 109 (November 1994): 1055 – 84.

7. Bernanke, Ben; Gertler, Mark; and Gilchrist, Simon. "The Financial Accelerator and the Flight to Quality." *Working Paper no.* 4789. Cambridge,Mass. : NBER, July 1994.

8. Bewley, Truman. "The Optimum Quantity of Money." In Models of Monetary Economies, edited by John H. Kareken and Neil Wallace. Minneapolis: Fed.

9. Reserve Bank, 1980.

10. Bhattacharya, Sudipto, and Gale, Douglas. "Preference Shocks, Liquidity, and Central Bank Policy." In New Approaches to Monetary Economics, edited by William A. Barnett and Kenneth J. Singleton. Cambridge: Cambridge Univ. Press, 1987.

11. Boot, Arnoud W. A. ; Thakor, Anjan V. ; and Udell, Gregory F. "Credible Commitments, Contract Enforcement Problems and Banks: Intermediation as Credibility Assurance." J. Banking and Finance 15 (June 1991): 605 – 32.

12. Menghua, Zhao ,Insurance (financial) Research Group's Financial Regulation – Based on Cash Flow Analysis of the Characteristics and Risk ,2009

13. Zhuyong Li , Qingsong Wang, and Xiaoquan Jin , The Study of Insurance Financial Group Economic Capital Approach—Based on Risk Management of the Comprehensive Management of the Situation ,*China Academic Journal Electronic Publishing House*,2012

14. Zhuyong Li and Qingsong Wang , The Study of Insurance Group's Overall Financial risk Management System Construction—Based on the Group's Strategic Management and Control Type, *China Academic Journal Electronic Publishing House*,2008

15. Zhuyong Li and Qingsong Wang , Insurance Group management for matching assets with liabilities—Risk Management under Insurance comprehensive Operations. *China Academic Journal Electronic Publishing House*,2012

16. Zhang Zijuan , Research on Risk Conduction Mechanism and Control Countermeasure of Financial Holding Company, 2008

An Empirical Investigation of Impact Factors for the Profit Performance of Regional Life Insurance Market of China[1]

Xiao Wei[2] Jun Yang[3]

Abstract: This paper tests the applicability of the structure – conduct – performance (SCP) hypothesis in the life insurance market of different provinces in China. Due to several factors, such as economy, policy, population, and geography, different provinces in China have formed diversified markets. As a result, the insurance companies in different provinces show an apparent difference in the performance of making profit. We apply a model based on the SCP hypothesis and employ a panel data regression model which includes data of 30 provinces and municipalities over the time period of 2005 to 2011. The purpose of this paper is to analysis the factors that influence the performance of making profit for life insurance companies and the relation of market structure and performance in China. The results reveal that the SCP hypothesis is not supported in the life insurance market of China. The life insurance market in China is highly centralized, while the high degree of concentration is not the consequence of competition but caused by some politic reasons. Although the SCP Hypothesis is not supported, there are several factors that influence the performance of making profit for life insurance companies in different provinces: the logarithmic form of GDP, one – year deposit interest rate of central bank, the average price earnings ratios of Shanghai Composite Index as well as the dummy variable for policy reform.

Key words: Structure – Conduct – Performance Hypothesis, Market Structure, Profit Analysis, Impact Factors, China life insurance market.

1. Introduction

1.1 Research Background and Motivation

The structure – conduct – performance (SCP) hypothesis is the main theoretical framework in the industrial organization theory, and it is mainly applied to analyze the relationships shared by the market structure, enterprise conduct and performance. The industrial organization theory is included

---

[1] 18th Asia – Pacific Risk and Insurance Association Annual Conference, Moscow, 2014.
[2] Xiao Wei is an associate professor of China Institute for Actuarial Science, Central University of Finance and Economics;
[3] Jun Yang is a graduate student of Central University of Finance and Economics. The address is Central University of Finance and Economics, 39 South College Road, Haidian District, 100081 Beijing, China, and email address is yjtthxq@163.com.

in the applied economic theory. It is generated in the 1930's and gradually developed. The main idea of this theory is applying microeconomic theory to analyze the relationships of competition as well as monopoly among the market, industry and enterprises. Since generated, the SCP hypothesis has gained much attention from international scholars, and it has been applied in insurance market. However, using this theory to analyze the relation of insurance market structure and performance in China is still under development, and there are still many valuable researches to do.

As the world's biggest developing country, China has experienced a rapid development in the life insurance industry in recent decades. However, in the progress of this rapid development, many problems have been exposed. One of the most important problems is that the low degree of performance of making profit for life insurance companies is not consistent with the rapid development. Another important problem is that the life insurance market has some apparent regional characteristics that the degree of development of life insurance companies is quite different from province to province. This significant difference may result from several impact factors, such as economy, policy, population, geography and so on. We want to find the factors that causing this phenomenon. Therefore, the purpose of this paper is to analyze the impact factors for the performance of making profit, especially to check the relation of market structure and performance in insurance market of China from the perspective of industry organization theory. If there exists such a logical relation, then we can improve the performance of life insurance companies in China by optimizing the market structure. Also we can explain the significance difference among provinces by analyzing the impact factors. Although there is some research about the validity of SCP hypothesis, but almost all using data of some companies or some provinces, while the analysis of the effects of the whole market structure on the performance is neglected. Therefore we will fill this gap and test the validity of the SCP hypothesis in the range of whole China systematically with all the provinces.

To test the validity of SCP hypothesis systematically and find out the impact factors for the performance of making profit of regional insurance market in China, we employ a panel data including records of all the life insurance companies in 30 provinces and municipalities in China[1] from 2005 to 2011. The result shows that the SCP hypothesis is not supported in the life insurance market of China. The life insurance market in China is highly centralized but it is not the consequence of competition. The performance of making profit for life insurance companies has an obvious regional character and it is significant influenced by several factors.

1.2 Literature Review

The development of the SCP hypothesis can be summarized as two main stages: one is the traditional industrial organization theory that is supported by researchers of the Harvard school, Chicago school, Neo-Austrian school, etc. The other one is the new industrial organization theory generated after the 1970s. As the representatives of the Harvard school, Bain (1951)[2] completely and sys-

---

[1] We don't include Hong Kong, Taiwan and Macao because of the characteristic which come from some politic reasons in those markets. Besides we exclude Tibet because of the incompleteness of the data.

[2] See Bain, J. S. (1951), Relation of Profit Rate to Industry Concentration: American Manufacturing, 1936–1940.

tematically discussed the theoretical frame of the industrial organization theory for the first time and put forward three basic concepts of the modern industrial organization theory: market structure, conduct and performance. The Harvard school and Chicago school hold different opinions on the relationship of market structure, conduct and performance. The Harvard school emphasize the effect of market structure on conduct and performance, and conclude that there exists a one – way causal relationship of the structure, conduct and performance. The internal mechanism is that the degree of market concentration determines the conduct of enterprises, and the latter determines the performance of enterprises. The representatives of the Chicago school are Stigler, Demset and Brozen. They believe that the performance of enterprise itself plays the crucial role: different performance of enterprises has formed the various market structures and it is concluded as the Efficient – structure (ES) hypothesis[1]. The enterprises with highly efficient performance can constantly enlarge their market share, and eventually lead to the market structure of high degree of concentration. Therefore, no matter the Harvard school or the Chicago school, they both regard the SCP hypothesis as the main theoretical framework, and the divergence is that they review the causal relationship between S, C and P differently.

In the aspect of empirical researches, both international and domestic literatures have enlightened our idea and methodology. Choi and Weiss (2005)[2] analyzed the relationships of structure, conduct and performance in the US property – liability insurance market and they found support for the ES hypothesis of the Chicago school. They believed that the regulation agency should pay more attention to the performance of enterprises instead of the market structure. Pope and Ma (2008)[3] tested the applicability of the SCP hypothesis in the international non – life insurance sector. They found that the expectations associated with the SCP hypothesis were supported when the level of liberalization were low. However, if the markets were highly liberalized, the presence of foreign competitors significantly changed the dynamics of nonlife insurance markets.

In the domestic literatures, Chen (2007) analyzed the relationship between market structure and performance in insurance market, both life insurance market and property insurance market using data of 15 life insurance companies and 14 property insurance companies which have the biggest market shares in the time period from 2002 to 2005. She drawn the conclusions that the insurance markets in China were a high monopoly markets, and the high degree of concentration and low efficiency of performance were the main characteristics of the industries. Thus the SCP hypothesis was not supported in both life and property insurance market in China. Because of some political factors, the ES hypothesis was not supported either. Wang (2007) also proved that neither the SCP hypothe-

---

[1] As Nat Pope and Yu – Luen Ma (2008) suggested the ES hypothesis had enjoyed significant support in the banking literature and to a lesser degree in the insurance literature. Thus, we limit our discussion in this article to test the SCP hypothesis but would further investigate the ES hypothesis in the later research.

[2] Choi, P. and M. Weiss (2005), An empirical Investment of Market Structure, Efficiency, and performance in Property – Liability Insurance.

[3] Nat, Pope and Yu – Luen, Ma (2008), The Market Structure: Performance Relationship in the International Insurance Sector.

sis nor the ES hypothesis was supported in the insurance market of China applying data of 22 companies with the biggest market shares in the time period from 1999 to 2004. Zhong (2009) tested the applicability of the SCP hypothesis in the life insurance market of China including data of all the life insurance companies in 2006 and data of three insurance companies in the time period from 1998 to 2007. The first conclusion he got was that life insurance market of China was classified into the highest degree of monopoly market, and it was the high degree of monopoly market that caused the imbalance of development in different provinces in China. Secondly, the relation between market structure and performance was a two – way interactive relationship, and the core of this relation was the market structure. Finally, from the macro level, market structure was the main factor that influenced the public performance in life insurance market in China; from the micro level, the ES hypothesis was supported in China's life insurance market. The above articles focus on the analysis for several insurance companies in the range of whole country; there are no researches consider the case with all provinces in China. Therefore, we fill the gap of in this area.

The rest of this paper is organized as follows. We introduce the basic model in SCP hypothesis and explain the variables in this paper in section 2. Section 3 is about the data and empirical model, and section 4 is the result of empirical analysis. At last, we summarize this paper in section 5.

2. Variable Declaration

The equation below is the basic model which mainly used in the empirical study of industry organization theory. The model was introduced by Berger (1995)[①] and can be applied to test both the SCP hypothesis and ES hypothesis, which is given as follows:

$$\prod_i = f(CONC_n, MS_i, X-EFF_i, S-EFF_i, Z_i) + v_i \qquad (1)$$

Where $\prod_i$ is the dependent variable representing the performance and usually measured by return on asset (ROA), return on equity (ROE), or price, etc. $CONC_n$ is an index measures the degree of market concentration. MS_i stands for the market share of each market participant. $X-EFF_i$ and $S-EFF_i$ are efficient variables, and the former one is the efficient variable which is influenced by management, techniques and such factors of an enterprise, and the latter one is determined by the scale of the enterprise. Z_i represents a group of control variables related to the market, such as the statue of market demands, the operation cost, the barriers to entry the market, etc. To test the SCP hypothesis analysis in the international insurance market, the paper of Pope and Ma (2008) proposed an adapted version based on model (1). They use the profit margin, which is proposed by Cowling and Waterson (1976)[②], as a new variable for measuring the performance of insurance companies. The profit margin is defined as:

$$PROFIT = \frac{premiums - Losses - Expenses + Investment}{premiums}$$

[①] Berger, A. N. (1995), The Profit – Structure relationship in banking: Test of Market – Power and Efficient – Structure Hypotheses.

[②] See Cowling, k. and M. Waterson (1976), Price – Cost Margins and Market Structure for detailed explanation.

$$= 1 - loss\ ratio - \exp ense\ ratio + return\ on\ investment \tag{2}$$

Pope and Ma (2008) used the (1 – loss ratio) to measure the profit since lack of data for expense ratio and return on investment. Besides, they added several control variables: degree of liberal, level of regulation, threat of substitution, economic factor and book of business to the basic model and delete the variable of MS for market share of each market participant for their model is market based but not companies based. Based on the model of Pope and Ma (2008) and the available data of Chinese case, we delete the variable representing the threat of substitution. And since we focus on life insurance companies, the variable for books of business is deleted as well. Since the whole insurance market in China is under the same regulation, we will not include this part. Meanwhile we add the variable of the population structure for representing the demand of life insurance, as well as the investment control variables, which we think it might have effect on the profit of life insurance market. Therefore we will use the profit margin as the dependent variable for measuring the performance and use Herfindahl – Hirschman Index, Degree of Liberal, Economy, Population Structure, Investment control variables and a dummy variable for policy as the independent variables. The detail explanation of the variables is given as follows.

2.1 PROFIT: Performance of making profit

Following Pope and Ma(2008), we also use the profit margin for measuring the performance of the life insurance companies. Since we can have the data for the expenses and investment, we will include the expenses and investment part in the calculation of the profit margin. Here we give the definition of the dependent variable: profit margin for the life insurance company and it is calculated as follows:

$$profit = \frac{premiums - Losses - Expenses + Investment}{premiums} \tag{3}$$
$$= 1 - loss\ ratio - \exp ense\ ratio + return\ on\ investment$$

We calculate the profit margin for each life insurance company in every regional market, and apply the weighted mean for measuring the profit of each market. The reason for using weighted mean is that the life insurance companies with different premium incomes contribute differently to the whole market profit margin. The weight we use is calculated as following:

$$weight = \frac{premium\ income\ of\ each\ life\ insurance}{Total\ premium\ income\ of\ all\ life\ insurance\ companies} \tag{4}$$

2.2 Herfindahl – Hirschman Index (HHI): Degree of market concentration

The degree of market concentration is the fundamental factor of the market structure, and it reflects the degree of competition and monopoly of the market. There are several commonly used indicators, such as the concentration ration (CR), HHI, Lorenz curve, etc. In this paper, we choose HHI to reflect the market structure as it is a good index to measure the market concentration and usually adopted by the government department and economists. HHI is calculated as follows:

$$HHI = \sum_{i=1}^{N}\left(\frac{X_i}{X}\right)^2 = \sum_{i=1}^{N} S_i^2,\ S_i = \frac{X_i}{\sum_{i=1}^{n} X_i} \tag{5}$$

Where X_i stands for premium income for each life insurance company of each province; N[①] stands for the number of all life insurance companies of each market. S_i means the premium income share of each life insurance company. HHI varies from 0 to 1, and the bigger the index is, the deeper the degree of concentration and monopoly is.

2.3 Foreign competitors (FC): Degree of liberal

As a factor of reflecting the degree of liberal of the market, Pope and Ma (2003) found that the presence of foreign competitors significantly influences the performance of insurance market. In China, although the foreign life insurance companies showed poor performance compared to local companies in the past ten years, they had a certain degree of impact on the domestic market. Therefore, we introduce an independent variable which is measured by the proportion of premium income earned by foreign competitors (full foreign invested insurance companies) to the total premium income of each market and it is calculated as follows:

$$FC = \frac{Premium\ income\ of\ foreign\ life\ insurance\ companies}{total\ premium\ imcome\ of\ all\ life\ insurance\ companies} \quad (6)$$

2.4 Economy (ECON)

Economy is one of the most important factors which determines the consumption capacity and insurance demand of people. In general, the more developed the economy of a region is, the greater the life insurance demand. In this paper, we choose the logarithmic form of GDP (Econ) to measure this variable. The reason of taking the logarithmic form is to normalize the data and make the explanation more meaningful.

2.5 Population Structure (PS)

As we know, China has stepped into the aging society, and the burden of the aging population will continue to increase in the following decades. People of old age will face the risk of losing the income resource, which stimulates the demand for life insurance in some degree. Therefore, in this paper, we add a variable which measuring the structure of population (PS), which can be considered as the source of demand for the life insurance. The computation of this variable is as follows:

$$Population = \frac{Population\ over\ the\ age\ of\ 65}{Total\ population} \quad (7)$$

2.6 Deposit Rate (DI) and Investment Return Rate (IRR)

A significant portion of profits in life insurance companies comes from the investment, especially the long-term fund of life insurance companies which lead to the investment income accounts for a large part of their total profit. In China, the main channels for insurance fund to invest are stock market and bond market. Also bank deposit is another method for life insurance companies to deal with their premium incomes. Therefore the control variables which measure the return rate of stock market, bond market as well as bank deposit should be included in the model. But the return rate of bond market has strong correlation with the return rate of the bank deposit, so we do not include it in

---

① Herfindahl – Hirschman Index calculates 50 competitors with the largest market share. If the number of competitors in the market is less than 50, then N is the number of the actual competitors.

the model. Therefore we use one-year deposit interest rate of central bank and the average price earnings ratios of Shanghai Composite Index to measure return rate of deposit and investment respectively.

2.7 Dummy Variable (DUM): Policy Reform

In 2006, the China's Ministry of Finance promulgated The New Accounting Standard[①], and the range of application covers insurance industry. According to the new standards, some important accounting issues have been changed, such as the confirmation of premium incomes. Therefore we introduce a dummy variable representing policy reform for the consideration that the New Accounting standards may have influence on the performance of making profit of life insurance companies. We set it equals to 0 for the year 2005 and 2006, while it equals to 1 after 2006.

3. Data and Empirical Methodology

The data we have are from various resources. The data of premium, losses, expenses, investment income are obtained from the website of insurance regulation commission in each province and Insurance Statistic Yearbook. We acquire the population data from the Demographic Yearbook. The data of GDP is gained from the website of National Bureau of Statistics. And the return rate related data comes from some relevant articles. We have the data of 30 provinces and municipalities over the time period from 2005 to 2011. For some missing data, we use the interpolation method to generate them. In the stage of data preprocessing and analysis, we make the descriptive statistics of the data. There are total 210 observations and the descriptive statistically analysis of the original panel data is showed in Table 1 below.

Table 1 Descriptive Statistic of original panel data

	PROFIT	HHI	FC	ECON	PS	DI	IRR
Mean	-0.022707	0.282517	0.027185	8.961524	0.090781	0.027129	0.267714
Median	0.061200	0.258400	0.000400	9.052700	0.089000	0.025200	0.216000
Maximum	0.351900	0.694000	0.297900	10.88200	0.144000	0.035000	0.592000
Minimum	-3.481100	0.091200	0.000000	6.297700	0.053000	0.022500	0.134000
Observations	210	210	210	210	210	210	210
Cross sections	30	30	30	30	30	30	30

[①] The New Accounting Standards of China was forced to be executed by all the public companies and encouraged to be executed by other enterprises. It is noteworthy that The New Accounting Standards basically realized the convergence with International Financial Reporting Standards.

An Empirical Investigation of Impact Factors for the Profit Performance of Regional Life Insurance Market of China

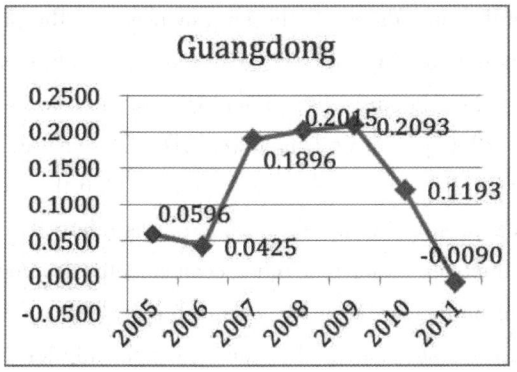
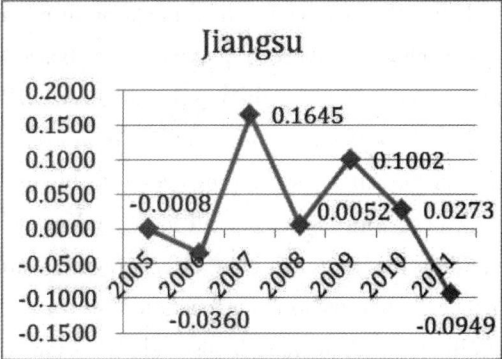
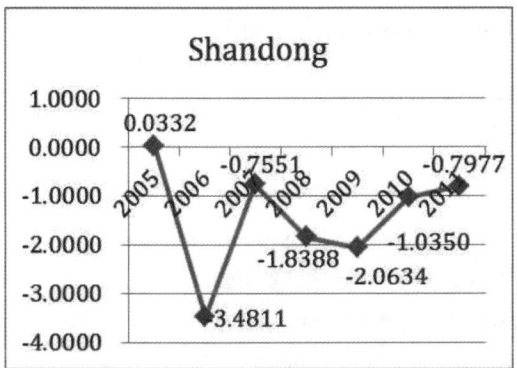
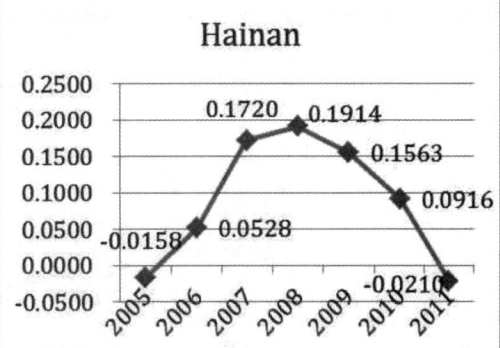
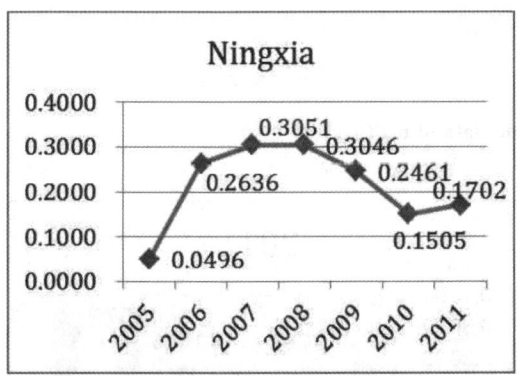
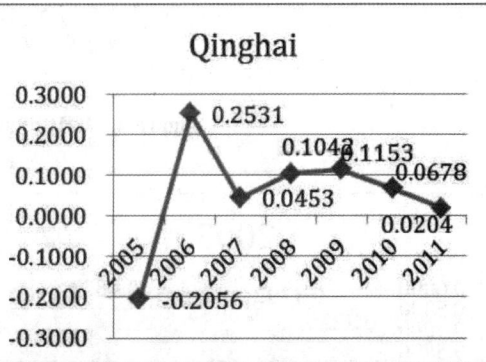

Figure 1   Weighted Average Profit Margin dynamic data of 6 Provinces

All the provinces from 2005 to 2011, as we can see, the value of profits margin for some provinces ranges from negative value to positive value, and the values are quite different from province to province, as well as the tendency during the study period. The largest value of profit margin from 2005 to 2011 among 30 provinces and municipalities is that of Xinjiang province with 35.19% in 2007, while the smallest value is that of Shandong province with −348.11% in 2006. Besides, the largest average value of profit margin from 2005 to 2011 is that of Ningxia province with 21.28%, while the smallest average value is that of Shandong province with −141.97%.

Figure 1 above is weighted mean profit margin dynamic data of 6 chosen provinces and the principles of choosing those 6 provinces are based on the ranking of GDP: Guangdong, Jiangsu and Shandong provinces are the top 3 of highest GDP, while Hainan, Ningxia and Qinghai are the last 3 in GDP. As we can see in Figure1, from 2005 to 2006 provinces with lower GDP all show an increase of the value, while provinces with higher GDP all show a decrease. Also after 2006 the value of provinces with lower GDP all have tendency of decreasing and the decreasing rate is relatively stable, while the value of other three provinces are fluctuate. Consider other economically developed provinces, contrary to our expectation, the value of profit margin in some other big provinces, such as Beijing and Shanghai, is also relatively low and fluctuate compared to some economically less developed provinces. Therefore, we speculate that there exists a relation between the degree of performance and degree of economic development and the correlation is negative.

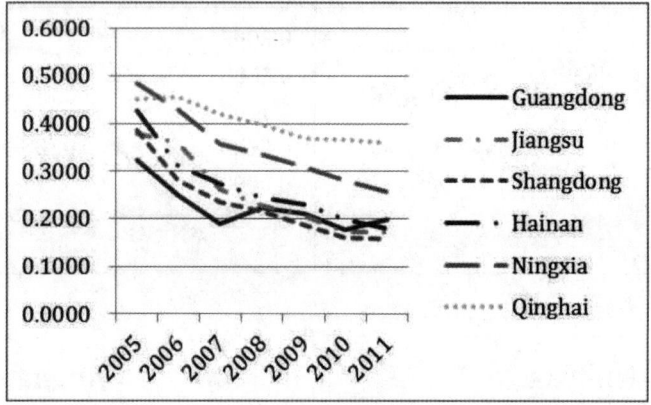

Figure 2   HHI dynamic data of 6 Provinces

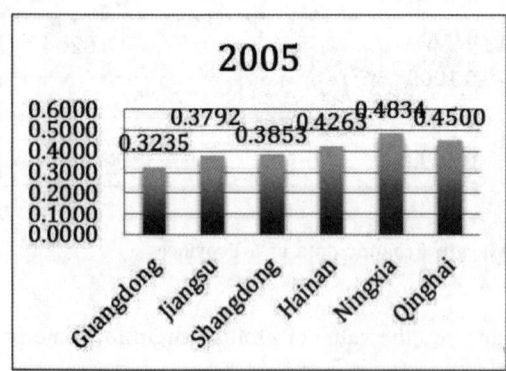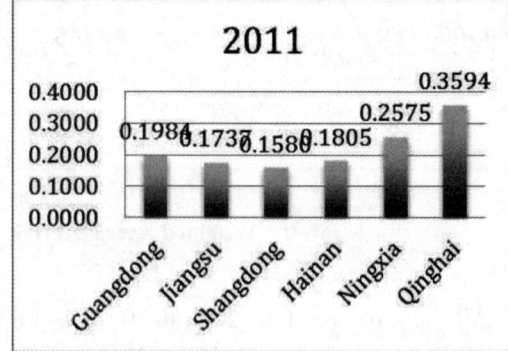

Figure 4   Column charts of HHI for 6 provinces

As the most important independent variable, from Table1 and Figure2 we can see that the values of HHI continue to decline during the time period from 2005 to 2011 for almost all the provinces. The greatest value of HHI from 2005 to 2011 is 69.40% of Inner Mongolia and the smallest

An Empirical Investigation of Impact Factors for the Profit Performance of Regional Life Insurance Market of China

mean is 9.12% of Beijing. Although the decline trend is similar, the value of HHI for provinces is quite different. As we can see in Figure3, the value of Qinghai province in 2011 is even greater than that of Guangdong province in 2005. According to the criterion set by Department of Justice of United State to judge the degree of concentration for a certain industry, the life insurance markets of China are classified into high oligopolistic type II and low oligopoly type I①. The data show that the life insurance market of China is highly centralized, especially in the economically less developed provinces. Also the degree of concentration varies from province to province, and the difference is quite big which means obvious difference exists among market structure of life insurance for different provinces.

From Table1, we can also get the information that the variable FC, the degree of liberal is generally low and also varies from province to province. There are 19 provinces with 0 premium income earned by foreign companies in 2005, and 11 provinces with 0 premium income earned by foreign companies in 2011. The provinces without foreign life insurance companies are generally distributed in the Midwest and Southwest. These provinces have not been opened to foreign insurance companies for as long as some southeast provinces have, and the markets of these provinces seem have less attraction to foreign investment. In conclusion, the life insurance of regional market in China is highly centralized and lowly liberally, especially in the economically less developed provinces.

The Model in this paper can be written as follows:

$$PROFIT_{p,t} = \alpha_p + \beta_1 (HHI)_{p,t} + \beta_2 (FC)_{p,t} + \beta_3 (ECON)_{p,t} + \beta_4 (PS)_{p,t} \\ + \beta_5 (DR)_t + \beta_6 (IRR)_t + \beta_7 (DUM)_t + C + \varepsilon_{p,t} \quad (8)$$

Where $PROFIT_{p,t}$ is the profit of companies of province p at year t as defined in (3), HHI stands for the concentration rate of each market; FC is the proportion of premium income earned by foreign life insurance companies to the total premium income earned by all life insurance companies in each market; ECON is the natural logarithm of GDP for each province; PS measures the proportion of population over 65 years old; DI and IRR are the control variables for return rate of bank deposit and stock market: one - year deposit interest rate of central bank and average price earnings ratios of Shanghai Composite Index respectively.

According to the preliminary analysis and economic common sense, we speculate the relation of variables as shown in Table 2 below:

Table 2   Expected signs of variables

Variable	HHI	FC	ECON	POPULATION	DI	IRR	DUM
PROFIT	+	±	−	±	−	±	+

---

① Department of Justice of United State set the criterion to judge the degree of concentration as: if HHI = 1, the market is classified into high oligopolistic type I; if 0.3 ≤ HHI < 1, the market is classified into high oligopolistic type II; if 0.3 ≤ HHI ≤ 0.18, the market is classified into low oligopoly type I; if 0.1 ≤ HHI ≤ 0.18, the market is classified into low oligopoly type II; if 0.1 ≤ HHI ≤ 0.14, the market is classified into competitive market type I; if HHI ≤ 0.1, the market is classified into competitive market type II.

4. Empirical Results

Before doing regression, several tests of panel data model are taken. First of all, in order to avoid the problem of multi-colinearity, we do the correlation analysis of the independent variables. The results show that the coefficients of independent variables are not statistically significant at 5% level, which indicate that there are no statistically significant relations among them. Secondly, since our data includes both time series data as well as panel data, so we should use the cross-section fixed model theoretically. We do the test of Redundant Fixed Effect, and the result verifies that cross-section fixed model is preferable than pooled model. The results of the empirical analysis are reported in Table 3 below. Besides, since generally there exists heteroscedasticity in cross-section data, therefore we apply cross-section weights method to eliminate it.

The results of the empirical analysis are reported in Table 3 where two models are presented. Model 2 makes the assumption that an AR (1) as a covariance structure of error terms, while Model 1 does not make that assumption. As we see, the value of Durbin-Watson test for model 2 is acceptable which means no autocorrelation exists. Also the coefficient of AR (1) is statistically significant. Therefore, we use the coefficients from Model 2 to illustrate the regression results. The weighted goodness of fit for Model 2 is 0.787278, which means the goodness of fit in this paper is acceptable. The significance of equation is tested by F-statistic and its value is 14.20369 as showed. And the equation is statistically significant at the level of 1%. The significance of coefficient is measured by t-statistic. As we see in table 3 below, variables of ECON, DI, IRR and DUM are statistically significant at the level of 1%.

Table 3 Parameters Estimates from the Cross-section fixed panel data model

Variable	Model 1 Cross-Section Fixed Effect		Model 2 Cross-Section Fixed Effect with AR(1) Error Structure	
	Coefficient	t-Statistic	Coefficient	t-Statistic
Intercept	-0.051901	-0.118760	1.113444***	2.443812
Herfindahl-Hirschman Index	0.189529	1.491035	0.162714	1.302073
Foreign Competitors	0.056256	0.122862	0.019239	0.051711
Economy	0.012588	0.261591	-0.119448***	-2.381890
Population Structure	-0.679732	-0.815680	-1.001310	-1.303958
Deposit Rate	-10.31981***	-7.169824	-7.403488***	-5.065346
Investment Return Rate	0.454037***	8.337788	0.268279***	3.787870
Policy Reform	0.114005***	5.471792	0.151855***	7.010199
AR(1)			-0.257892***	-3.198741
Weighted R-squared	0.723061		0.787278	
Unweighted R-squared	0.537295		0.705395	

续表

Variable	Model 1		Model 2	
	Cross – Section Fixed Effect		Cross – Section Fixed Effect with AR(1) Error Structure	
	Coefficient	t – Statistic	Coefficient	t – Statistic
F – statistic	12.54687		14.20369	
Durbin – Watson stat	2.143853		1.843164	

Note: Cross – section fixed intercepts are omitted from the table. *** indicates statistically significance at 1% level.

As we can see in Table 3, the coefficient of HHI is not statistically significant which means that the degree of concentration has no significant relation with profit, therefore the SCP hypothesis is not supported in the life insurance market of China. We can explain this result that the highly concentration rate of life insurance market in China is not the consequence of competition, but the result of some political reasons and phenomenon left over from the past. Therefore, the highly centralized market structure does not lead to a high profit rate of enterprises.

The coefficient of FC is not statistically significant. Although Pope and Ma (2003) found that when the market is highly liberalized, the presence of foreign competitors significantly influence the domestic market, in this paper, the result show that the presence of foreign competitors has no remarkable impact on the life insurance market of China.

The coefficient of ECON is statistically significant and the coefficient is negative. The result is consistent with the analysis of the descriptive statistic, which shows that the markets with lower GDP have a better performance of making profit. The reason for explaining this result may be that the markets with lower GDP have a bigger space for developing and a relative faster speed of development in recently years, therefore, they show a better performance of making profit compared to those relatively high developed markets such as Beijing, Shanghai and Guangzhou which have constructed for many more years. What's more, the more developed markets may undertake much more risk either domestic or international, which leads to the bigger fluctuation in the performance of making profit. Thus this may be a clue for the insurance companies who want to open new business in some region of China, and it also confirms that the west and north of China have a great market potential for insurance.

The coefficient of PS is not statistically significant. The variable of PS measures the proportion of population over 65 years old and we thought the population structure might affect the demand for life insurance products, and then affect the performance of making profit. However, the results show that no significant relation exists between population structure and performance.

The coefficient of DI is statistically significant and it represents one – year deposit interest rate of central bank. As we know, the insurance fund is usually divided into two main parts: deposit and investment, and investment incomes account for a large part of profit for life insurance companies in China. The coefficient of DI is negative which conforms to principles of economics. The more insurance fund life insurance companies deposit into banks, the less they could invest in stock market.

Also the interest rate of bank has a positive relation with the amount of deposit. Therefore, it is reasonable that the one – year deposit interest rate of central bank has a negative relation with the performance of making profit for life insurance companies. The coefficient of IRR is statistically significant and the coefficient is positive. It represents the average price earnings ratios of Shanghai Composite Index. It has a positive influence on profit and the result is quite consistent with the reality that the stock market is a main channel for long – term life insurance fund to invest. The higher the return rate is, the better the performance of making profit.

The coefficient of Dummy variable for policy reform is statistically significant and the coefficient is positive. The result means that the New Accounting Standards do have some positive effect on domestic insurance market. Therefore, it is better for the Regulatory Administration to establish normative standards in order to regulate the industry as well as improve performance of making profit for enterprises.

In conclusion, the result of regression shows that the SCP hypothesis is not supported in the life insurance market of China. As it is verified in other scholars' articles, for example, Chen (2007) and Wang (2007) proved in their thesis that the SCP hypothesis was not supported in the insurance market of China by test with data of insurance companies of top market share. The reasonable explanation may be that the highly centralized life insurance market in China is not the consequence of competition, but the result of some politic reasons and phenomenon left over from the past. And also the highly centralized market structure does not lead to a high profit rate of enterprises. Besides, according to the result of regression, several factors influence the profit: the logarithmic form of GDP, one – year deposit interest rate of central bank, the average price earnings ratios of Shanghai Composite Index as well as the dummy variable for policy reform. Since one – year deposit interest rate of central bank, the average price earnings ratios of Shanghai Composite Index as well as the dummy variable for policy reform are all time series data, according to the results of regression, the main factor that influence the performance of making profit for life insurance companies in different provinces is economy. However, contrary to our expectation, the degree of economic development has negative relation with performance of making profit. The result can be explained, but it may also be influenced by the time period we choose.

5. Conclusion

This paper tests the validity of the SCP hypothesis in the life insurance market of different provinces in China. We apply the model based on the SCP hypothesis and employ a panel data which includes data of 30 provinces and municipalities over the time period of 2005 to 2011 to analysis the factors that influence performance of making profit for life insurance companies. The results reveal that the SCP hypothesis is not supported in life insurance market of China. The life insurance market in China is highly centralized, while it is not the consequence of competition. The performance of making profit for life insurance companies also has an obvious regional character and they are significant influenced by several factors: the logarithmic form of GDP, one – year deposit interest rate of central bank, the average price earnings ratios of Shanghai Composite Index as well as the dummy variable for policy reform.

It would be interesting to introduce the variable of efficiency to test whether the ES hypothesis is supported in China's market or not. However, it needs to choose deliberately to generate a proper proxy variable to measure the operate efficiency of the insurance companies. Our future work will continue to explore this topic and try to include the efficiency variable in the model. Hopefully the result of this paper may have the inspiration for subsequent studies and ideas for both regulators and operators of enterprises.

References

1. Anne M. Carroll, An Empirical Investigation of the Structure and Performance of the Private Workers'Compensation Market: The Journal of Risk and Insurance, 1993, 60(2), 185 – 207.

2. Bain, J. S. , Relation of Profit Rate to Industry Concentration: American Manufacturing, 1936 – 1940, Quarterly Journal of Economics, 1951, 65, 293 – 324.

3. Byeongyong Paul Choi and Mary A. Weiss, An Empirical Investigation of Market Structure, Efficiency, and Performance in Property – Liability Insurance: The Journal of Risk and Insurance, 2005, 72(4), 635 – 673.

4. Bin Lu, A study of China's insurance market based on the SCP paradigm Journal of Huainan Normal University, General 2012, 1.14(75).

5. Choi, P. , and M. Weiss, An empirical Investment of Market Structure, Efficiency, and performance in Property – Liability Insurance, Journal of Risk and Insurance, 2005, 72(4), 635 – 673.

6. Cummins, J. D. , and N. A. Doherty, The Economics of Insurance Intermediaries, The Journal of Risk and Insurance, 2006, 73(3), 359 – 396.

7. Cheng Yuan and Run Yu, Study of relation of the Chinese insurance market structure and performance – – – based on the SCP hypothesis: Journal of Jiangxi University of Finance and Economics, 2013.

8. Feng Lin, The literature review of SCP paradigm applied in insurance industrial organization: Journal of Jinan Vocational College, 2011, 1(84).

9. Fan Zhong, The Research on the life insurance industry of China based on the SCP theory: Central South University, Dissertation, 2009.

10. Hifza Malik, Determinants of insurance companies profitability: an analysis of insurance sector of Pakistan: Academic Research International, 2011, 1(3).

11. Maofu Zhuo, Analysis of Market structure and Performance about China Insurance Industry: Jilin University, Master's Dissertation, 2009.

12. Nat Pope and Yu – Luen Ma, Market Deregulation and Insurer Pricing Strategies: The Japanese Experience, The Geneva Papers on Risk and Insurance: issues and practice, 2005, 30, 312 – 326.

13. Nat Pope and Yu – Luen Ma, The Market Structure: Performance Relationship in the International Insurance Sector: The Journal of Risk and Insurance, 2008, 75(4), 947 – 966.

14. Vickie L. Bajtelsmit and Raja Bouzouita, Market Structure and Performance in Private Passenger Automobile Insurance: The Journal of Risk and Insurance, 1998, 65(3), 503 – 514.

15. William W. Cooper1, Lawrence M. Seiford2 and Joe Zhu, Data Envelopment Analysis: history, models and interpretations.

16. Xinwei Jiang, An Empirical Research on the Insurance market structure, Conduct and Performance of China: Southwestern University of Finance and Economics, Master's Dissertation, 2002.

17. Yubo Wang, Study of the relation of Chinese insurance market structure and performance: Chongqin Univer-

sity, Master's Dissertation, 2007.

18. Yu Wang, A study of China's life insurance market based on SCP paradigm: Jiao Tong University of East China, Master's Dissertation, 2011.

19. Yanhua Chen, Study of the relation of Chinese Insurance Market structure efficiency and Performance: Shandong University, Master's Dissertation, 2007.

Acknowledgement

The authors would like to thank Yujia He for her contributions on collecting the data and the valuable comments and suggestions from the participants of the 2014 Annual conference of APRIA in Moscow.

Addendum for Three Formulae in Section 3.2 of Lectures on Macroeconomics[①]

Zaigui Yang[②] Mengjie Zhang[③]

Abstract: The monograph, Lectures on Macroeconomics written by Blanchard and Fischer (1989) explains the theory of macroeconomics by the numbers. Chapter 3 of the monograph elaborates overlapping – generations model wholly. Section 3.2, Social Security and Capital Accumulation explains the overlapping – generations models with a Fully Funded System and a Pay – As – You – Go System of social security. However, there are omissions in three formulae of this section, which are equations (30, (32) and (34). Unfortunately, two translated versions in Chinese of this monograph, "Macroeconomics: Advanced Text Book" in 1992 and "Macroeconomics: Advanced Text Book" in 1998, have the same problems as the original work. And some citations in Chinese scholars' research works such as the paper titled "Social Security Tax and Optimization of Social Security System" published in two famous Chinese journals of economics have made analogous mistakes. The paper was cited by many other papers or books because it was published by the impacted journals. To avoid the error spreading in the future, this paper discusses the omissions at the headstream and fetches them up.

JEL code: C51

Key words: Lectures on Macroeconomics; Social security; OLG model; Omission

1. Introduction

Most researchers present their research results by publication to allow others to examine and refer to. When writing the research reports, the author may draw some incorrect conclusions due to a slip of the pen or problems existing in the process of calculation. If other researchers who quote the incorrect results to advance their study do not examine them, the errors would mislead much more readers and lead to the enlargement of the influence of the problematic results. And this would reduce the study efficiency of the researchers to a certain extent. Once the references are the error for-

---

[①] CES 2014 China Annual Conference, Guangzhou, June 14 – 15, 2014.

[②] Professor of China Institute for Actuarial Science and School of Insurance, Central University of Finance and Economics, Beijing, China.

[③] Graduate student of School of Insurance, Central University of Finance and Economics, Beijing, China.

mula, the series of inferences based on them would problematic, too. Besides, if the researchers doubt and reconsider their research results, they would review the derivation processes to find the source of the error. Then it may take a much longer time to do research. More seriously, the misinformation happens as mentioned above if the researcher found no problems.

The paper is aimed at rectifying the cited errors existing in the articles quoted frequently. Lectures on Macroeconomics written by Blanchard and Fischer describes and evaluates macroeconomic theory systematically for the first time. The main issue of the work is to explain output, unemployment and volatility of the price change. The section 3.2 mainly explains the OLG model (Overlapping – generation Model) which is the second fundamental model of the macroeconomics based on microeconomics.

2. Formulae (30), (32) and (34) lack the part $(1 + r_{t+1})$

Section 3.2 Social Security and Capital Accumulation of Lectures on Macroeconomics analyzes the OLG Model under Fully Funded System and Pay – as – You – Go System respectively. And three formulae of Section 3.2 have problems. Analyze as follows:

Before the illumination of the problems, we should figure out some related concepts to get a better understanding about the errors.

Everyone is indiscriminate in the same generation and they all go through the Work Period and Retirement Period. And every person acquires utility from the consumption of Work Period c_t and Retirement Period c_{2t+1} which is described through separable additive general utility function (except for altruism).

$$\max\{c_{1t} + c_{2t+1}\} \quad U_t = u(c_{1t}) + (1+q)^{-1}u(c_{2t+1})$$
$$s.t. \quad c_{1t} = w_t - s_t$$
$$c_{2t+1} = (1 + r_{t+1})s_t$$

$(1 + \theta)^{-1}$ is the discount factor and utility function $u(.)$ is monotonically increasing function of consumption and is strictly concave function. wt is the salary. s_t is the savings. r_{t+1} is the rate.

Based on the differences of the social security scheme supplying the retirement income, namely the Fully Funded System and the Pay – as – You – Go, we discuss about the maximization problem according to different types as follows:

1.1 The Fully Funded System

The contribution of the young at time t is invested. At time t + 1 the sum combined with the interest is b_{t+1} ($b_{t+1} = (1 + r_{t+1})d_t$) and it is returned to the old at that time.

In this way, the maximization problem transformed as follows:

$$\max\{c_{1t} + c_{2t+1}\} \quad U_t = u(c_{1t}) + (1+q)^{-1}u(c_{2t+1})$$
$$s.t. \quad c_{1t} = w_t - (s_t + d_t)$$
$$c_{2t+1} = (1 + r_{t+1})s_t + b_{t+1} = (1 + r_{t+1})(s_t + d_t)$$

Construct a Lagrange function:
$$L = u(c_{1t}) + (1+\theta)^{-1}u(c_{2t+1}) + \lambda_1[w_t - (s_t + d_t) - c_{1t}] + \lambda_2[(1 + r_{t+1})s_t + b_{t+1} - c_{2t+1}]$$

Take the partial derivative of c_{1t}, c_{2t+1}, s_t:

Addendum for Three Formulae in Section 3.2 of Lectures on Macroeconomics

$$\frac{\partial L}{\partial c_{1t}} = u'(c_{1t}) - \lambda_1 = 0$$

$$\frac{\partial L}{\partial c_{2t+1}} = (1+\theta)^{-1} u'(c_{2t+1}) - \lambda_2 = 0$$

$$\frac{\partial L}{\partial s_t} = -\lambda + \lambda_2(1+r_{t+1}) = 0$$

Rewrite the formulas:

$$u'(c_{1t}) = (1+\theta)^{-1}(1+r_{t+1}) u'(c_{2t+1})$$

Namely,

$$u'[w_t - (s_t + d_t)] = (1+\theta)^{-1}(1+r_{t+1}) u'[(1+r_{t+1})(s_t + d_t)] \qquad (1)$$

1.2 Pay-As-You-Go System

Transferring the current contribution of the young to the old contemporary, and the social security do not behave the form of the fund. Under the circumstance, $b_{t+1} = (1+n) d_{t+1}$

In this way, the maximization problem transformed as follows:

$$\max\{c_{1t} + c_{2t+1}\} \quad U_t = u(c_{1t}) + (1+q)^{-1} u(c_{2t+1})$$
$$s.t. \quad c_{1t} = w_t - (s_t + d_t)$$
$$c_{2t+1} = (1+r_{t+1}) s_t + b_{t+1} = (1+r_{t+1}) s_t + (1+n) d_{t+1}$$

Construct a Lagrange function:

$$L = u(c_{1t}) + (1+\theta)^{-1} u(c_{2t+1}) + \lambda_1 [w_t - (s_t + d_t) - c_{1t}]$$
$$+ \lambda_2 [(1+r_{t+1}) s_t + (1+n) d_{t+1} - c_{2t+1}]$$

Take the partial derivative of c_{1t}, c_{2t+1}, s_t

$$\frac{\partial L}{\partial c_{1t}} = u'(c_{1t}) - \lambda_1 = 0$$

$$\frac{\partial L}{\partial c_{2t+1}} = (1+\theta)^{-1} u'(c_{2t+1}) - \lambda_2 = 0$$

$$\frac{\partial L}{\partial s_t} = -\lambda + \lambda_2(1+r_{t+1}) = 0$$

Rewrite the formula:

$$u'(c_{1t}) = (1+\theta)^{-1}(1+r_{t+1}) u'(c_{2t+1})$$

Namely,

$$u'[w_t - (s_t + d_t)] = (1+\theta)^{-1}(1+r_{t+1}) u'[(1+r_{t+1}) s_t + (1+n) d_{t+1}] \qquad (2)$$

Meantime the savings of the consumer of the tth period forms the capital stock of the beginning of the t+1th period. $N_t s_t = K_{t+1}$, both sides are divided by the N_t at the same time:

$$s_t = (1+n) k_{t+1} \qquad n = \frac{N_{t+1}}{N_t} - 1$$

Considering the influence of private savings on social security and suppose the wage and the interest rate are known, we could figure out (2) using implicit function:

$$\frac{\partial s_t}{\partial d_t} = -\frac{u''_1 + (1+\theta)^{-1}(1+n) u''_2 (1+r_{t+1})}{u''_1 + (1+\theta)^{-1} u''_2 (1+r_{t+1})^2} \qquad (3)$$

The form of the implicit function is:

$$\frac{\partial F}{\partial s_t}ds_t + \frac{\partial F}{\partial x}dx = 0 \quad \text{(x means dt)}$$

But Blanchard and Fischer concluded the formulae (30), (32), (34):

$$u'[w_t - (s_t + d_t)] = (1 + \theta)^{-1} u'[(1 + r_{t+1})(s_t + d_t)] \tag{30}$$

$$u'[w_t - (s_t + d_t)] = (1 + \theta)^{-1}(1 + r_{t+1})u'[(1 + r_{t+1})s_t + (1 + n)d_t] \tag{32}$$

$$\frac{\partial s_t}{\partial d_t} = - \frac{u''_1 + (1 + \theta)^{-1}(1 + n)u''_2}{u''_1 + (1 + \theta)^{-1}u''_2(1 + r_{t+1})} \tag{34}$$

Compared with the correct equations with Lagrange function, the tree formulae all leave out the $(1 + r_{t+1})$

3. Add the correction in the corresponding position of the Chinese version to avoid the misinformation

The three formulae above all are lacking in $(1 + r_{t+1})$ and the errors are also existing in the corresponding position of the two Chinese versions. As the advanced book of "macroeconomics", this book takes priority of mathematical models for the analysis of the theory. In this way, the books are mainly used as the graduate students' teaching material or as the reference reading books of the professional researchers. At the same time, the book is also the advanced tutorial of "macroeconomics" translated into Chinese version for the first time. Because of the important role of this book, the errors in the Chinese version should be corrected timely so that they would influence the learning of the students or the in-depth study of the researchers. The two Chinese versions are:

3.1 "Macroeconomics: Advanced Text Book" translated by Shucheng Liu, Economic science press, (1992)

The content from page 119 to page 124 is the translation of the original version Section 3.2. And the formulae (34) (36) (38) in this book correspond to the original version (30) (32) (34):

The three equations all exist the same error with the original version, namely lack of $(1 + r_{t+1})$

$$u'[w_t - (s_t + d_t)] = (1 + \theta)^{-1} u'[(1 + r_{t+1})(s_t + d_t)] \tag{34}$$

$$u'[w_t - (s_t + d_t)] = (1 + \theta)^{-1}(1 + r_{t+1})u'[(1 + r_{t+1})s_t + (1 + n)d_{t+1}] \tag{36}$$

$$\frac{\partial s_t}{\partial d_t} = - \frac{u''_1 + (1 + \theta)^{-1}(1 + n)u''_2}{u''_1 + (1 + \theta)^{-1}u''_2(1 + r_{t+1})} \tag{38}$$

3.2 "Macroeconomics: Advanced Text Book" translated by Shucheng Liu, Economic science press, (1998)

The content from page 119 to page 124 is the translation of the original version Section 3.2. And the formulae (34) (36) (38) in this book correspond to the original version (30) (32) (34):

$$u'[w_t - (s_t + d_t)] = (1 + \theta)^{-1} u'[(1 + r_{t+1})(s_t + d_t)] \tag{34}$$

$$u'[w_t - (s_t + d_t)] = (1 + \theta)^{-1}(1 + r_{t+1})u'[(1 + r_{t+1})s_t + (1 + n)d_{t+1}] \tag{36}$$

$$\frac{\partial s_t}{\partial d_t} = - \frac{u''_1 + (1 + \theta)^{-1}(1 + n)u''_2}{u''_1 + (1 + \theta)^{-1}u''_2(1 + r_{t+1})} \tag{38}$$

Addendum for Three Formulae in Section 3.2 of Lectures on Macroeconomics

Chinese versions have not corrected the three formulae. In order to avoid the errors to mislead more people, the paper demonstrates the right forms here.

4. Errors in domestic research for quotation of the corresponding content in Section 3.2

As the classical tutorial of "Macroeconomics", this book is often quoted by researchers in their writing. Because the original and the corresponding Chinese translation both have the errors, other researchers make some mistakes quoting these formulae. For example: Shaoguang Li: "Social Security Tax and Optimization of Social Security System Economic" Research 2004,8 and Tax Research 2004,8

The article analyzed tax incidence of the payroll tax and influence of the elasticity of the labor supply. The fourth part of the article quoted the formulae (30) (34) of Lectures on Macroeconomics when explaining some fundamental conclusions about fund accumulation system.

$$u'[w_t - (s_t + d_t)] = (1 + \theta)^{-1} u'[(1 + r_{t+1})(s_t + d_t)]$$

(Shaoguang Li)

$$s_t + d_t = (1 + n)k_{t+1}$$

$$\frac{\partial s_t}{\partial d_t} = -\mu \Box \frac{u''_t + (1 + \theta)^{-1}(1 + n)u''_{t+1}}{u''_t + (1 + \theta)^{-1}(1 + r_{t+1})u''_{t+1}}$$

(Shaoguang Li)

Due to the errors existing in the original version, the reference is incorrect. Wish to correct it sooner.

This article is published in the Economic Research 2004,8 from page 35 to page 41. The main readers of Economic Research are economy theory researchers, policy makers, policy research department personnel, directors of enterprises or teachers and students in university and so on. It has a wide range of aspects. At the same time, Tax Research is the academic journals in area of taxation. Both journals have much more important influence in domestic economy and industry. In order to maintain the academic rigor, it is necessary to make this revision.

5. Conclusion

To sum up, the researchers would inevitably have some flaws when writing their articles. And we could not be hard on the authors to make sure all the interpretation is perfect. Meanwhile, the printing errors may occur so that it leads that the content of the article is flawed. To some extent, these errors may affect other researchers' further study and lead to the enlargement of the original errors for the continuous quotation. However, it is the imperfect that inspires others to find out the truth and tries to solve the problems and even acquires the new thoughts during the process. Research process sometimes may be a constantly exploring process by standing on predecessors' shoulders upward. But we still need to examine the content of quotation so that we could avoid the spread of the misinformation. Researcher should timely point out the errors in some important articles and correct them to avoid the expansion of the problem and low efficiency of the study.

Acknowledgement:

Financial support from the Major Program of the Key Research Institute on Humanities and Social Science of China Ministry of Education (10JJD790038), the Program for New Century Excellent Talents in Universities of China Ministry of Education (NCET-11-0755), and the Beijing Philosophy and Social Science Programming Project (11JGB089) is gratefully acknowledged.

References:

1. Blanchard O J, Fischer S. Lectures on Macroeconomics[M]. MIT press, 1989.

2. Blanchard OJ and Fischer S. Macroeconomics Advanced Textbook[M]. Translated by Liu Shucheng, et al. Economic Science Press, 1992.

3. Blanchard OJ and Fischer S. Macroeconomics Advanced Textbook[M]. Translated by Liu Shucheng, et al. Economic Science Press, 1998.

4. Yang Z. OLG model analysis on public pension: principles and applications[M]. Beijing: Guangming Daily Publishing House, 2010.

5. Li Shaoguang. Social Security Tax and Optimization of Social Security System. Economic Research[J], 2004,8:004.

6. Li Shaoguang. Social Security Tax and Optimization of Social Security System. Tax Research[J], 2004 (008):35-41.

Rural Consumption, Capital Accumulation and Pension Benefits in China[①]

Zaigui Yang[②]　Yuan Cao[③]

Abstract: This paper investigates the rural public pension in China by employing an overlapping-generations model. We examine the effects of the individual contribution rate, village subsidy rate, local government allowance rate, basic pension benefit rate and population growth rate on the capital-labor ratio, per capita consumption and pension benefits. Raising the individual contribution rate only increases the per capita pension benefits, and has no effect on the capital-labor ratio and per capita consumption. Raising both the village subsidy rate and local government allowance rate increases the capital-labor ratio, per capita consumption and pension benefits. Raising the basic benefit rate decreases the capital-labor ratio and per capita consumption, while increases the pension benefits. A rise in the population growth rate decreases the capital-labor ratio, per capita consumption, and pension benefits. In accordance with the effects and their intensities, it will do more good than harm to raise the individual contribution rate and village subsidy rate, maintain the present basic benefit rate and accordingly raise the local government allowance rate by adjusting the structure of fiscal expenditures, and control the population growth rate.

Key words: Rural public Pension; Consumption; Capital accumulation

1. Introduction

The "State Council Guidance on New Type Rural Public Pension Pilots" (Chinese State Council Document 32 in 2009) stipulates: Peasants make pension contributions, villages subsidize and local governments allowance the individual contributions. Individual contribution standards include five levels, 100, 200, 300, 400 and 500 Yuan per participant per year. Peasants can choose one of the levels as they like. Villages subsidize the individual contributions according to the decision of villagers' meeting. Local governments allowance the individual contributions with a standard not less

---

① 3rd International Agricultural Risk, Finance, and Insurance Conference, Zurich, Switzerland, June 22 – 24, 2014.
② Professor of China Institute for Actuarial Science and School of Insurance, Central University of Finance and Economics, Beijing, China.
③ PhD student of School of Insurance, Central University of Finance and Economics, Beijing, China.

than 30 Yuan per participant per year. The individual contributions, village subsidies and local government allowances are accumulated in the peasants' individual accounts. Each retiree (peasant above the age of 60) can draw individual account benefits from her/his individual account and get basic pension benefits from the central government and local government. The central government pays full basic benefits decided by the central government to the retired peasants in western and central areas, and a half of that to those in eastern areas (this is not explained explicitly, maybe it is because the later is richer than the former). The full basic benefits decided by the central government are 55 Yuan per retiree per month. Local governments can pay more basic benefits to retired peasants according to local circumstances. The rural public pension system is expected to reduce rural poverty, narrow the gaps between urban and rural areas, and promote domestic consumption.

However, the present rural public pension has the following problems: the pension benefits are very low; most participants choose the lowest pension contribution grade; the village subsidies and local government allowances are also very low; and the incentive mechanism is inefficient. In addition, village collective economy offers less competitive products and declines with the upgrading and adjustment of national industrial structure. Hence, it is difficult for villages to subsidize individual contributions and to provide sufficient incentives for participants to choose higher contribution level. Although there are additional subsidy policies on basic pension benefits, the power of these policies is small. These problems, such as insufficient village subsidies and local government allowances, as well as lack of significant incentive mechanism for the long - term participants, will eventually impede the sustainable development of the rural pension system. Therefore, the new system should strengthen incentive mechanism, and gradually upgrade the financing ability and pension benefit level.

Research on the rural public pension should take into account the concrete situations in China. Firstly, the pension benefit level should be raised. The per capita annual net income of rural residents is 7916.6 Yuan. The basic pension benefits are 55 Yuan per month, which only provides the replacement rate of 8.3%. Secondly, world economy has been recovering slowly after the international financial crisis. China's economy is also affected. The growth rate has come down significantly in the last two years, and the downside pressure remains. Although the quality and efficiency of economic development have got unparalleled attention now, the economic growth should not be ignored, because it affects employment, income and social stability. It relies on expanding domestic demand, including consumption demand and investment demand, to maintain the stable, sustainable and healthy growth of China's economy after the financial crisis. Finally, although China is implementing new population policy which allows two children per family if husband or wife is a single child in their own families before getting married, the new policy is unlikely to result in dramatic increase in the rural population growth rate.

Overlapping - generations (OLG) model has been used widely in the literature to investigate the relationship between public pension system and consumption and capital accumulation. Barro (1974) argues that if individuals in successive generations were linked by bequests, changes in the stock of government debt or in social security programs would have no effect on the steady state capital stock. Feldstein (1974) uses an extended life – cycle model to analyze the impact of social security on the individual's simultaneous decision about retirement and saving, and concludes that social security would reduce the capital – labor ratio in models that do not admit a bequest motive. Blanchard and Fischer (1989) use the OLG model to study PAYG and fully funded social security system. It is shown that a PAYG social security system prevents the rate of capital accumulation and reduces the steady state capital stock. A fully funded social security system has no effect on total savings and capital accumulation. The reason is that the increase in social security savings is exactly offset by a decrease in private savings in such a way that the sum of the two is equal to the previous level of private savings. Zhang and Zhang (1998) analyze the effects of social security on savings, fertility, and per capita income growth with three specifications of utility functions. The literature studies PAYG or fully funded public pensions based on developed countries.

There is also some domestic literature to study the public pension system for urban enterprise employees in China with OLG model. Wang et al., (2001) use computable general equilibrium model to examine the impacts of various design options for pension system reform on the sustainability of the system and on overall economy growth. Within a framework of an endogenous growth OLG model, Yang (2009) examines the effects of the public pension system on the fertility, economic growth and family old – age security. Kang (2012) compares the effects of improving the contribution rate and postponing the retirement age on capital stock per worker, personal and social pooling account pension level and other economic variables within a general equilibrium OLG model. However, what the literature study is the basic pension system for enterprise employees in China. It is hard to find the studies regarding on the rural public pension system. Employing an endogenous growth model, Yang (2011) investigates the rural public pension by examining the effects of the individual contribution rate, village subsidy rate, local government allowance rate and basic benefit rate on the labor income growth rate, population growth rate, consumption rate, saving rate and education expense rate. But the model is an endogenous growth model. In this paper, we aim to establish an exogenous OLG model to study the rural public pension.

According to the literature mentioned above and the reality of rural public pension, we develop an exogenous overlapping – generations model, examine whether and how the individual contribution rate, village subsidy rate, local government allowance rate, basic pension benefit rate and population growth rate affect the capital – labor ratio, per capita consumption and pension benefits. We estimate relevant parameter values according to the actual situation in the rural areas, and simulate the effects and their strengths. We hope to look for suitable policies to enhance the local government allowances and village subsidies, raise the individual contribution level and pension benefit level, and promote domestic consumption and capital accumulation. Most of the studies are based on the assumption that only individual participant pays pension contributions. The exogenous OLG model in this paper considers not only the individual contributions, but also the village subsidies and local government allowances.

2. The Model

This paper adopts Diamond's (1965) two-period OLG model. There are numerous individuals and villages and a government in a closed economy. Each individual lives for two periods: working period and retirement period. At the beginning of period t, N_t identical individuals of generation t enter the workforce. The population grows at a rate of $n = (N_t/N_{t-1}) - 1$.

2.1 Individuals

In working period each individual earns wage by supplying inelastically one unit of labor, makes pension contributions, consumes part of her income, and saves the remainder of the income. In retirement period, she consumes her savings with accrued interest, individual account benefits and basic pension benefits. Each individual derives utility from the working-period consumption $c_{1,t}$ and retirement-period consumption $c_{2,t+1}$. The utility is described by a logarithmic function. Each individual maximizes her utility by choosing savings and consumption. Hence, the utility maximization problem is:

$$\max_{\{s_t, c_{1,t}, c_{2,t+1}\}} U_t = \ln c_{1,t} + \theta \ln c_{2,t+1}, \tag{1}$$

$$s.t. \quad c_{1,t} = (1 - \tau)w_t - s_t, \tag{2}$$

$$c_{2,t+1} = (1 + r_{t+1})s_t + I_{t+1} + J_{t+1} \tag{3}$$

where $\theta \in (0,1)$ denotes the individual discount factor, $\tau \in (0,1)$ the individual contribution rate, w_t the wage, s_t the savings, r_{t+1} the interest rate, I_{t+1} the individual account benefits, J_{t+1} the basic pension benefits. The first-order condition is:

$$\theta(1 + r_{t+1})c_{1,t} = c_{2,t+1} \tag{4}$$

This equation implies that the utility loss from reducing one unit of working-period consumption is equal to the utility gain from increasing $(1 + r_{t+1})$ units of retirement-period consumption.

2.2 Villages

Villages produce homogenous commodities in competitive markets. The production is described by Cobb-Douglas function $Y_t = AK_t^\alpha N_t^{1-\alpha}$ or $y_t = AK_t^\alpha$, where Y_t is the output in period t, K_t the capital stock, $\alpha \in (0,1)$ the capital share of income, A the productivity, y_t the output-labor ratio and $k_t = K_t/N_t$ the capital-labor ratio.

Based on the total labor income, villages provide pension contribution subsidies at a rate of $\eta \in (0,1)$, the local government allowance rate is $\zeta \in (0,1)$, and the basic pension benefit rate is $j \in (0,1)$. In the long term, the village subsidies, local government allowances and basic pension benefits paid by the central government and local governments together are all from the peasants' achievement, which is a part of the labor income. According to the product distribution, we can get that $AK_t^\alpha N_t^{1-\alpha} = r_t K_t + (1 + \eta + \zeta + j)N_t w_t$. By virtue of Euler's theorem, we have:

$$r_t = \alpha A k_t^{\alpha-1}, \tag{5}$$

$$w_t = \frac{(1 - \alpha)Ak_t^\alpha}{1 + \eta + \zeta + j} \tag{6}$$

2.3 The government

The individual pension contributions, village subsidies and local government allowances are saved in the individual accounts by governments. The accumulation in the individual account is used to pay the individual when she/he retires in the next period:

$$I_{t+1} = (1 + r_{t+1})(\tau + \eta + \zeta)w_t \qquad (7)$$

Based on the total labor income of working generation, the governments pay the basic pension benefits to retirees at the basic pension benefit rate: $N_{t-1}J_t = jN_tw_t$, or

$$J_t = (1 + n)jw_t \qquad (8)$$

2.4 The goods market

The savings, individual contributions, village subsidies and local government allowances in period t generate the capital stock in period $t+1$: $K_{t+1} = N_t[s_t + (\tau + \eta + \zeta)w_t]$, or

$$(1 + n)k_{t+1} = s_t + (\tau + \eta + \zeta)w_t \qquad (9)$$

2.5 Dynamic Equilibrium

Substituting equations (2), (3) and (5) – (9) into equation (4) gives the following dynamic equilibrium system:

$$k_t^\alpha = \frac{(1 + \eta + \zeta + j)(1 + \theta)(1 + n)}{\theta(1 + \eta + \zeta)(1 - \alpha)A}k_{t+1} + \frac{(1 + n)jk_{t+1}^\alpha}{\theta(1 + \eta + \zeta)(1 + A\alpha K_{t+1}^{\alpha-1})} \qquad (10)$$

Assume that there is unique, stable and nonoscillatory steady state equilibrium. In order to find the stability condition, we linearize Dynamic System (10) around the steady-state (k) gives

$$p(k_{t+1} - k) + q(k_t - k) = 0$$

where

$$p = -\frac{(1 + \eta + \zeta + j)(1 + \theta)(1 + n)}{\theta(1 + \eta + \zeta)(1 - \alpha)A} - \frac{(1 + n)j\alpha k^{\alpha-1}(1 + Ak^{\alpha-1})}{\theta(1 + \eta + \zeta)(1 + A\alpha k^{\alpha-1})^2} < 0,$$

$$q = \alpha k^{\alpha-1} > 0.$$

The assumption that the equilibrium is unique, stable and nonoscillatory implies $0 < \dfrac{k_{t+1} - k}{k_t - k} = -\dfrac{q}{p} < 1$, Therefore, the stability condition is

$$p + q = -\frac{(1 + \eta + \zeta + j)(1 + \theta)(1 + n)}{\theta(1 + \eta + \zeta)(1 - \alpha)A}$$
$$- \frac{\alpha k^{\alpha-1}[j(1 + n)(1 + Ak^{\alpha-1}) - \theta(1 + \eta + \zeta)(1 + \alpha Ak^{\alpha-1})^2]}{\theta(1 + \eta + \zeta)(1 + \alpha Ak^{\alpha-1})^2} < 0.$$

3. Comparative Statics

Since the individual contributions (compulsory savings) crowd-out the voluntary savings, the individual contribution rate did not appear in equation (10) and has no effect on the capital-labor ratio. Totally differentiating equation (10) around the steady state gives

$$(p + q)dk + md\eta + gd\zeta + hdj + ldn = 0 \qquad (11)$$

where

$$m = \frac{(1 + \theta)(1 + n)j}{\theta(1 - \alpha)A(1 + \eta + \zeta)^2}k + \frac{(1 + n)jk^\alpha}{\theta(1 + \eta + \zeta)^2(1 + A\alpha k^{\alpha-1})} > 0$$

$$g = \frac{(1+\theta)(1+n)j}{\theta(1-\alpha)A(1+\eta+\zeta)^2}k + \frac{(1+n)jk^\alpha}{\theta(1+\eta+\zeta)^2(1+A\alpha k^{\alpha-1})} > 0$$

$$h = \frac{(1+\theta)(1+n)}{\theta(1+\eta+\zeta)(1-\alpha)A}k - \frac{(1+n)k^\alpha}{\theta(1+\eta+\zeta)(1+A\alpha k^{\alpha-1})} < 0$$

$$l = \frac{(1+\theta)(1+\eta+\zeta+j)}{\theta(1+\eta+\zeta)(1-\alpha)A}k - \frac{jk^\alpha}{\theta(1+\eta+\zeta)(1+A\alpha k^{\alpha-1})} < 0$$

Define $c_t = \frac{N_t c_{1t} + N_{t-1} c_{2t}}{N_t} = c_{1t} + \frac{c_{2t}}{1+n}$ as per capita consumption, $B_t = I_t + J_t$ as pension benefits per retiree. When the economy converges to the steady state equilibrium, the per capita consumption and pension benefits become:

$$c = Ak^\alpha - nk \tag{12}$$

$$B = [(1+\alpha Ak^{\alpha-1})(\tau+\eta+\zeta) + (1+n)j]\frac{(1-\alpha)Ak^\alpha}{1+\eta+\zeta+j} \tag{13}$$

3.1 Effect of individual contribution rate

The individual contribution rate has no effect on the capital-labor ratio, i.e. $\frac{\partial k}{\partial \tau} = 0$. Partially differentiating c and B with respect to τ, gives:

$$\frac{\partial c}{\partial \tau} = 0$$

$$\frac{\partial B}{\partial \tau} = (1+\alpha Ak^{\alpha-1})\frac{(1-\alpha)Ak^\alpha}{1+\eta+\zeta+j} > 0$$

According to equation (12), individual contribution rate has no effect on the capital-labor ratio, thus has no effect on per capita consumption. The pension benefits are composed of the individual account benefits and basic pension benefits, hence a rise in the individual contribution rate increases the individual account pension, and furthermore the pension benefits.

3.2 Effect of village subsidy rate and local government allowance rate

Partially differentiating k, c and B with respect to η, gives:

$$\frac{\partial k}{\partial \eta} = -\frac{m}{p+q} > 0$$

$$\frac{\partial c}{\partial \eta} = (A\alpha k^{\alpha-1} - n)\frac{\partial k}{\partial \eta}$$

$$\frac{\partial B}{\partial \eta} = (1-\alpha)\frac{\alpha Ak^{\alpha-1}}{(1+\eta+\zeta+j)}\frac{\partial k}{\partial \eta}[(\tau+\eta+\zeta)(1+(2\alpha-1)Ak^{\alpha-1}) + (1+n)j]$$
$$+ (1-\alpha)\frac{Ak^\alpha}{(1+\eta+\zeta+j)^2}[(1+\alpha Ak^{\alpha-1})(1+j-\tau) - (1+n)j]$$

Raising the village subsidy rate increases the capital-labor ratio. According to equation (9), raising the village subsidy rate increases capital-labor ratio directly, and decreases labor income indirectly. The direct effect is greater than the indirect effect, thus raising the village subsidy rate increases the capital-labor ratio. When $A\alpha k^{\alpha-1} > n$, according to equation (12), raising the village subsidy increases per capita consumption. According to equation (13), raising the village subsidy rate decreases the labor income and increases the individual account benefits directly, increases the capital – labor ratio and decreases the interest rate indirectly. Hence, the overall effect of village subsidy rate on the pension benefits is ambiguous.

According to equations (10) – (11) and the expressions of m and g, the effect and function of ζ and η in the model are consistent. So the effects of the local government allowance rate on k, c and B are as the same as that of the village subsidy rate. That is, raising the local government allowance rate increases the capital – labor ratio, and increases per capita consumption if the interest rate is higher than the population growth rate, but the effect on the pension benefits cannot be determined.

3.3 Effect of basic pension benefit rate

Partially differentiating k, c and B with respect to j, gives:

$$\frac{\partial k}{\partial j} = -\frac{h}{p+q} < 0$$

$$\frac{\partial c}{\partial j} = (A\alpha k^{\alpha-1} - n)\frac{\partial k}{\partial j}$$

$$\frac{\partial B}{\partial j} = (1-\alpha)\frac{Ak^{\alpha-1}}{(1+\eta+\zeta+j)}\left[\alpha(\tau+\eta+\zeta)[1+(2\alpha-1)Ak^{\alpha-1}]\frac{\partial k}{\partial j} + (1+n)\left(k+j\alpha\frac{\partial k}{\partial j}\right)\right]$$

$$- (1-\alpha)\frac{Ak^{\alpha}}{(1+\eta+\zeta+j)^2}[(\tau+\eta+\zeta)(1+\alpha Ak^{\alpha-1}) + (1+n)j]$$

Raising the basic pension benefit rate decreases the capital – labor ratio. A rise in the basic pension benefit rate decreases the labor income and voluntary savings, and both of which decrease the capital – labor ratio. According to equation (12), raising the basic pension benefit rate decreases per capita consumption if the interest rate is higher than the population growth rate. According to equation (13), raising the basic pension benefit rate has a positive impact on the basic pension benefits, and decreases the labor income directly, decreases the capital – labor ratio indirectly and increases the interest rate. The overall effect of the basic pension benefit rate on the pension benefits is ambiguous.

3.4 Effect of population growth rate

Partially differentiating k, c and B with respect to n, gives:

$$\frac{\partial k}{\partial n} = -\frac{l}{p+q} < 0$$

$$\frac{\partial c}{\partial n} = (\alpha Ak^{\alpha-1} - n)\frac{\partial k}{\partial n} - k$$

$$\frac{\partial B}{\partial n} = \frac{(1-\alpha)\alpha Ak^{\alpha-1}\{[1+(2\alpha-1)Ak^{\alpha-1}](\tau+\eta+\zeta) + (1+n)j\}}{1+\eta+\zeta+j}\frac{\partial k}{\partial n} + j\frac{(1-\alpha)Ak^{\alpha}}{1+\eta+\zeta+j}$$

A rise in the population growth rate decreases the capital – labor ratio because of the dilution effect of population growth. According to equation (12), a rise in the population growth rate decreases the per capita consumption if the interest rate is higher than the population growth rate. According to equation (13), a rise in the population growth rate decreases the capital – labor ratio and labor income indirectly, increases the interest rate and has a positive impact on the basic pension benefits. The overall effect of the population growth rate on the pension benefits cannot be determined.

Since some effects of the exogenous variables on the endogenous variables cannot be determined, we check the effects by simulations below.

4. Numerical Experiment

4.1 Parameter setting

Because one period is usually assumed to be 25 – 30 years in OLG model, and the data of National Population Census in 1982 and 2010 are used in this model, we set each period as 28 years in this paper. The individual discount factor per year is assumed to be 0.985, which is similar to that used by Pecchenino and Pollard (2002). Hence, the individual discount factor per period is $\theta = 0.985^{28}$.

The capital share of income is usually estimated as 0.3 in developed countries (e.g., Zhang *et al.*, 2001; Pecchenino and Pollard, 2002). The labor in China is comparatively cheaper, thus the labor share of income is lower, while the capital share of income is higher than that in developed countries. Hence, we assume that α in China could be 0.35. Since the technological progress is not reflected in this model, and what we want to see here is how the endogenous variables change with the exogenous variables, the constant A can be normalized as 1.

There are several statistical calibers for population in China. The public pension system is divided between urban and rural areas, and this paper only examines the rural public pension system, so the "Rural employed population" is selected as statistical caliber. According to China Statistical Yearbook, the rural employed population growth rate in the period from 1984 to 2012[①] is computed to be $n = 39602/35968 - 1$.

At present, the annual contributions per participant are 183 Yuan and the monthly pension benefits per retiree 82 Yuan (Gao, 2013). Calculated with 7916.6 Yuan of net annual income per capita in rural areas, the individual contribution rate is computed to be $\tau = 183/7916.6$. According to the annual pension benefits per retiree $J = 12 \times 82$ Yuan and equation (8), the basic pension benefit rate is computed to be $j = J/[(1+n)w] \approx 11.289\%$. The State Council Document 32 in 2009 stipulates: Local government allowances participant no less than 30 Yuan per person per year; village subsidy standards should be democratically determined by villagers' committee. Because the allowances in different regions are different and there is no authorized data, we assume the local government allowances to each participant per year are 45 Yuan. Thus, the local government allowance rate is $\zeta = 45/7916.6$. The village subsidies are lower than the local government allowances, thereby we assume the subsidies are 30 Yuan per participant per year, hence the village subsidy rate is $\eta = 30/7916.6$. These are benchmark values of the parameters.

4.2 Simulation

Other things are equal, raising the individual contribution rate gradually to 7.0%, simulating

---

[①] The rural public pension came out in 2009. But the peasants above the age of 60 have gotten pension benefits because they had contributed to the pension system when they were young through price scissors of industrial and agricultural products, agriculture taxes, etc.

with them gives the result shown in Table 1. Obviously, raising the individual contribution rate only increases the pension benefits, and has no effect on the capital – labor ratio and per capita consumption.

Table 1	Effect of individual contribution rate				
τ	2.3%	4.0%	5.0%	6.0%	7.0%
k	0.0815	0.0815	0.0815	0.0815	0.0815
c	0.4075	0.4075	0.4075	0.4075	0.4075
B	0.0518	0.0631	0.0698	0.0765	0.0832

Other things are equal, raising the village subsidy rate gradually to 2.0%, simulating with them gives the result shown in Table 2. Raising the village subsidy rate increases the capital – labor ratio, per capita consumption and pension benefits.

Table 2	Effect of village subsidy rate				
η	0.4%	0.7%	1.0%	1.5%	2.0%
k	0.0815	0.0815	0.0816	0.0817	0.0818
c	0.4075	0.4077	0.4078	0.4079	0.4081
B	0.0518	0.0538	0.0557	0.0588	0.0618

Other things are equal, raising the local government allowance rate gradually to 2.5%, simulating with them gives the result shown in Table 3. Raising the local government allowance rate increases the capital – labor ratio, per capita consumption and pension benefits.

Table 3	Effect of local government allowance rate				
ζ	0.6%	1.0%	1.5%	2.0%	2.5%
k	0.0815	0.0816	0.0817	0.0818	0.0819
c	0.4075	0.4077	0.4079	0.4080	0.4082
B	0.0518	0.0545	0.0576	0.0607	0.0637

Other things are equal, raising the basic pension benefit rate gradually to 20.0%, simulating with them gives the result shown in Table 4. Raising the basic pension benefit rate decreases the capital – labor ratio and per capita consumption, while increases the pension benefits.

Table 4		Effect of basic pension benefit rate			
j	11.3%	14.0%	16.0%	18.0%	20.0%
k	0.0815	0.0767	0.0735	0.0704	0.0675
c	0.4075	0.3994	0.3936	0.3879	0.3825
B	0.0518	0.0569	0.0604	0.0636	0.0667

Other things are equal, raising the population growth rate gradually to 18.0%, simulating with them gives the result shown in Table 5. A rise in the population growth rate decreases the capital – labor ratio, per capita consumption and pension benefits.

Table 5		Effect of population growth rate			
n	10.1%	12.0%	14.0%	16.0%	18.0%
k	0.0815	0.0797	0.0778	0.0760	0.0743
c	0.4075	0.4029	0.3982	0.3937	0.3892
B	0.0518	0.0517	0.0516	0.0514	0.0513

According to Tables 1 – 5, we calculate the elasticity of the endogenous variables with respect to the exogenous variables, which is shown in Table 6. They reflect the sensitivities of the endogenous variables with respect to the exogenous variables. The sign reflects the direction of the effect and the absolute value reflects the strength of effect. Comparing the absolute values of the elasticity gives the following result: each parameter affects capital – labor ratio to different extent, with the basic pension benefit rate the strongest, followed by the population growth rate, and the village subsidy rate and government allowance rate weakest. As to the per capita consumption, the impact of basic pension benefit rate is greatest, followed by the population growth rate, and the village subsidy rate and government allowance rate have little impact. In regard to the pension benefits, the impact of individual contribution rate is greatest, followed by the basic pension benefit rate, local government allowance rate, village subsidy rate and population growth rate.

Table 6 Elasticity of endogenous variables with respect to τ, η, ζ, j and n

	τ	η	ζ	j	n
k	0	0.3%	0.4%	-33.7%	-16.4%
c	0	0.1%	0.1%	-11.4%	-8.2%
B	46.2%	12.9%	16.4%	45.1%	-1.6%

5. Conclusions

This paper investigates the rural public pension system in China by developing an exogenous overlapping generations model. It examines the effects of the individual contribution rate, village subsidy rate, local government allowance rate, basic pension benefit rate and population growth rate on the capital – labor ratio, per capita consumption and pension benefits. According to the circumstances in rural areas of China, we estimate the values of relevant parameters, and simulate the effects and the sensitivities of the endogenous variables with respect to the exogenous variables. The differences from the previous studies are that this paper uses an exogenous overlapping generations model to analyze the rural public pension. In addition, except from participants pay pension contributions, villages subsidize and local governments allowance the contributions.

The results are as follows. Raising the individual contribution rate only increases the pension benefits, and has no effect on the capital – labor ratio and per capita consumption. Both raising the village subsidy rate and local government allowance rate increase the capital – labor ratio, per capita consumption and pension benefits. Raising the basic pension benefit rate decreases the capital – labor ratio and per capita consumption, while increases the pension benefits. A rise in the population growth rate decreases the capital – labor ratio, per capita consumption and pension benefits. The basic pension benefit rate has the strongest effect on the capital – labor ratio, followed in descending order by the population growth rate, local government allowance rate and village subsidy rate. The effects of the four exogenous variables on the per capita consumption rank in the same order. The effect of the individual contribution rate on the pension benefits is the greatest, followed by the basic pension benefit rate, local government allowance rate, village subsidy rate and the population growth rate.

The recovery of world economy is slow after the international financial crisis. China's economic growth rate also falls, and the downside pressure remains. It must rely on expanding domestic demand, including consumption and investment, to maintain a balanced, sustainable and healthy growth of China's economy in the era of post financial crisis. To enhance attraction of the rural public pension system, we should strengthen the incentive mechanism by increasing subsidies at the entrance and pension benefits at the exit of the system. According to the above results, the following statements can be made. In order to increase the capital accumulation and consumption, it is necessary to reduce the basic pension benefit rate and population growth rate, and raise the local government allowance rate and village subsidy rate. To increase the pension benefits, it is necessary to raise the individual contribution rate, local government allowance rate, village subsidy rate and basic pension benefit rate, while reduce the population growth rate. In accordance with the effects of the five exogenous variables on the endogenous variables and their strengths, it will do more good than harm to raise the individual contribution rate, local government allowance rate and village subsidy rate, maintain the present basic pension benefit rate, and moderately reduce the population growth rate.

Increasing the local government allowance rate and maintaining the present basic pension benefit rate can be fulfilled by adjusting the present fiscal expenditure structure. Local governments can lower the growth rate of additional basic pension benefits or even temporarily do not increase the amount of it. The saved resources can be used to increase the local government allowances to the individual contributions, namely, transform part of allowances from the exit to the entrance. This can increase the local government allowance rate. When the rural residents notice the increased government allowances to pension participants, and become aware of the fact that the more each participant contributes, the more government allowances, they will experience the growth of their own benefits, be more confident about future pension benefits, and then consciously raise contribution level. As a result, the individual contribution rate increases. Rise in the village subsidy rate relies on growth and grandness of village collective economy. Population growth rate control is still relying on the Chinese special population policy. Based on the above results, the population policy is not suitable to be relaxed greatly.

Acknowledgement:

Financial support from the Major Program of the Key Research Institute on Humanities and Social Science of China Ministry of Education (10JJD790038), the Program for New Century Excellent Talents in Universities of China Ministry of Education (NCET – 11 – 0755), and the Beijing Philosophy and Social Science Programming Project (11JGB089) is gratefully acknowledged.

References

1. Barro R. J., (1974) "Are government bonds net wealth?" [J], Journal of Political Economy 82, 1095 – 1117.
2. Blanchard O. J. and Fischer S., (1989) Lectures on Macroeconomics [M], London: MIT Press.
3. Diamond P. A., (1965) "National debt in a neoclassical growth model" [J], American Economic Review 55, 1126 – 1150.
4. Feldstein, M., (1974) "Social security, induced retirement, and aggregate capital accumulation" [J], Journal of Political Economy 82, 905 – 926.
5. Gao, F., (2013) "Basic Situations of the New – Type Rural and Urban resident Public Pension", Urban and Rural Resident Social Public Pension Seminar proceedings: 1 – 10.
6. Kang, C., (2012) "Improving the Contribution Rate or Postponing the Retirement Age?", Statistical Research 12, 59 – 68.
7. Pecchenino R., and Pollard P., (2002) "Dependent children and aged parents: funding education and social security in an aging economy" [J], Journal of Macroeconomics 24, 145 – 169.
8. Wang, Y., Xu, D., Wang, Z., Zhai, F., (2001) "The Implicit Debt, Transition Cost, Reform Forms and the Influence of China's Pension System", Economic Research Journal 2001, (5), 3 – 12.
9. Yang, Z., (2009) "Urban public pension, fertility and endogenous growth in China", Statistical Research 26(5), 77 – 81.
10. Yang, Z., (2011) "New – style rural old – age insurance and peasant income growth". Beida CCISSR Forum 2011 Annual Conference. In: The Twelfth Five – year Plan · New Challenge: Comprehensive Risk Management for Economy and Society. Edited by CCISSR. Peking University Press, 356 – 369.
11. Zhang J. and Zhang J., (1998) "Social security, intergenerational transfers, and endogenous growth" [J], The Canadian Journal of Economics 31, 1225 – 1241.
12. Zhang J., Zhang J., and Lee R., (2001) "Mortality Decline and Long – Run Economic Growth" [J], Journal of Public Economics 80, 485 – 507.

Effects of China's Enterprise Employee Public Pension on Investment and Consumption

Yan Gao Zaigui Yang

Abstract: Employing an overlapping-generations model within general equilibrium framework, this paper analyzes China's public pension system for enterprise employees. We examine the effects of the firm contribution rate, individual contribution rate and the share of individual contributions going to individual account on the capital-labor ratio, pension benefits and per capita consumption. The results are as follows: Both increases in the firm contribution rate and individual contribution rate decrease the capital-labor ratio and per capita consumption, and the firm contribution rate has greater impact. Both increases raise the pension benefits, and the individual contribution rate has greater impact. An increase in the share of individual contributions going to individual account will increase the capital-labor ratio, pension benefits and per capita consumption. In the post-crisis era we should reduce the firm contribution rate to increase social investment and consumption, and increase the individual contribution rate and the share of individual contributions going to individual account simultaneously to raise the pension benefits. Meanwhile the government should provide preferential fiscal and taxation policies.

Key words: Enterprise employee public pension; Capital-labor ratio; Per capita consumption; Pension benefits

1. Introduction

The Chinese State Council Document 38 in 2005, "Decision on Improving Basic Pension System for Enterprise Employees" indicates: In order to make the individual accounts get full real assets, each firm contributes 20% of its payroll to the social pool, while each employee contributes 8% of her wage to her individual account from January 1, 2006 on. More than a dozen provinces have been trying to make the individual accounts get full real assets. The Ministry of Human Resources and Social Security conducted a special study on making individual accounts be full of real assets and oper-

---

① CES 2014 China Annual Conference, Guangzhou, June 14-15, 2014.
② PhD student of School of Insurance, Central University of Finance and Economics, Beijing, China.
③ Professor of China Institute for Actuarial Science and School of Insurance, Central University of Finance and Economics, Beijing, China.

ating and managing the funds. But the problem of individual accounts without full real assets, which is often called empty individual accounts running, is still serious. "China Pension Development Report 2012", issued by Chinese Academy of Social Sciences shows: By the end of 2011, the individual account balance of the basic pension system for enterprise employees all over China should be 2.5 trillion yuan, but the individual accounts have only real assets 270.3 billion yuan. The ratio of the individual contributions entered the individual accounts, which can be called the individual account real asset ratio, is only 10.8%. Guangdong province has the largest pension funds among all provinces of China, and its individual account real asset ratio is 75.8%, which is far from the goal of individual accounts with full real assets.

The third quarter press conference in 2013 of the Ministry of Human Resources and Social Security comes out the ministry's voice: China will insist on the partially funded public pension system combined social pooling account and individual accounts, and continue to make the individual accounts get full real assets. What are the effects of making the individual accounts get full real assets on the pension benefits, consumption and capital accumulation, and how about the effect intensities? This relates to the vital interests of the enterprise retirees, the enormous pressure of pension payments during the population aging, and the balanced, sustainable and healthy development of China's economy in the post – crisis era. Firstly, the pension benefit level of enterprise retirees is lower than that of institution retirees. In the last decade, the Chinese government raises the pension benefit level of enterprise retirees annually. Although it has made significant progress, there is still a large gap to the expectations of enterprise employees. It is the direction of future efforts to further narrow the gap between enterprise and institution retirees' pension benefit levels. Secondly, the world economy recovers slowly and grows weakly after the international financial crisis. Affected by it, the growth rate of China's economy in the last two years falls evidently. The economy development speed must also be taken seriously while the quality and efficiency of economy development has been attached unprecedented importance, because it relates to employment, income and social stability. Maintaining balanced, sustainable and healthy development of China's economy in the post – crisis era has to rely on expanding domestic demand, including the demand of consumption and investment.

There are a large number of literature do research on public pension system and pension benefits, consumption and capital accumulation with overlapping – generations (OLG) model, e.g., Diamond (1965), Barro (1974), Feldstein (1974), Blanchard and Fischer (1989), Fuster (2000), etc. These studies are based on developed countries' economic background and public pension systems, including pay – as – you – go (PAYG) and fully funded systems. A common feature of these studies is their models contain only individual contributions but no firm contributions. Yang (2009a) studies Chinese partially funded public pension system combined social pooling account and individual accounts by assuming both individuals and firms make pension contributions, but does not consider the problem of making individual accounts get full real assets.

There is also some domestic literature to study public pension system with OLG model, e.g., Wang et al., (2001), Yang (2009b, 2011), etc. These studies inspire this paper although they do not involve the individual account real asset problem. Yang (2010) studies the optimal combination of the contribution rates and ratios of firm contributions and individual contributions entering respectively the social pooling account and individual accounts. But the model is based on the Chinese State Council Document 26 in 1997, "Decision on Establishing Basic Pension System for Enterprise Employees". This paper will establish a model based on the Chinese State Council Document 38 in 2005, "Decision on Improving Basic Pension System for Enterprise Employees", to match the implementing basic pension system.

Facing the status quo that the individual accounts have not full real assets, this paper investigates the public pension system for enterprise employees in China. It examines the effects of the firm contribution rate, individual contribution rate and individual account real asset ratio on the capital – labor ratio, per capita consumption and pension benefits. The significant difference of this paper from the previous studies is that it explicitly introduces the factor of making the individual accounts get full real assets, based on the partially funded public pension system stipulated by the Chinese State Council Document 38 in 2005.

2. The model

A closed economy is composed of numerous individuals and firms, and a government. This paper adopts Diamond's (1965) two – period OLG model. The generation born at the beginning of period t is called generation t. The workforce grows at rate $n = N_t/N_{t-1} - 1$, where N_t is the workforce size of generation t.

2.1 Individuals

Individuals live for two periods: working period and retirement period. Each individual earns wage by supplying inelastically one unit of labor, makes pension contributions, consumes part of her income, and saves the remainder of the income during her working period. In the retirement period, she consumes her savings with accrued interest, funded pension benefits and PAYG pension benefits.

Each individual derives utility from the working – period consumption c_{1t} and retirement – period consumption c_{2t+1}. The utility is described by a constant relative risk aversion utility function. Each individual maximizes her utility by selecting savings and consumption:

$$\max_{\{c_{1,t}, c_{2,t+1}, s_t\}} U_t = \frac{c_{1,t}^{1-\sigma}}{1-\sigma} + \theta \frac{c_{2,t+1}^{1-\sigma}}{1-\sigma}, \sigma > 0, \sigma \neq 1, \quad (1)$$

$$s.t. \quad c_{1,t} = (1-\tau)w_t - s_t, \quad (2)$$

$$c_{2,t+1} = (1 + r_{t+1})s_t + I_{t+1} + P_{t+1} \quad (3)$$

where $\theta \in (0,1)$ is the individual discount factor, σ the coefficient of relative risk aversion, τ the individual contribution rate, w_t the wage, s_t the savings, r_{t+1} the interest rate, I_{t+1} individual account pension, P_{t+1} social pool benefits. The first – order condition is

$$[\theta(1 + r_{t+1})]^{\frac{1}{\sigma}} c_{1t} = c_{2t+1} \quad (4)$$

This familiar expression implies that the utility loss from reducing one unit of working – period consumption is equal to the utility gain from increasing $(1 + r_{t+1})$ units of retirement – period consumption.

2.2 Firms

Firms produce homogenous commodity in competitive markets. The production is described by Cobb–Douglas function $Y_t = AK_t^\alpha N_t^{1-\alpha}$ or $y_t = AK_t^\alpha$, where Y_t is the output in period t, K_t the capital stock, $\alpha \in (0,1)$ the capital share of income, A the productivity, $k_t = K_t/N_t$ the capital-labor ratio, and y_t the output-labor ratio.

Firms make pension contributions at rate $\eta \in (0,1)$ on their payroll. According to the product distribution, one can get that $AK_t^\alpha N_t^{1-\alpha} = r_t K_t + (1+\eta) w_t N_t$. Firms act competitively. By virtue of Euler's theorem, we get

$$r_t = \alpha A K_t^{\alpha-1} \quad (5)$$

$$w_t = \frac{(1-\alpha) A K_t^\alpha}{1+\eta} \quad (6)$$

2.3 The government

Only a small part of individual contributions enters the individual accounts because the social pooling account overdraws the individual accounts to pay current retirees. Assume the ratio of individual contributions entering individual accounts, i.e., the individual account real asset ratio, is $v \in (0,1)$, then

$$I_{t+1} = (1 + r_{t+1}) v \tau w_t \quad (7)$$

All the firm contributions and most of the individual contributions are used to pay current retirees' pension benefits: $N_{t-1} P_t = N_t [(1-v)\tau + \eta] w_t$, or

$$P_t = (1+n)[(1-v)\tau + \eta] w_t \quad (8)$$

2.4 The goods market

The workers' savings and individual contributions entered individual accounts in period t generate the capital stock in period $t+1$ (see Barro and Sala-I-Martin, 2004):

$$s_t + v\tau w_t = (1+n) k_{t+1} \quad (9)$$

2.5 Dynamic Equilibrium

Given the initial condition k_0 and the policy parameters τ, η and v, a competitive equilibrium for the economy is a sequence as $\{c_{1t}, c_{2t+1}, s_t, w_t, r_t, I_{t+1}, P_t, k_{t+1}\}_{t=0}^{\infty}$ that satisfies equations (1)–(9) for all t.

Substituting equations (2), (3) and (6)–(9) into (4) gives the following dynamic equilibrium system:

$$[\theta(1+\alpha AK_{t+1}^{\alpha-1})]^{\frac{1}{\sigma}}\left[(1-\tau+v\tau)\frac{(1-\alpha)AK_t^\alpha}{1+\eta} - (1+n)k_{t+1}\right]$$
$$= (1+\alpha AK_{t+1}^{\alpha-1})(1+n)k_{t+1} + (1+n)\frac{(1-v)\tau+\eta}{1+\eta}(1-\alpha)AK_{t+1}^\alpha \quad (10)$$

Assume that there exists a unique, stable and nonoscillatory equilibrium. In order to find the stability condition, we linearize Dynamic System (10) around the steady state (k),

$$i dk_{t+1} + j dk_t = 0$$

where

$$i = \frac{1}{\sigma}[\theta(1 + \alpha AK^{\alpha-1})]^{\frac{1-\sigma}{\sigma}} \times \theta A\alpha(\alpha - 1)k^{\alpha-2} \times \left[(1 - \tau + v\tau)\frac{(1-\alpha)AK^\alpha}{1+\eta} - (1+n)k\right]$$

$$- [\theta(1 + \alpha AK^{\alpha-1})]^{\frac{1}{\sigma}}(1+n) - (1+n)(1+\alpha^2 AK^{\alpha-1}) - (1+n)(1-\alpha)\alpha AK^{\alpha-1}\frac{\tau - v\tau + \eta}{1+\eta}$$

$$j = [\theta(1 + \alpha AK^{\alpha-1})]^{\frac{1}{\sigma}}(1 - \tau + v\tau)\frac{(1-\alpha)A\alpha}{1+\eta}k^{\alpha-1} > 0$$

The assumption that the equilibrium is unique, stable and nonoscillatory is equivalent to $0 < \frac{k_{t+1} - k}{k_t - k} = -\frac{j}{i} < 1$. Therefore, the stability condition is

$$i + j < 0.$$

3. Comparative Statics

Totally differentiating equation (10) around the steady state gives
$$(i+j)dk + md\eta + \gamma d\tau + \chi dv = 0 \tag{11}$$

where

$$i+j = \frac{1}{\sigma}E^{\frac{1-\sigma}{\sigma}} \times \theta A\alpha(\alpha-1)k^{\alpha-2} \times [(1-\tau+v\tau)F - (1+n)k] - E^{\frac{1}{\sigma}}(1+n)$$

$$- (1+n)(1+\alpha^2 Ak^{\alpha-1}) - (1+n)\alpha(\tau - v\tau + \eta)F + E^{\frac{1}{\sigma}}(1-\tau+v\tau)\frac{F}{k}$$

$$m = \frac{\partial\phi}{\partial\eta} = -F\frac{(1-\tau+v\tau)}{1+\eta}[E^{\frac{1}{\sigma}} + 1 + n] < 0,$$

$$\gamma = \frac{\partial\phi}{\partial\tau} = (-1)[E^{\frac{1}{\sigma}} + 1 + n](1-v)F < 0,$$

$$\chi = \frac{\partial\phi}{\partial v} = [E^{\frac{1}{\sigma}} + 1 + n]\tau F > 0,$$

and $[\theta(1 + \alpha Ak^{\alpha-1})] = E$, $\frac{(1-\alpha)Ak^\alpha}{(1+\eta)} = F$

Define $c_t = \frac{N_t c_{1t} + N_{t-1} c_{2t}}{N_t} = c_{1t} + \frac{c_{2t}}{1+n}$ as per capita consumption, and $B_t = I_t + P_t$ as pension benefits of each retiree. After the economy converging to the steady state equilibrium, the per capita consumption and pension benefits become:

$$c = c_1 + \frac{c_2}{1+n} = AK^\alpha - kn$$

$$B = [(1+n)(\tau - v\tau + \eta) + (1 + \alpha Ak^{\alpha-1})v\tau]\frac{(1-\alpha)Ak^\alpha}{1+\eta}$$

3.1 Effect of firm contribution rate

Partially differentiating k, c and B with respect to η, respectively, and using equation (11) and the stability condition gives

$$\frac{\partial k}{\partial \eta} = \frac{-m}{i+j} < 0$$

$$\frac{\partial c}{\partial \eta} = (\alpha Ak^{\alpha-1} - n)\frac{\partial k}{\partial \eta}$$

$$\frac{\partial B}{\partial \eta} = \frac{(1-\alpha)Ak^{\alpha}}{(i+j)(1+\eta)}$$

$$\left\{(1+n)(i+j) + [(1+n)\tau + (1+n)\eta + (\alpha Ak^{\alpha-1} - n)v\tau]\left[\alpha k^{-1}(-m) - \frac{(i+j)}{1+\eta}\right]\right\}$$

Raising the firm contribution rate decreases the capital – labor ratio. A rise in the firm contribution rate decreases the wage, furthermore the voluntary savings and the individual account principal, hence the capital – labor ratio falls. A fall in the capital – labor ratio decreases the wage and voluntary savings; hence the per capita consumption falls if the interest rate is higher than the workforce growth rate, and vice versa. According to equations (7) and (8), a rise in the firm contribution rate decreases the wage and individual account benefits. But the rise directly increases the social pooling benefits. Hence, the effect of the firm contribution rate on the pension benefits cannot be determined.

3.2 Effect of individual contribution rate

Partially differentiating k, c and B with respect to τ, respectively, and using equation (11) and the stability condition gives

$$\frac{\partial k}{\partial \tau} = \frac{-\gamma}{i+j} < 0,$$

$$\frac{\partial c}{\partial \tau} = (\alpha AK^{\alpha-1} - n)\frac{\partial k}{\partial \tau},$$

$$\frac{\partial B}{\partial \tau} = \frac{F}{i+j}[(1+n) + (\alpha Ak^{\alpha-1} - n)v]$$

$$\left\{\begin{array}{l}\frac{1}{\sigma}E^{\frac{1-\sigma}{\sigma}}\theta A\alpha(\alpha-1)k^{\alpha-2}[(1-\tau+v\tau)F - (1+n)k] \\ -(1+n)[E^{\frac{1}{\sigma}} + 1 + \alpha^2 Ak^{\alpha-1} + \alpha(\tau-v\tau+\eta)F] \\ + E^{\frac{1}{\sigma}}(1-\tau+v\tau)F\frac{1}{k}\end{array}\right\}$$

$$+ \frac{F}{i+j}[(1+n)\tau + (1+n)\eta + (\alpha Ak^{\alpha-1} - n)v\tau]\alpha k^{-1}(E^{\frac{1}{\sigma}} + 1 + n)(1-v)F$$

Raising the individual contribution rate decreases the capital – labor ratio. A rise in the individual contribution rate decreases the voluntary savings, furthermore the capital – labor ratio. A fall in the capital – labor ratio decreases the wages and disposable income. Hence the per capita consumption falls if the interest rate is higher than the workforce growth rate, and vice versa. According to equations (7) and (8), a rise in the individual contribution rate and a fall in the wage exist in the same time, so the effect of the individual contribution rate on the pension benefits cannot be determined.

3.3 Effect of individual account real asset ratio

Partially differentiating k, c and B with respect to v, respectively, and using equation (11) and the stability condition gives

$$\frac{\partial k}{\partial v} = \frac{-\chi}{i+j} > 0$$

$$\frac{\partial c}{\partial v} = (\alpha A k^{\alpha-1} - n)\frac{\partial k}{\partial v}$$

$$\frac{\partial B}{\partial v} = \frac{F}{i+j}(\alpha A k^{\alpha-1} - n)\tau$$

$$\left\{ \frac{1}{\sigma} E^{\frac{1-\sigma}{\sigma}} \theta A\alpha(\alpha-1) k^{\alpha-2}[(1-\tau+v\tau)F - (1+n)k] \right.$$
$$\left. - (1+n)[E^{\frac{1}{\sigma}} + 1 + \alpha^2 A k^{\alpha-1} + \alpha(\tau-v\tau+\eta)F] + E^{\frac{1}{\sigma}}(1-\tau+v\tau)F\frac{1}{k} \right\}$$

$$- \frac{F}{i+j}[(1+n)\tau + (1+n)\eta + (\alpha A k^{\alpha-1} - n)v\tau]\alpha k^{\alpha-1}(E^{\frac{1}{\sigma}} + 1 + n)\tau F$$

A rise in the individual account real asset ratio increases the individual account principal, furthermore the capital – labor ratio. Hence the per capita consumption rises if the interest rate is higher than the workforce growth rate, and vice versa. According to equations (7) and (8), a rise in the individual account real asset ratio increases the individual account benefits and decreases the social pooling benefits, so the effect of the individual account real asset ratio on the pension benefits cannot be determined. Some effects on the endogenous variables are not determined, thus we will check the effects by simulations below.

4. Simulations

4.1 Parameter setting

The capital share of income is usually to be estimated as 0.3 in developed countries (e.g., Zhang et al., 2001; Pecchenino and Pollard, 2002). The labor in China is comparatively cheaper, thus, the labor share of income is lower, while the capital share of income is higher than that in developed countries. Hence, it is proper to assume that α in China is 0.35.

There are several calibers for population statistics in China. Since the public pension system in urban area is different from that in rural area, and only the former is studied in this paper, so the caliber of "Urban employed population" in China Statistical Yearbook is selected. One period is usually assumed to be 25 – 30 years in the literature; hence we set each period as 28 years. The urban work force growth rate in the period from 1982 to 2010 is computed to be $n = 2.035$ according to the Third National Population Census in 1982 and the Sixth National Population Census in 2010 in China Statistical Yearbook.

Assume that the individual discount factor per year is 0.98, which is similar to that used by Pecchenino and Pollard (2002). Hence, the individual discount factor per period (28years) is $\theta = 0.98^{28}$. Since the technological progress is not reflected in this model, and what we want to see is how the endogenous variables change relatively with the exogenous variables, the constant A can be normalized as 1.

According to the "Decision on Improving Basic Pension System for Enterprise Employees", the firm contribution rate is 20% and the individual contribution rate is 8%. As mentioned in the Introduction, the individual account real asset ratio is only 10.8%. The above values are the benchmark values of the parameters.

4.2 Simulation

Simulating with the benchmark parameter values but raising the firm contribution rate from 16% gradually to 20% gives the result shown in Table 1. The arc elasticity of k, c and B with respect to η are also shown in the table. It is shown that raising the firm contribution rate decreases the capital – labor ratio and per capita consumption, and increases the pension benefits.

Table 1 Effect of firm contribution rate

η	16%	17%	18%	19%	20%	elasticity
k	0.0023	0.0022	0.0021	0.0020	0.0019	-0.7876
c	0.1151	0.1135	0.1119	0.1103	0.1088	-0.2563
B	0.0582	0.0591	0.0599	0.0607	0.0615	0.2460

Simulating with the benchmark parameter values but raising the individual contribution rate from 6% gradually to 10% gives the result shown in Table 2. The arc elasticity of k, c and B with respect to τ are also shown in it. Raising the individual contribution rate decreases the capital – labor ratio and per capita consumption, and increases the pension benefits.

Table 2 Effect of individual contribution rate

τ	6%	7%	8%	9%	10%	elasticity
k	0.0022	0.0021	0.0020	0.0019	0.0018	-0.3936
c	0.1123	0.1105	0.1088	0.1070	0.1053	-0.1288
B	0.0568	0.0591	0.0615	0.0638	0.0661	0.3035

Simulating with the benchmark parameter values but raising the individual account real asset ratio from 10% gradually to 30% gives the result shown in Table 3. The arc elasticity of k, c and B with respect to v are also shown in it. Raising the individual account real asset ratio increases the capital – labor ratio, per capita consumption and pension benefits.

Table 3 Effect of individual account real asset ratio

v	10%	15%	20%	25%	30%	elasticity
k	0.00195	0.00199	0.00203	0.00208	0.00213	0.0881
c	0.1086	0.1094	0.1102	0.1110	0.1118	0.0287
B	0.0607	0.0654	0.0701	0.0747	0.0792	0.2644

Comparing the elasticity gives that the effect of the firm contribution rate on the capital – labor ratio is the strongest, the individual contribution rate takes second place, and that of the individual account real asset ratio is the weakest. The effects of the three policy variables on the per capita consumption rank in the same order. The effect of the individual contribution rate on the pension benefits is the strongest, the individual account real asset ratio takes second place, and that of the firm contribution rate is the weakest.

5. Conclusion

Aiming at the status quo of the individual accounts without full real assets, this paper uses OLG model to investigate the partially funded public pension system for enterprise employees in China. We examine the effects of the firm contribution rate, individual contribution rate and individual account real asset ratio on the capital – labor ratio, per capita consumption and pension benefits. This paper explicitly introduces the factor of making the individual accounts get full real assets, and prominently reflects that raising the individual account real asset ratio can increase the pension benefits for enterprise retirees.

The main results are as follows. Raising individual account real asset ratio increases the capital – labor ratio, per capita consumption and social pool benefits. Raising both the firm contribution rate and individual contribution rate decreases the capital – labor ratio, per capita consumption and increases the pension benefits. The effect of the firm contribution rate on the capital – labor ratio and per capita consumption is the strongest, the individual contribution rate takes second place, and that of the individual account real asset ratio is the weakest. The effect of the individual contribution rate on the pension benefits is the strongest, the individual account real asset ratio takes second place, and that of the firm contribution rate is the weakest. Therefore, in order to increase the pension benefits, it is necessary to raise the individual contribution rate, individual account real asset ratio and firm contribution rate. To increase the demands of consumption and investment, it is necessary to reduce the firm contribution rate and individual contribution rate, and raise the individual account real asset ratio.

The Chinese government pledges to continue to raise pension benefits for enterprise retirees, and further narrow the gap between enterprise and institution retirees' pension benefit levels. Dragged down by the international financial crisis, China's economy still exist downside risk. In order to maintain the balanced, sustainable and healthy development of the economy, China needs to expand domestic demand. The above results indicate that the measures of raising the individual account real asset ratio and individual contribution rate and reducing the firm contribution rate can increase the pension benefits, consumption and investment, and are helpful to increase the pension benefits for enterprise retirees and domestic demand. The negative effect of reducing the firm contribution rate can be covered by the positive effect of raising the individual account real asset ratio. Moreover, the positive effect of raising the individual contribution rate on the pension benefits is greater than that of raising the individual account real asset ratio. The total effects of raising the individual account real asset ratio, reducing the firm contribution rate and raising the individual contribution rate are increasing the pension benefits greatly. The positive effects of reducing the firm contribution rate and raising the individual account real asset ratio on the consumption and investment are much greater than the negative effects of raising the individual contribution rate on the consumption and investment. Thus, the total effects of raising the individual account real asset ratio, reducing the firm contribution rate and raising the individual contribution rate are increasing the consumption and investment greatly.

Acknowledgement:

Financial support from the Major Program of the Key Research Institute on Humanities and Social Science of China Ministry of Education (10JJD790038), the Program for New Century Excellent Talents in Universities of China Ministry of Education (NCET-11-0755), and the Beijing Philosophy and Social Science Programming Project (11JGB089) is gratefully acknowledged.

References

1. Barro, R. J., (1974) "Are government bonds net wealth?" *Journal of Political Economy* 82, 1095 – 1117.
2. Barro, R. J. and X. Sala-I-Martin, Economic Growth, 2nd ed., Cambridge: MIT Press, 2004.
3. Blanchard, O. J. and S. Fischer, Lectures on Macroeconomics, London: MIT Press, 1989.
4. Diamond, P. A., (1965) "National debt in a neoclassical growth model", *American Economic Review* 55, 1126 – 1150.
5. Feldstein, M., (1974) "Social security, induced retirement, and aggregate capital accumulation", *Journal of Political Economy* 82, 905 – 926.
6. Fuster, L., (2000) "Capital accumulation in an economy with dynasties and uncertain lifetimes", *Review of Economic Dynamics* 3, 650 – 674.
7. Groezen, B., T. Leers and L. Meijdam, (2003) "Social security and endogenous fertility: pensions and child allowances as siamese twins", Journal of Public Economics 87, 233 – 251.
8. Pecchenino, R., and P. Pollard, (2002) "Dependent children and aged parents: funding education and social security in an aging economy", *Journal of Macroeconomics* 24, 145 – 169.
9. Wang, Y., D. Xu, Z. Wang, F. Zhai, (2001) "The Implicit Debt, Transition Cost, Reform Forms and the Influence of China's Pension System", *Economic Research Journal* 2001, (5): 3 – 12
10. Yang, Z., (2009a) "Urban public pension, replacement rates and population growth rate in China", *Insurance: Mathematics and Economics* 45 (2), 230 – 235.
11. Yang, Z., (2009b) "Urban public pension, fertility and endogenous growth", *Statistical Research* 26 (5), 77 – 81.
12. Yang, Z., "OLG Model Analysis on Public Pension: Principles and Applications", Guangming Daily Press, 2010.
13. Yang, Z., (2011) "A Theoretical and Empirical Study on the Optimal Replacement Rate of Urban Public Pension under Uncertain Lifetime" *Management Review* 23(2), 28 – 32.
14. Zhang, J., J. Zhang, and R. Lee, (2001) "Mortality Decline and Long-Run Economic Growth". *Journal of Public Economics* 80: 485 – 507.